Library of Congress Cataloging in Publication Data

Frankl, Ludwig August, 1810-1894.
  The Jews in the East.

  Translation of Nach Jerusalem.
  Reprint of the 1859 ed. published by Hurst and Blackett, London.
  1.  Palestine--Description and travel.  2.  Jews in
the Levant--Social life and customs.  3.  Jews in Pal-
estine--Social life and customs.  4.  Frankl, Ludwig
August, 1810-1894.  I.  Beaton, Patrick.  II.  Title.
DS107.F813  1975        915.69'04        78-97278
ISBN 0-8371-2596-0

Originally published in 1859 by Hurst and Blackett, Publishers,
London

Reprinted in 1975 by Greenwood Press,
a division of Williamhouse-Regency Inc.

Library of Congress Catalog Card Number 78-97278

ISBN 0-8371-2596-0 (Set)
ISBN 0-8371-2600-2 (Vol. II)

Printed in the United States of America

# THE JEWS IN THE EAST.

BY

## THE REV. P. BEATON, M.A.

CHAPLAIN TO THE FORCES.

[FROM THE GERMAN OF DR. FRANKL.]

IN TWO VOLUMES.

VOL. II.

GREENWOOD PRESS, PUBLISHERS
WESTPORT, CONNECTICUT

# CONTENTS.—VOL. II.

## CHAPTER III.

## CHAPTER IV.

## CHAPTER V.

## CHAPTER VIII.

## CHAPTER IX.

## CHAPTER X.

# THE JEWS IN THE EAST.

## CHAPTER I.

REB JIZCHAK, who joined us before Ramleh, and whom
we saw expelled from the monastery, had hastened on

before our caravan, for the purpose, as I afterwards learned, of announcing my arrival. I was now some hundred yards in advance of the caravan, and quite close to the walls of the city. Suddenly a man, whom I had not previously observed, rushed upon me, and seized the collar of my great-coat with his left hand, while he brandished a long glittering knife in his right. My reverie, from which I was suddenly roused by this unexpected attack, gave place to a feeling of indescribable terror, and I was almost mechanically drawing my pistols from the holster, when the man quickly loosened his hold, lowered his arms, and, with pale lips, exclaimed:—

"Schema Israel! what are you going to do?"

All this happened in less than a minute, and recognising one of the same creed, I, who may have been just as pale with terror myself, could not help bursting into a laugh. He explained to me that every Jewish pilgrim, before he enters the city, must tear his dress from sorrow at its destruction, in the same way as on the occasion of the death of a relative. So I allowed Mr. Mosche Kural, who derives a small income from this office, "a krie cut," i.e., I allowed him to make a rent in my dress, while I repeated after him the usual formula—"Zion is turned into a desert, it lies in ruins." Then I rode through the Jaffa gate to the house of Dr. Fraenkel, the director of Sir Moses Montefiore's dispensary, which was hospitably opened for my reception.

Feeling rather feverish from my long ride and ex-

posure to the sun, I rested till the cool of the evening,
during which interval the Austrian Consul sent his dragoman to pay me his respects; the representatives of the
Spharedisch and German-Dutch communions bade me
welcome; and the Rabbis of the community " Chassi-
den" sent a letter to inquire at what hour they should
wait upon me.

My first walk in Jerusalem led me through the lively
bazaar with its motley picturesque population—through
steep, narrow, unpaved lanes, which grew lonelier and
quieter as I left the bazaar behind.  As I passed between lofty stone houses, with closed doors, and narrow
wooden latticed windows, stumbling at times over
dead cats and dogs, and finding, in one place, the street
barricaded with the body of a dead camel, I felt the
utter incongruity between the feelings which I had
cherished as a pilgrim and the objects which surrounded
me.  It was only at rare intervals that I met a horseman, or a woman, with her face not veiled, but muffled
up, a white-turbaned Mussulman, a black slave, or a
Jew in the Polish costume.  I felt as I walked through
the city that I was in a place where the plague was
almost endemic, and could not banish the thought from
my mind that a large portion of its inhabitants had been
recently swept away by this scourge.  At length I saw
on my right an arched, half-ruinous bath, and a street
which gradually ascends and passes by the side of it.
This, I was informed by my guide, is the Via
Dolorosa.  On the left are some ruinous houses,
and opposite to me stands the Damascus Gate, with its

lofty arch and its picturesque roof of tin.    Close to it
is a small path which ascends a heap of ruins, on the
left of which is the city wall—a good specimen of
Saracenic architecture, while to the right, on the other
side of the Via Dolorosa, may be seen some lofty cypresses, and two palm-trees which spring from Mount
Moriah, and cast their shade over that part of the
temple court which was devoted to sacrifice.    On a
small platform before me stood the buildings of the
Austrian Consulate.    I ascended to it by a small flight
of stairs, having a plot of garden ground newly laid out
on both sides, and planted with all kinds of trees, among
which the red blossom of the pomegranate was conspicuous.    On arriving at the gate, I turned round and
enjoyed a splendid view of the city spread out at my feet,
and glittering with its numerous domes in the rays of
the sun.    On entering the house, I found that the Consul was out, but I was received by his lady, who held by
the hand a little girl of three years of age, who addressed
me in Arabic.    At some little distance stood her ayah,
a native of Bethlehem, in the picturesque dress of the
country.

I then waited upon Mr. Chajim Nissim Abulafia,
Head Rabbi of Jerusalem.

In former years the Turkish Government, which
shows all due respect to the Chacham Baschi, as one of
its recognised officials, stationed a double guard of
honour before his house, which, about ten years ago,
was gratefully dispensed with, on account of the
expense.    I found the old man, who is more than eighty

years of age, seated on a divan in a spacious apartment. His hair was covered by the light blue turban, which was wound round his head, while his long white beard flowed over a wide woollen *talar*. He made two of his servants lift him up, to enable him to salute me. A truly venerable, patriarchal figure. He laid his right hand on his breast and forehead, and motioned me to a seat beside him.

" Excuse us," he began, in the Spanish language, " for not having gone out to meet you before the gate of the city."

" I should have been ashamed if a venerable old man like you had come out to meet a younger man."

" When offerers came to Jerusalem, the High Priest always went to meet them. And you bring an offering."

" It is not I, it is a noble lady."

" Have you not travelled this great distance ?"

" The great desire of my life to see Jerusalem is now accomplished. Look at my signet ring, and you will see along with the shield of David the motto with which we conclude our prayers at the Passover,—' Leschono habo be Jeruschalaim.' "

" You have reason to rejoice ; you are more fortunate than our teacher Moses. He could only see the promised land from a distance. You have entered it ; but we that have been born here are waiting, full of longing and of sorrow, for the Messiah."

Saluting him by applying my hand to my breast and my forehead, I then handed to him my letters of introduction. Meanwhile, several Rabbis, in Oriental costumes, had assembled and taken their places, in order by their presence to show respect to the guest of the master of the house. Two servants handed round chibouques and coffee, and also preserved fruits and lemonade in silver cups. Before partaking of these delicacies, I uttered the brief prayer used before eating and drinking, bowed to the master of the house, and applied my hand to my breast and forehead.

Meanwhile the Chacham Baschi, while enjoying a chibouque himself, had read over my letters attentively, and promised to aid me in every way. I took my leave, taking care to apply my hand to the *mesusa* of the doorpost and to my lips, as I had done on entering —a pious custom which is universally observed at Jerusalem.

Two days after, the Chacham Baschi, preceded by his servants, and accompanied by his reverend Besdin or college of Rabbis, returned my visit, and I then observed that all of them, though it was the Sabbath, carried Spanish sticks, as they are called, mounted with silver, while the German Jews look upon it as a sin to use a stick of any kind upon the Sabbath. Before his arrival, the Chacham Baschi sent me a present of sweet cakes, with the wish that my journey to the holy city might prove agreeable to me.

Soon after this I had a visit from the presidents of the " Chassidim " community, headed by Mr. Nissim Back, from Galicia, who is the proprietor of the only printing-press in Jerusalem, which was provided by Sir Moses Montefiore, and, I am sorry to say, enjoys a general holiday.

These gentlemen, while expressing their regret at the want of educational etablishments, and their joy at the prospect of one being opened, offered me their services in the most friendly manner. They then made known to me their painful position in having been engaged for years in collecting money to erect a synagogue, a site for which has been already purchased, without any successful result. When I referred them to the Curator at Vienna, whose special duty it is to transmit alms to the Holy Land, they disposed of him by observing that he excluded all who are Austrians by birth from participating in the money collected in Austria, and bestowed it solely on the "Peruschim" community, who enjoy the protection of Russia. The Austrian Consul confirmed this fact. These gentlemen afterwards sent me an appeal, drawn up under the direction of the Consul, and addressed to their co-religionists in the west, begging them to assist them in accomplishing the object which they have in view.

The following morning I was honoured with several other visits, which furnished me with a passing but characteristic sketch of individuals and affairs at Jerusalem. My sitting-room was an apartment with a roof composed of a lofty vaulted cupola, similar to that with which every room in Jerusalem is provided, which, with its two windows looking into a narrow lane, commanded an extensive view of a large portion of the town, of the Mount of Olives, and of the Jewish burying-place in the Valley of Jehoshaphat. In my mouth was generally to be found a beautiful amber-mouthed chibouque, used here even before breakfast as soon as one awakes, filled with *tombak*, the yellow tobacco of Persia, and emitting clouds of fragrant smoke. The housemaid, Chanula, a Spanish Jewess, only fifteen years of age, but already married, with a still, subdued expression, a turban round her head, and her whole face chastely covered, while her breast is quite exposed, brings me my breakfast. Every room has a small elevated floor—a sort of stage about a foot high, covered with carpets, on which the divans are placed. Before this elevation, Chanula, in true Oriental fashion, always reverently takes off her slippers, and approaching barefooted, salutes me by placing her right hand on her heart, her forehead, and her mouth. Then she places the breakfast on the table—black coffee and goat's milk, white bread, honey, and butter quite liquid with the heat. Thus I am literally in a land flowing with milk and honey.

I little suspected that my first visitor should be an associate of the royal harper of Israel, a member of the immortal fraternity of bards—a poet.

There entered a small, pale, sickly-looking man, with reddish, inflamed eyes, marked by a dull ascetical expression. Down both sides of his head, which was covered by a dirty little satin cap, flowed the "Peies," the long, unkempt locks characteristic of the Polish nation. His silk *talar*, or so-called "Schubeze," retained few traces of its long-departed splendour, and all the dust in the valley of Jehoshaphat seemed to be collected on his dilapidated slippers. Mr. Jacob Sapir, from Wilna, after shaking hands with me in silence, without any further preface, thus addressed me :—

" Here all is dust.  After the destruction of the city, the whole earth blossoms from its ruins ; but here there is no verdure, no blossom, and yet there is ripening here a fruit of bitter taste—sorrow—because Jerusalem has perished.  Look for no joy here, neither from men nor from mountains."

" I am delighted to make your acquaintance ; I have already heard of you at Vienna, how you wander through the ruins of the Holy City, and draw from them material to feed the lamp of poetry."

" Say rather the shade, for all is darkness here.  But I am surprised that in such a noble city as Vienna people should condescend to speak of a poor Jewish minstrel at Jerusalem. After this, nothing is wonderful."

" Have you not made a collection of your poems ?"

" Do men gather withered leaves ?  When I finish a song I give it to my friends, and thus it escapes from me, or I burn it, and much is lost.  What can be permanent when Jerusalem has perished ?"

" Bring me a song."

" If God permits me."

" Write an elegy on Zion, and show yourself worthy of Don Jehuda Halewi, the great poet."

" Who is great after David the King ?"

A haggard-looking man, with an unsettled expression and very abrupt manners, then entered, and introduced himself as correspondent to a newspaper from the holy city.  Mr. M. S. is a native of a small town in central

Germany. To show his refined taste, or his piety, he wore a Polish Schubeze, and an abundant crop of hair, which covered his temples. After devoting some time to the study of the Talmud, he had attended the medical classes at Munich and Vienna. In the latter city, as he informed me, he had exerted himself for twenty years in vain, to find sympathy and assistance for those engaged in the cultivation of the soil in Palestine. Scarcely had Ibraham Pasha's despotic rule begun to introduce law and order, when he was obliged to evacuate Syria, and thus all hope of security in the country was removed.

"And why," continued my guest, "should the Jew till the ground in the sweat of his brow, when the Bedouin comes with violence, at the time of harvest, and carries off with impunity, on his camels, what he has not sowed, from the place where he has not ploughed. But the Rabbis, also, are opposed to agriculture, though from a very different reason; they are afraid, that if agriculture were pursued, people in Europe, instead of sending alms here, might take it into their heads to buy lands and estates, by which, as their ambition is to be pious, and not laborious, the large stream of gold that now flows into their hands, without any effort on their part, would be dried up. For the same reason, when Sir Moses Montefiore proposed to establish a soup kitchen, they stoutly resisted, candidly stating as one of their objections: 'Why, the poor would be running there, and eating, and we should receive less money.' And where are our schools?

There is not a single one in the whole of the holy city. In some miserable dens may be found the "Chedorim" of the poorest communities in Galicia, and ignorant teachers. And yet I, a poor man, must pay for the ruin of my own children! Why do the Rabbis not care for schools? Why do the wealthy not contribute money? In Jerusalem there is not one Talmud Thora! In Jerusalem! Does not this cry aloud to God?"

He took his leave, with this advice:—"Listen to all, but believe no one; not even me."

A fourth visitor produced a more pleasant impression. It was Reb Jechiel, a joiner, from Mogolnitz, near Warsaw, who offered for sale different objects, made with the greatest skill, of olive wood—sticks, rulers, boxes, cups, letter-holders, &c. On all these objects was inscribed, in beautiful Hebrew characters, the year, and Jerusalem.

I asked him why he did not use the Latin letters, as being more generally known, on which he explained to me that the English, who are his chief customers, show a decided preference for the Hebrew inscriptions. I had more intercourse afterwards with this industrious man.

The glowing heat of the day grew milder. My thermometer, during a residence of forty days, from the end of May to the beginning of July, varied from 22° to 32° R. Sometimes the South East wind, known as "the wind of Arabia," was prevalent. During this time, the atmosphere, on the other side of the Red Sea, towards the Arabian mountains, had a murky appearance, the sun was overcast, and everything seemed covered with smoke. The heat was then intolerable. After 1 o'clock, P.M., the cool north breeze begins to blow. During the period above specified, I did not see a cloud on the pale blue sky, and observed but little dew.

Under the direction of a guide, I visited the still conspicuous wall which surrounded the temple, to see the wailing place of the Jews, where they assemble every Friday evening to pray, and to lament over the destruction of the sanctuary.

The Jews have a *firman* from the Sultan, which, in return for a very small tax, ensures them the right of entrance for all time to come. The road conducted us through several streets, till, entering a narrow, crooked lane, we reached the wall, which has been often described. There can be no doubt but the lower part of it is a real memorial of the days of Solomon, which, in the language of Flavius Josephus, is "immovable for all time." Its Cyclopic proportions produce the positive conviction, that it will last as long as the strong places of the earth.

Before we reached the wall, we heard a sort of howling melody, a passionate shrieking, a heart-rending wailing, like a chorus, from which the words came sobbing forth—" How long yet, O God ? "

Several hundreds of Jews, in Turkish and Polish costumes, were assembled, and with their faces turned towards the wall, were bending and bowing, as they offered up the evening prayer. He, who led their devo-

tions, was a young man in a Polish *talar*, who seemed
to be worn out with passion and disease. The words
were those of the well-known *Mincha* prayer, but
drawled, torn, shrieked, and mumbled, in such a way,
that the piercing sound resembled rather the raging
phrensy of chained madmen, or the roaring of a
cataract, than the worship of rational beings. At a
considerable distance from the men, stood, about a hundred women, all in long white robes, the folds of which
covered the head and the whole figure—white doves,
which, weary of flight, had perched upon the ruins.
When it was their turn to offer up the usual passages
of the prayer, they joined the men's tumultuous chorus,
and raised their arms aloft, which, with their wide
robes, looked like wings, with which they were about to
soar aloft into the open sky, and then they struck their
foreheads on the square stones of the wall of the temple. Meanwhile, if the leader of their prayers grew
weary, and leaned his head against the wall in silent
tears, for a moment there was a death-like silence.

I happened to be near him, and I could mark the
sincerity of his agitated soul. He gave a rapid glance
at me, and, without stopping short in his prayer, said
to me, "Mokem Kodesch"—*i. e.*, holy place, and
pointed to my covered feet. My guide had forgotten
to inform me that I must take off my shoes. I now
did so, and was drawn into the vortex of raging sorrow
and lamentation.

After this, accompanied by the Austrian Consul, I waited
upon the Pasha of Jerusalem, who had already received

notice that I had a letter for him from Baron von
Bruck. His house stands on Mount Moriah, on the
ancient site of the temple. On entering it, all my
preconceived ideas of eastern magnificence were
speedily dispelled. The court was filled with soldiers,
slaves, and prisoners, forming the most picturesque
groups. The large room which we entered was destitute of any furniture, except divans covered with
dirty calico, and a table, on which lay a crucifix and a
Bible. His Excellency entered, placed the Consul on
his left—the place of honour among the Turks—and
provided seats for us opposite to himself, as he comfortably seated himself, with his legs crossed.    His
dress was of the simplest description, and all of canvas,
except the vest, which was made of light blue silk.
His appearance was prepossessing.    The Consul had
informed me that it was contrary to etiquette to talk
of business before partaking of coffee and the chibouque.
After these refreshments, I gave the Pasha the letter
from the Austrian Minister of Finance, which he
applied to his heart, his forehead, and his mouth, and
then handed over to the interpreter.    The latter
bowed, opened it, and, on finding that it was written
in Turkish, returned it to the Pasha.    He took the
letter, and read it with a feeling of satisfaction, which
increased as he proceeded.    He was evidently flattered,
and said to me, through the interpreter, " I am ready
to fulfil all your wishes and commands."

Meanwhile, I had been seized with a strange feeling
of uneasiness.    On my right was a lofty bow-window,

which commanded a view of localities, which were covered with cupolas, arches, pillars, niches, ruins, porches, and gigantic cypress-trees. It was the platform of Mount Moriah, and the ever-sacred place where the temple of Jehovah stood. I was so overpowered with excitement and sorrow, that I only seemed to listen to the conversation. The Consul, on observing this, asked what was the matter. I explained to him the cause of my emotion, and asked the Pasha to allow me to gaze upon the scene for a little.

" Look at it as long as you like," was his answer; " and if you wish to descend, my armed retainers shall accompany you."

I rose from my seat, and gazed upon the wonderful scene. There are moments in our existence, when the past and the future are blended into one—when the mind realizes all that is separated by time and space as actually present, and is borne along on the unfettered wing of fancy as in a waking dream. The soul floats on an ocean of sensations, in the midst of which may be discerned the dark outline of mighty thoughts. We are swept away, as it were, by the flood of joy and of sorrow, that seizes upon us. All that had been done in past generations and centuries passed in review before me; I saw a father preparing to offer up his own son as a sacrifice; I saw the pillar of fire marching through the wilderness, and the mountain of thunder, with its flames; I stood as a listener in the temple of Jehovah; I heard the Royal bard of Israel strike the harp inspired of God. A countless multitude was thronging in the court of the temple, and the High Priest, in his white robes, brought forth the sacrifice of atonement. I witnessed apostacy and treason against God, and weak kings rising in rebellion, and devouring flames licking the beams of cedar in Jehovah's temple! The anger of the Lord burst forth, and brought all to destruction, and it has not yet ceased to pour down darkness and misery on His chosen people.

After this we took our leave. The Pasha is benevolent, far superior to any feeling of fanaticism, and particularly friendly to Austria, ever since the Grand Cross of one of her orders was bestowed upon him. He got involved, however, in great difficulties, on account of the outbreak at Nablous, in April, 1856, which threatened, at one time, to grow so serious, from being accused of having accepted a bribe of 300,000 piastres. The Austrian and French consuls exerted themselves in his behalf. "If we get a new Pasha, he also will accept presents, and we do not know whether he will be so friendly and favourable to the Christians as this one."

At six o'clock, A.M., on the first Sabbath which I spent at Jerusalem, I visited the synagogue of Zion, which, according to tradition, was the "Midrasch," or school-house, of Rabbi Johannan ben Sakai, at the time of the destruction of Jerusalem. The great synagogue is the property of the Sepharedisch community, and consists of four synagogues, which are built together, and form rather an extensive building. We descended by a stone stair to the first synagogue, and passed through it into the three others.

The ancient building was in a very ruinous condition. The local authorities did not allow any repairs to be made till it was rebuilt under Ibrahim Pasha. On this occasion, a tablet of stone was found, which proved the building to be 460 years old; but it had, probably, been only built on the site of the former synagogue. The halls are lofty, airy, and well lighted; the furniture plain, but decent.

I was shown to the seat of honour on the Almemer. I was honoured with the same distinction in all the synagogues; and in each of them I had to take part in Divine service. The thora rolls were kept in the ark — I observed this to be the case in all the synagogues—in a sort of round wooden case, which was mounted with silver or copper, or beautifully varnished. When you open the door of the holy ark, which is usually painted, you have to draw aside a silk curtain, adorned with inscriptions in gold or silver; then you see the thora rolls, from which the lessons for the day are to be read, in the open case, which it requires some little effort to lift, and to carry through the synagogue. The attendant, as he advances, points out to the different worshippers in succession, with the silver *Jad*, the places at which the lessons for the day begin. The rolls, which project over the *thora*, are adorned with " Ezchajim " trees of life, which usually represent pomegranates worked in silver.

When I wished to buy a similar pair for the new temple at Vienna, I was only allowed to do so because I myself had brought a *thora roll* to the holy city. The exportation of a thora roll, or of any sacred vessel, is not allowed. Great excitement, therefore, was occasioned by Rabbi E. having sold a thora to the Princess of Holland. In order to ward off the storm, which was gathering over him, the Consul addressed a letter to the Princess's chamberlain, requesting him to return the *thora*, but as yet this has not produced any effect.

During the "hagbaha," the elevation and exhibition of the thora, all stand up, just as we do, from their seats; but the women who are seated behind latticed wooden galleries, present a peculiar appearance. They spread out their arms repeatedly towards the thora, and, applying their hands to their lips, throw kisses to it with an expression of ardent devotion. This is almost the only real part—for only a very few of them can read—which the *Sepharedisch* women take in divine service.

A peculiar ceremony took place while the thora was being carried forward. In the middle of the synagogue, beneath a canopy, sat a boy of some fifteen years of age, who a week before was a bridegroom, and to-day was accompanied to the thora by his two groomsmen, who sat near him. After the reading of the lessons for the day, he listened devoutly to the passage read for his especial behoof, beginning " And Abraham was old," and ending, " thou shalt take a wife unto thy son." Meanwhile the attendant in the synagogue sprinkled all the worshippers with rose-water, while he who recited the prayer chaunted a benediction.

It is a beautiful custom for sons to stand up when their father is called to the thora, and to remain standing during the reading; in the same way the whole congregation stands up when a Rabbi rises. The same honour was shown to me.

Before leaving the synagogue, the attendant gives each of the worshippers a bouquet or some kind of fruit, the fragrance of which is inhaled during the benediction.

The following day the Chacham Baschi sent me a document through the Austrian Consul, in which he announced that he was about to excommunicate U——, an Austrian subject, for having grossly insulted the head of religion at Jerusalem. To understand this notice, it is necessary to explain that sentence of excommunication at Jerusalem involves very serious consequences for the party against whom it is pronounced. No Jew will venture to sell him provisions, and if he is a merchant, no one will buy his goods. All intercourse with him ceases; he is excluded from the synagogue; wife and children desert him, his very touch is pollution. As this sentence is now sometimes pronounced on trifling grounds, and its victim is deprived at the same time of all his political rights, the consuls make it a preliminary condition, that, when it affects any of their subjects, they shall receive previous notice before giving it their sanction. I hurried at once to the Chacham Baschi, and mentioned that, while I had no wish to interfere with him in the discharge of his official duties, I thought it might be better not to invite the interference of the civil authorities in a purely religious affair. I contrived to appease him, and it was matter of self-congratulation to me to have warded off the thunderbolt with which my enemy was threatened. Contrary to my expectation of receiving such an intimation at so early a period, I received next day, the 2nd of June, a circular note from the Chacham Baschi, to the effect that the meeting would take place at 12 o'clock at noon. He himself, accompanied by his Chachams, honoured me with another visit, and assured me of his friendly feelings towards myself and the object which I had in view.

In order to convey to the reader a clear idea of the religious, moral, and social condition of the Jews at Jerusalem, and explain the attitude which they assumed towards the proposed institution, it is necessary, beforehand, to give a more minute explanation of the terms Sepharedim, Aschkenasim, Peruschim, and Chassidim, which have been frequently employed in this work, and to give at least an outline of the statistics connected with the different communities, and of the social relations which exist between them.

According to official reports, the Jewish population of the Holy City amounts to 5,700 souls;[*] it thus forms

---

[*] The accuracy of the following statement of the Jewish population of Palestine and Syria, may be relied on :—Jerusalem, 5,700; Safed, 2,100; Tiberias, 1,514; Hebron, 400; Jaffa, 400; Saida, 150; St. Jean D'Acre, 120; Khaifa, 100; Schafamer, 60; Prkyin,

one-third of the whole population, which is 18,000 souls, and is twice as large as the Christian. Jerusalem contains 3,000 Christians, of whom 1,000 are Latins, and 2,000 Greek and Armenian Christians. Of the Jews 1,700 are Austrian subjects, and enjoy her protection, while she has only 100 Christian subjects, including every sect in the Holy City. The title " His Apostolic Majesty, King of Jerusalem," is therefore as correct in this respect, as in matters of diplomacy and history.

The Jews are distinguished as Separedisch and Aschkenasisch. The name Sepharedim was applied to the Spanish-Portuguese Jews, who were expelled from Spain under Isabella II. and scattered over the whole world. The Sepharedim in Jerusalem again had their origin in the Turkish provinces, in Egypt, Tunis, Tripoli, Morocco, Algiers, India, Persia, &c., and they use the Spanish language. They constitute by far the largest portion of the Jewish population, being 4,000 in number, and form the largest community at Jerusalem. At their head is the Chacham Baschi, chosen by the Chachams, *i.e.* by the Rabbis, who is recognised by the Turkish Government. He, aided by his Besdin, decides all religious questions. The Chachams again— the members of the community have no voice in the matter—choose three " Pakidim " or presidents for the

50; Nablous, 40; Rameh, 5—in all, 10,639. Damascus, 5,000; Beyroot, 180; Deir el Kamar, 100; Chasbeia, 100; Tripolis, 40; in all 5,420. The entire Jewish population of Palestine and Syria thus amounted in 1856 to 16,059 souls.

management of secular and economical affairs ; there are three others subordinate to them. The accounts of all the presidents are audited by three "Maschkichim;" these are chosen by the Chacham Baschi from his college of Rabbis. There is thus a kind of representative government, but its members are in no respect responsible to the commmunity, who do not elect them. The consequence is, that most of the " Balebatim" or heads of families, are dissatisfied with the conduct of the Chachams, who are 100 in number, and are exclusively occupied in learning the Talmud, to the neglect of all those studies that would enlarge their views. But the greatest amount of dissatisfaction exists among the labourers and the "Moghrebim," the Jews from Morocco, Tunis, and Algiers, who are suspicious about the management of pecuniary affairs, and the distribution of the money by the Chachams, and have been recently trying to secede from the chief community, so as to secure a more equitable division of the alms contributed from their respective countries. There is reason, therefore, to dread the same disaster which, as we shall afterwards see, has caused a disruption among the Aschkenasim, and divided them into four communities.

The community possesses the four synagogues, to which we have already alluded in this work, six houses, one of which is in Jaffa, and several sites for building, which are as yet unoccupied.

There are thirty-six "Jeschibot," or pious institutions, most of which have been endowed with a certain capital by foreigners, the interest of which is drawn by those Chachams who study the Talmud and offer up prayers in remembrance of the founders.

The Jeschiba "Perera" is endowed with 16,386 piastres, the smallest one with only 1,000 piastres. There is no accurate statement of the resources of the community; no tax is levied. New settlers must purchase their entrance, by paying the exact amount of their annual income. When they die, the community takes possession of all their property, without any regard to their heirs in foreign countries, but this is always done with their free consent.

It is the duty of the Padekim to be present at every death-bed; they seal the property of the deceased, and convey it to the "Auda," the community's place of assembly, where it is sold for the benefit of the community to the highest bidder. Widows, who immigrate here in great numbers, and are without heirs, choose Chachams to be their heirs, in order that they may have some one to offer up the "Kadisch," the prayer in memory of the dead, and burn a taper for them on the anniversary of their death. On their arrival, they are obliged to come to terms with the community, the same as others. The community sends abroad messengers to collect alms throughout the whole world, with the exception of Russia and Poland, but chiefly in Africa.

In addition to the revenues derived from foreign sources, the community receives 20,000 piastres annually from selling ground for graves, of which they possess the exclusive right, and other 20,000 piastres from their privilege of killing animals used as food.

But all these revenues are not sufficient to pay even the interest of the debt, with which the community has been burdened for generations, and which is always increasing, chiefly from the numerous direct disbursements that are made.

The community owes :—

|  | Ducats. |
|---|---|
| A direct capital, which must be repaid . . | 12,000 |
| Interest on the capital which is presented to them by immigrants, payable so long as the latter are alive . . . . . . | 8,000 |
| The interest of legacies for the "Jeschibot" | 10,000 |
| Whole amount of debt . . . ducats | 30,000 |

The community's direct disbursements are :—

|  | Piastres. |
|---|---|
| To the village of Siluan, near the valley of Jehoshaphat, for guarding, or rather for not injuring the burying-ground . . . | 10,000 |
| Gifts to Turks of high rank, especially for the privilege of free access to the west wall of the temple . . . . . . | 30,000 |
| To the inhabitants of Bethlehem for the right of access to Rachel's sepulchre . . . | 5,000 |
| For the Talmud Thora school . . . | 20,000 |
| Salary of the Chacham Baschi . . . | 5,000 |
| Salary of the secretary and servant . . | 5,000 |
| Support of the poor, widows, and orphans . | 30,000 |
| piastres | 105,000 |

According to the budget of the previous year, the community receives :—

| | |
|---|---|
| From deaths ⎫<br>Tombstones ⎪<br>Marriages ⎬ . . . . 500,000 piastres.<br>Goods imported ⎪<br>Duty on wine ⎪<br>Duty on meat ⎭ | |
| Alms from Amsterdam . . . . . 80,000 | |
| The collections from Turkey and other countries vary, but in good years the whole revenue amounts to . . 1,000,000 piastres. | |

The poll tax was not paid during the Eastern war, a new distribution of taxes was expected; it was hoped that, in consequence of the Hat Humayoum, at least the gifts to the Effendis would be dispensed with. It is lamentable to state that the community has saved 20,000 piastres for several years, by giving up the Talmud Thora, and in order to pay the current interest has sold the establishment to the Rothschild family for the erection of a hospital, for the sum of 96,000 piastres.

But what do the Chachams and the presidents do with the capital? Have they expended it partly in payment of the interest in arrears, and put aside the balance as a fund for the future support of educational establishments? They have done neither. They simply divided the money in true Turkish fashion among themselves, though they were in comfortable circumstances, on the ground that it was their forefathers, who collected the money for the purchase of the house.

However incredible this fact may appear, it is surpassed by another. At the period of my arrival in that city, which the Jews esteem to be the holiest on the earth, there was not even a single school, such as the smallest and poorest community of Europe would be ashamed not to possess.

## ASCHKENASIM.

Only a small number of Aschkenasim had their origin in Germany, *i.e.* in Aschkenes and Holland; the most of them are from Russia, Galicia, Hungary, Bohemia, and Moravia. The term German is so far justly applied to them, as they all understand the German language, of which they speak a strange dialect, with a still stranger accent. Their want of union is a further proof of their claims to the character of Germans; as about thirty years ago, they separated from their Sepharedisch co-religionists, along with whom they had previously constituted one community, and are now divided into six different communities, which hate one another *à outrance*. The number of the Aschkenasim in the Holy city is 1,700. We shall here introduce them according to their different communities.

### PERUSCHIM.

The word "porisch" means separated; the members of this community, 850 in number, proudly separate themselves from the rest of their co-religionists. They are also called Pharisees.

Fanatical, bigoted, intolerant, quarrelsome, and, in truth, irreligious, with them the outward observance of the ceremonial law is everything; the moral law little binding, morality itself of no importance; and thus they have contributed, as we shall afterwards prove, by far the largest quota of those, whom the Missionary Society regards as converts to Christianity.

They call themselves the scholars of Rabbi Elja Gaon, who lived, half-a-century ago, at Wilna. Their chief seat was formerly at Zafet, but after the earthquake in the year 1837, they fled, with few exceptions, to Jerusalem.

They have no spiritual head; their president is Rabbi Schaje Bordaki, from Minsk in Russia; all of them are natives of Russia, and as this state, some years ago, ordered them to return, and they refused to obey that order, she renounced them. Some of them placed themselves under the protection of England, but most of them under that of Austria. The seat of their government is at Wilna, from which they annually receive about 15,000 rubles, that is 300,000 piastres, and about 80,000 more from other countries; so that, altogether, they receive 380,000 piastres for their support.

As they have only been taken under the protection of Austria, and are not in any sense Austrian subjects, it was with surprise that I learned from the Austrian consul, that the alms collected at Vienna and in the surrounding country among Austrian subjects, and honestly intended for the relief of their Austrian co-religionists in this country, are appropriated by the

Peruschim community.    None but the respectable
Rabbis of Vienna and Eisenstadt send money to the
Austrian community through the consul.

The Peruschim are connected with Hungary through
the Rabbis of Presburg, with Germany through the
Rabbis of Altona, with Prussia through the Rabbis of
Königsberg, with Bavaria through the Rabbis of Würz-
burg, and with Holland through the mercantile house
of Leeren.

### 'VOLHYNIAN CHASSIDIM.

The members of this community had their origin in
Volhynia, in Moldau, in Bessarabia ; they have settle-
ments at Zafet and Tiberias, and about 12 or 16 years
ago, established a community at Jerusalem.

The seat of government, by which the communities
of the three holy cities are ruled, is at Berditchew and
Sardagura in Buckowina, which is also the seat of their
spiritual head.    Mr. Nissim Back holds the office of
president at Jerusalem.    In their religious views they
are closely allied to the Peruschim, only they adhere to
the Sepharedisch ritual, while the latter are attached to
the Aschkenasisch.    They are not so fanatical as the
Peruschim, and much purer in their morals.    With
them the study of the Talmud. is not the chief object,
they attach a higher value to idealism, which gives
them a tendency to cabalism.

They receive annually 5,000 rubles, 100,000 piastres,
from their native land, 50,000 from other countries,
altogether 150,000 piastres.

## AUSTRIAN CHASSIDIM.

These had their origin in Galicia and Cracow, and separated from the Volhynian Chassidim, whom they closely resemble in character, six years ago, in consequence of quarrels about money. Since that period, they have formed a distinct community, which contains 150 souls. A small number of them live also at Zafet and Tiberias. Lemberg is the seat of their government. Mr. Rabbi Mosche Schmelke Horwitz holds the office of president at Jerusalem.

They receive from Galicia 7,000 florins, or 80,000 piastres, about 6,000 from other countries, in all, 86,000 piastres.

## CHASSIDIM CHABAT.

When the consonants of the word Chbt Chochim, viz., (wisdom), Bine (reason), Deie (knowledge) are placed beside one another, C. B. D.,* omitting the vowels, they form the word " Chabat." This community has its chief settlement at Hebron, where its members are the only Aschkenasim. There is only an affiliated branch at Jerusalem, containing 40 or 50 souls, under the local presidency of Mr. Salamon Epstein. The president of the whole community is Rabbi Schimon Menasche, who resides at Hebron. Libawiz, in Russia, is the seat of their spiritual head, who also manages their civil affairs. The religion and morality of the Chabat are similar to those of the Peruschim.

The chief community and its affiliated branch receive

* ת כ ר

from Russia 2,000 rubles, 40,000 piastres, from other countries 5,000, in all, 45,000 piastres.

### WARSOVIANS.

This community is composed partly of Peruschim and partly of Chassidim; some of them follow the Aschkenasisch, others the Sepharedisch ritual; it contains about 150 souls. In consequence of quarrels about money, they erected themselves into a separate community 8 years ago. They are partly under the protection of England, partly under that of Prussia and Austria. Rabbi Juda Elia Deiches and Mr. Mordachai Maier Robinson are their presidents.

They receive from Poland 4,500 rubles, 90,000 piastres, from other countries 5,000, in all, 95,000 piastres.

### ANSCHE HOD.

A and H, the first letters of this name, are a contraction for Aschkenes, Germany, and Hod, Holland; then for men who have come from these two countries. They are only 60 in number, and formed themselves into a separate community about 6 or 7 years ago. Their German descent is scarcely perceptible; they wear the Oriental or Polish costume, and long hair, which covers their temples; the Peruschim, with whom they intermarry, are their model of imitation. Rabbi Josef Schwarz and Mr. Juda Leb Goldschmied hold the office of presidents.

While the sums sent by private individuals are not always known, the whole amount of the alms transmitted to Jerusalem every year, may be estimated, without exaggeration, at 818,000 piastres.

The Aschkenasim have no spiritual head at Jerusalem; but the community of the Peruschim and Warsovians have a "Besdin." The presidents are chosen in Europe, and not by the communities; their meetings are held privately, and men worthy of confidence are excluded.

The Aschkenasim have only one synagogue at Jerusalem, which is known by the name of Churba. When Nachmaindes came to Jerusalem in the 13th century, he bought "a handsome but ruinous building, with marble pillars and a splendid cupola," which really consisted of several buildings, and formed a large court, like that of a monastery: he converted part of it into a synagogue. The finer part of the building, that which still remains, was afterwards taken from the Jews, and changed into a wine-press.

Both the Sepharadim and Aschkenasim worshipped in this synagogue, till the former restored the synagogue of Zion, which was in a ruinous condition.

The possession of it by the Aschkenasim was afterwards disputed by the Mohammedans. Though they adduced documents, which placed their claims beyond a doubt, they had to pay 260 ducats to the Cadi before he decided that the synagogue had been their property for centuries. Notwithstanding this, some parts of the building were taken from them and used for dishonourable purposes. At the close of the 17th century, the Rabbi Jehudah Hachaszid, a native of Poland, arrived

at Jerusalem, and, in consequence of his many excellent
qualities, was chosen president of the Aschkenasim.
He enlarged the synagogue, and richly ornamented it;
and, in memory of their pious head, it was called the
synagogue of Rabbi Jehudah Hachaszid.    The Aschkenasim were afterwards reduced, by pestilence and
Mohammedan oppression, to such poverty, that the
munificent sum of 25,000 ducats, collected by their
president, Rabbi Moscheh Hakohen, in the course of a
pilgrimage which he made through the whole of Europe,
at the beginning of the 18th century, was not sufficient
to clear off the debt with which the community was
burdened.    In the year 1721, those of the creditors
who were most dissatisfied attacked the synagogue,
burned it to the ground, and expelled the Aschkenasim,
who were dispersed to Zafet, to Hebron, and throughout the whole world.

The walls and arches of the synagogue became gradually filled with rubbish to such an extent, that they
could scarcely be distinguished from it.    It was only
when the plague broke out at Zafet, in 1812, that about
twenty Aschkenasim ventured to return to Jerusalem
in disguise.    A firman, which was obtained at Constantinople four years after this event, declared that
the debt incurred by the forefathers of the Aschkenasim
had fallen under the right of prescription, and thus
absolved them from all further claims on the part of the
Mohammedans.    At the same time, they received permission to build a school-house and a *midrasch*, with an
oratory.    A later firman of Mehmed Ali in Egypt, in

the year 1836, replaced the Aschkenasim in the possession of their synagogue, which was soon after re-conse-
crated.

While I was at Jerusalem, the Persuchim were
rebuilding this synagogue. Mr. Jecheskiel, a pious
man from Bagdad, bequeathed 100,000 piastres to aid
in building this synagogue. A sum of 400,000 piastres
has already been expended on it, part of which has
been lent by the Peruschim from their reserved fund.
It will take a million of piastres to finish the synagogue. The pious task of laying the foundation stone
of what, we trust, will be a handsome and durable
building was assigned to Baron Rothschild.

Besides the chief synagogue of the Aschkenasim,
there is a considerable number of *midraschim* and
*jeschibot*, most of which have oratories connected with
them, where the Talmud is studied by adults, and theo-
logical discussions are carried on.

The Aschkenasim have never had a school of the
higher class for the education of youth, not even a
Talmud Thora; they rather allow the minds and bodies
of their children to be cramped by the Rabbis in those
filthy, damp, little rooms, which are known as
" Chedorim." I shudder at the remembrance of these
hotbeds for the growth of ignorance—of these dark dens
of disease and misery.

When any knowledge of the Talmud is found to
exist among the Aschkenasim at Jerusalem—the Peruschim enjoy the highest reputation in this branch—it has
never been acquired in the Holy City, but been brought

by the immigrants from their native land.  They never study the Bible, and derive all their knowledge of it from the Talmud, to which they have recourse without any previous knowledge of grammar.  But all study here is a mere mechanical exercise of memory, and in the land of the Tamaim and Amoraim there is not a single person engaged in learned researches.  I happened to mention to a Rabbi, who enjoys a high reputation for learning, that I was about to visit Mount Gerizim and Ebal, and expected to reach them in the course of two days.  " What ! are they not a thousand miles from this ? "  asked the Rabbi in astonishment.  Another did not know in which quarter of the globe he was living, and was ignorant that there is one particular part of the earth that bears the name of Europe.  All other parts of the world, apart from Palestine, were known to him as " Chuzelorez," *i. e.*, outside the Holy Land, in the same way as all other men were known to the Greeks as barbarians.  One of their Presidents learned in his old age to sign his name in Hebrew, and he did so only because he had to certify that he had received the chaluka and the kadima.

The Aschkenasim regard the Sepharedim as latitudinarian, unlearned, and ignorant; on the other hand, the Sepharedim give the Aschkenasim credit for piety, learning, and the most artful cunning.  They do not visit one another's Besdins, and only the poorest members of the two communities intermarry.  There is just as little unanimity and friendliness of disposition among the Sepharedim themselves.

When a Choszid wishes to employ the worst term of reproach, he says, " You are a Porisch," *i. e.*, one of the Peruschim.  On the other hand, the Porisch exclaims, in indignation, " What can be worse than a Choszid ? " *i. e.*, than one of the Chassidim.

The Sepharedi has quite a distinguished appearance, with his picturesque, flowing, eastern robes, his imposing walk and bearing; and the whole outline of his countenance has something noble in it.  Example and the influence of climate have made him resemble his Mohammedan neighbour in outward dignity and inward repose—perhaps, also, in indolence.

The Aschkenasim, especially the Russians and Poles, are hasty, restless in every movement, full of grimace, keen in assertion and reply.  Their appearance, in consequence of their wearing the well-known, ugly, Polish dress with all the filth that adheres to it, is, to say the least, unwholesome.

It is amusing to observe how great political events are sometimes reflected through a small, distorted medium.  Just in the same way as Russia tried to destroy Turkey, her Jewish sons at Jerusalem try gradually to undermine the power of the Turkish Jews, and, if possible, to oust them.  The Czar could scarcely have expected that his former subjects would serve as unpaid auxiliary forces in the East.

We have pointed out the debts and the disbursements with which the Sepharedim are burdened— disbursements for things, which the Aschkenasim share in common with them.  But the latter are not satisfied with merely paying nothing; their restlessness, their skill in writing, and their innate love of intrigue impel them to oppose and to overreach their Oriental brethren, who are not so active, or so quick-witted.

One of the chief sources of revenue to the Sepharedim, by which they are enabled to cover the expenses of the community, is the burying-ground, as they possess the right to sell graves and tombstones. We will not positively assert that their demands were always just, and this, perhaps, may have been the reason why the Peruschim, about three years ago, bought a separate place for the interment of their dead, and the Volhynians are now about to follow their example.

But the Peruschim have also tried to deprive the Sepharedim of the profits derived from the monopoly of slaughtering animals, and this attempt gave rise to a singular incident. As the Sultan formerly threatened to cover up the cupola of the church of the Holy Sepulchre, because the Christian sects would not yield to one another in rank and material pre-eminence, in this case, also, the Mohammedan authorities intervened between the contending Jewish sects, and gave the decision in favour of their Oriental fellow citizens. It happened in this way. The Mohammedans purchase at the stall of the Jewish butcher the hind part of the animal which the Jew is forbidden to use. The cadi, however, must give the butcher a certificate, that he and his forefathers have always been regular and strictly orthodox Jews, and that they are direct descendants of Israel. Before slaughtering the animal, the butcher must not only offer up the usual Hebrew prayer, but, turning the animal's head towards Mecca, he must, at the same time, offer up in Arabic a Mohammedan prayer, which is called " Bissem Alah agbar." Otherwise, no Mohammedan would eat his meat. When the Peruschim, jealous of the monopoly of the Sepharedim, opened a butcher's stall of their own, the cadi refused to grant this certificate to their butcher. The Mohammedan does not look upon the Aschkenasim as being veritable Jews. Notwithstanding, the Peruschim began to kill meat; the butcher turned the animal's head toward Mecca, and offered up the usual Mohammedan prayer. Most of the Mohammedans objected to buying his meat, because he had not received the proper certificate. Then the pious Scheik Assib suddenly raised the cry, that the Aschkenasim plucked the wool from the neck of the sheep before killing it, and thus tortured the animal. The Mohammedans, who believe that this animal will be admitted to Paradise, would buy no more meat, and the butcher's stall of Vordaki and Co. was closed, with a loss of 40,000 piastres—part of the alms sent from Europe.

The Jews at Jerusalem are still obliged, when they slaughter an animal, to give the priest the right shoulder, a part of the head without the tongue, and the maw, while the " truma " of wine, oil, and rakee is buried, because the priests are not considered to be quite clean.

One day, during my residence, there was no meat to be had in Jerusalem; the butcher refused to kill, because the Besdin declined to grant a certificate to his nephew, a lad of nineteen years of age, that he was a deeply-learned Rabbi. If he had obtained this certificate, it was his intention to proceed to Europe for the purpose of begging. The Jews cried, as on a former occasion in the wilderness, " Would to God we had died in the land of Egypt, when we sat by the flesh-pots." I could not understand the affair, and had the following conversation regarding it.

" Is not the butcher chosen by the community, and consequently their servant, subject to their orders ? "

" He is our servant."

" Then order him to do his duty."

" He will not obey."

" Then keep back his salary, and if he will not yield, dismiss him."

" We dare not do that."

" You dare not discharge a refractory servant ? "

" He has the Chasaka."

Every one has the Chasaka who holds an office, occupies a house, or enjoys a pension, after he has been in possession for six months. It is a common saying at Jerusalem, and perfectly true, " Happy are those who are in possession, for no one can deprive them of the right of possession, and it is hereditary to their children and grandchildren." There are many of the Chachams who are exactly in the same position, as regards some of the Jeschibots, and other profitable rights, and they take very good care never to dispute the time-honoured legitimacy of the Chasaka.

The contributions from Europe, of which we have only given an outline in the preceding pages, are naturally dependent on accidental circumstances, in consequence of which they sometimes reach a higher figure, and at other times are smaller in amount. There are two ways of distributing the money : as " Chaluka," *i.e.* at so much per head, without regard to sex or age, and of course a family blessed with many children receives a considerable sum, and as " Kadima," according to the rank and importance of the individual. The Ansche Hod, who receive the money for their support in the way we have first mentioned, are best off, and are, in fact, almost richly provided for; they are the only community without poor.

But all the money, which is contributed from pious and benevolent motives, does not find its way to Jerusalem, with the exception of the sum that is sent from Lemberg. In consequence of the expense of management and distribution, the want of every kind of control, and the difference in the value of money, the whole contribution does not reach those who are really in want. We shall afterwards return to this subject.

The poverty of some is so great that it cannot fail to excite surprise and compassion, while the wives of the presidents, who came there at first quite as poor, are dressed in silk, and decked with gold and precious stones. The daughter of one of them, on the day of her marriage, wore a dress which cost 1,000 piastres ; and the marriage feast, to which all the more dis-

tinguished members of society at Jerusalem were
invited, cost 1,500 piastres.

When that active philanthropist, Mr. Albert Cohen,
paid his second visit to Jerusalem, the wives of the
Rabbis were expressly forbidden to wear their jewels
during his stay.    We have often heard the poor, when
speaking of their contributions, and the way in which
they are applied by their rulers, use the characteristic
expression, "They devour them!"    We would not go
quite so far as this, or assert that the highly-honoured
presidents are guilty of embezzlement.    We would take
a charitable view of the subject, and say that they have
an over-weening idea of their own rank and importance,
which is all quite natural and pardonable.    But then
rank must be supported, and they perhaps deduct a
little  too  much  for  themselves  in  the  shape  of
"Kadima."

With what feelings of veneration is a Scheliach, a
begging delegate from Palestine, greeted, when he
enters our houses to collect money for our poor co-religionists at Jerusalem!    Does not the dust of the
sacred soil still adhere to his dress?    His eye has
lingered and wept over the ruins of the temple, and
tearing himself from the bosom of his family, he has
gone forth and exposed himself to the dangers of the
stormy ocean and of a long journey by land.    He tells
us of those who are languishing in poverty and starving
with hunger in Jerusalem, who are weeping and praying for us.

But how should we greet him if we knew that this

collecting of alms is simply a trade, and that the delegate himself will pocket the greater part of the money, which is contributed in perfectly good faith for the relief of those who are languishing and starving at Jerusalem?

The office of delegate is sold in the holy city to the highest bidder; usually to some respectable Chacham or Rabbi, to enable him to amass a fortune. It is quite true that he is bound to pay a certain sum to the community. The highest bidder continues to enjoy his right; he is not bound to enter on his journey immediately; he may put it off for months, or even for years, provided always that he pays the interest of the sum, which increases according to a fixed scale. This interest often amounts to a considerable sum, and there are cases where it has been paid for five or eight years. On his return, the delegate receives the third part of the proceeds of his journey, but he does not receive the sum originally deposited; it is therefore quite natural and pardonable that he should repay this sum to himself, and hand over only the balance to the community, which pays him the third part of the balance also.

A few years ago, on the day of atonement, an entrance was effected into the shop of a Jewish goldsmith, situated in the bazaar, and different articles of gold carried off. After a year, on a certain day, the son of a president of one of the most strictly orthodox communities, retired from the synagogue in white penitential robes, and after being absolved for the crime of housebreaking, returned again, and, penetrated with grief, began to beat upon his breast, confessed the offence of which he had been guilty, and besought the forgiveness of the community. From respect to the father, the crime was overlooked, and compensation was made to the goldsmith by the Jews themselves.

While this crime, perpetrated on that day which the Jews regard as the most sacred of all, excites our horror and affords a melancholy proof of the way in which the father brought up his children, still it is not our wish that the crime of the son should be reckoned against the father. But there is one thing that we must mention, though our pen is reluctant to write it down, because it gives us an insight into the fearful corruption of morals, which exists in the midst of the strictest religious observances; this same man, this housebreaker, this thief, this hypocrite, this blasphemer, was soon afterwards sent as a delegate to Europe, to collect money for the poor. Of course he was armed with a circular from the Besdin, addressed to all believers, and certifying that this pious, honourable, learned Rabbi had been selected from many others, &c., &c.

An incident of a more humorous character occurred in the case of a delegate who was sent to America. On his arrival at Smyrna he bought some wine, which had been made by Christians, and sold it to his co-religionists in America as a real genuine article from Hebron, grown in the immediate vicinity of the graves of the patriarchs. But it must be mentioned to the praise of the people of Jerusalem, that this Rabbi belonged to Jaffa.

The following still more amusing event, as it tends

to illustrate the character of the people, may here be introduced. Sir Moses Montefiore brought with him in wooden barrels dollars in specie, and resolved, with his usual kindness of disposition, to give with his own hand a dollar to every poor person. It took many hours before his task was done and the miserable exhibition of poverty concluded. It so happened that the noble distributor, forgetful of himself, gave away the sum which he required to pay his travelling expenses home. He was obliged to borrow money. A man was soon found, who expressed his readiness to oblige him—for a consideration—and supplied him with the necessary sum, the amount of which was considerable, in specie. And yet this man, the previous day, seemed to be the neediest of the needy, and had received a silver dollar from the hand of the benefactor of Palestine.

This incident proves the propriety of the advice which I received from our ambassador at Constantinople. "If you have money to distribute, take good care that all the presidents' relations are not dressed in rags, and introduced to you as the poorest members of the community.".

A wicked and satirical joke was perpetrated by a German physician at the expense of a president of the Chassidim, remarkable for his idle and begging propensities. He found a dead sheep, such as is often to be seen in the streets of Jerusalem, and had it conveyed to the house of the rich beggar. On arriving there himself, he called the president by name, and asked him, "Will you do a 'mizwe,' a pious deed?" The president expressed his readiness, on which he said to him, "Then skin this sheep, for it is written in the Talmud, 'It is better to support oneself by skinning carcasses, than by receiving alms.'"

# CHAPTER II.

MY host, to whom I had given an account of my visit
to the Karaites in Constantinople, and expressed a
desire to visit their community at Jerusalem, invited
me one Sabbath to accompany him to the house where
they all dwell together.

I may mention in a word, for the benefit of those

readers who are not familiar with these subjects, that the Karaites, who are also called Karäers or Jerusalemites, are Jews, who regard the text of the Bible with a sacred feeling, as alone containing the law, in consequence of which they are called Karäer, *i.e.* sticklers for the text, in contradistinction to the Mekebalim, *i.e.* the sticklers for a traditional faith. The latter assert that God favoured Moses with oral revelations of doctrine, which have been handed down by tradition and are contained in the Talmud.

We entered a very cleanly kept house, with a court in front, in the walls of which are inserted marble tablets, containing Hebrew inscriptions in gold letters, to the effect that such and such Karaite pilgrims have visited the Holy City. After ascending a staircase, adorned with marble pillars, we were kindly received by the President, who, surrounded by his wife and children, was reading a book in a room which was covered with carpets of different colours. His wife wore handsome gold ornaments round her fez, and her little girls had flowers in their loose, flowing hair, which was adorned with gold spangles.

When I asked the master of the house for some historical information regarding the Karaite community at Jerusalem, he gave me the following narrative :—

" We are the oldest inhabitants of Jerusalem since the destruction of the second temple. Two hundred and seventy years ago, there were two hundred Karaites in the Holy City, which they were obliged to leave, in consequence of the plague having broken out, so that for twenty years there was not a single Karaite to be found in Jerusalem. It is now a hundred and fifty years since we settled here again. Our oldest tombstone is only a hundred and ten years old; but there may be many buried in the ground. We now only number thirty-two souls, and four heads of families. It is painful that your countrymen, the Aschkenasim, despise us; the Sepharedim sometimes visit us, and we return their visits; still we only take wives from our own community, and we do not bury our dead with theirs. We are accustomed to industry and labour, because the assistance we receive from our brethren in the Crimea is very small. But in consequence of the famine of last year, our rich men have become poor, and the poor are without bread. You ask about books; we have none; the one book, which contains the wisdom of the whole world, is sufficient for us. I will show you our thora."

He then invited us to visit the synagogue. We first descended the stairs by which we had ascended, and then another flight of steps, which conducted us to a small subterraneous apartment, which was lighted by a square opening in the roof. A small glass lustre, with four burning lamps, mingled its rays with the light of day, without robbing the small synagogue, which was covered with beautiful carpets, of the charm of its magic gloom.

A silver plate is inserted behind the prayer-desk, over the holy ark, towards the east. It contains an incription in large letters of gold, through which the

Jewish confession of faith is brought under the notice
of every one who enters—"Hear, O Israel, the Lord
our God is one Lord." Their thora does not consist of leaves rolled together, as among all other sects,
but is written on parchment, in the form of a book,
with gold or painted initials and arabesques. The last
page contains information regarding the origin, the age,
and the writer of the manuscript in the following words,
"I, Moses, son of the blessed Menachem Dalbures,
have written this book, which is called 'Maknische,'
and given it to the honoured Rabbi Mordechai, the son
of the blessed Isack, as a worthy present, in the month
Siwan, in the 82nd year of the six thousandth year,
(5082.) May God grant that he meditate on the book,
he, and his children, and his children's children, to the
end of all generations. Amen. And may the word,
which is written, be verified: 'This book of the law
shall not depart out of thy mouth, but thou shalt meditate therein day and night, that thou mayest observe to
do according to all that is written therein; for then
thou shalt make thy way prosperous, and then thou
shalt have good success. Be strong. Amen. Selah.'"

Besides this book, there is also a thora on parchment
leaves rolled together, which has been written at a more
recent date.

When we came out of the synagogue and entered
the court, we found the whole community assembled.
All were dressed in their sabbath clothes. My host
directed my attention to the friendly bearing exhibited
by all; they evidently considered themselves honoured

by our visit. All of them bade us adieu, as if it were
with one mouth, while the President invited me to
repeat my visit.

Though they are perfectly independent in religious
matters, the Turkish Government regards the Chacham
Baschi as their spiritual head. All that he requires of
them is, that they shall at least outwardly observe and
respect the different Jewish festivals. Thus they would
not dare, even if it were permitted, to open their shops
on certain days.

A singular and mysterious event occurred in connection with the Karaites at Jerusalem. When, in the
year 1762, the Jews at Jerusalem were labouring under
great depression, and subjected to an exorbitant tax
by the Turkish Government, the Chacham Baschi
ordered a meeting to be held in the synagogue of the
Karaites, which, being subterraneous, as we have seen,
is in a manner concealed. When the Chacham Baschi
was descending the stairs, he suddenly became faint,
and stumbled. All were struck with this, and convinced that the place was haunted by evil spirits. They
soon removed the steps of the staircase, and found the
writings of Maimonides, which the Karaites had concealed under the staircase that they might tread upon
them with their feet. In consequence of this crime,
the Chacham Baschi condemned them to pay the tax,
and cursed them, that they should never have in their
community a Minjam, *i.e.* the ten men necessary for
prayer.

Rabbi Joseph Schwarz also gave me an account of

this tradition, and mentioned a remarkable circumstance which had come under his own observation. About twenty years ago several Karaitish families immigrated to Jerusalem from the Crimea. Great joy was felt in consequence in the small community, as they would now be sufficiently numerous to celebrate divine service as a congregation. But their joy was soon converted into horror. The immigrants were attacked by the plague before the city, and the men fell down dead from the city gate to the house of the Karaites; the rest died soon after in the house itself, and in this way again they had no Minjam.

The Literary Society, founded by Mr. Finn, the English Consul, has already a considerable library, containing valuable and learned works in the principal languages of Europe and Asia. The Museum is first in importance. One of the most interesting objects is a bas-relief of an old man in a sitting posture. The right hand is raised in an attitude of command; the head has the expression and formation of that of a Polish Rabbi; a slave is holding a parasol over it. It was presented by Layard, and Robinson was of opinion that it was a Sennacherib. Lamps, bracelets, heads of spears, &c., which were found on Lebanon, fragments of columns, capitals, volutes, shells, minerals, &c., were lying among one another in strange confusion. I was most attracted by several cwts. of heavy lumps of stone, which, on closer inspection, I found to be a mass of hundreds of thousands of very small purple shells, which had been sent here from Sidon. Mr. Finn promised, at my request, to send after me a similar specimen for the Imperial Museum of Vienna.

I visited the Anglican church, a plain, but handsome building, in the Gothic style. It rises with three pointed arches, between which are joists of brown wood. There is no cross on the altar. Instead of it there are two tablets of black marble, on which the Ten Commandments are engraven in Hebrew characters of gold. The pews are of plain, dark wood. The church is lighted in the evening by coloured glass globes supported on posts of oak. On one of the pews I found a prayer-book, which had been forgotten, in the Hebrew language. It contained the usual ancient Jewish prayers, with slight omissions, and interlineations on matters connected with the Christian faith. Thus the opinions and feelings of the recent convert to Christianity are not only spared, but, to speak more correctly, homage is done to them, and the neophyte is thus gradually habituated to the other faith. When all the Jewish converts residing in Jerusalem are assembled in this church, they form an imposing and numerous congregation. What other Jewish congregation in the world, even when all its members are assembled, can boast, like that at Jerusalem, of having a hundred and thirty baptized Jews in one church!

The Aschkenasim regard the Sepharedim as being less strictly orthodox, and this renders it all the more surprising that the Russian Jews alone have contributed 71 converts, or more than the half of the whole number, while the remaining 60 belong to almost every country

under the sun.  Conversion to Mohammedanism is very
rare.  The wife of an Austrian Jew fell in love with a
Turk, and when he brought her before the Pasha she
declared that she wished to become a Mohammedan.
The loving, and consequently most miserable, husband
had recourse to the consul, and requested him to
prevent his wife from becoming a convert to Islamism.
It happened that there was a flaw in the form ; when she
expressed her desire, in the presence of the Pasha,
there was not a dragoman present, and in consequence
of this her conversion was declared null and void.
After some time—in the interval the beautiful Pole had
been taught by her Turkish lover to read the Koran—
she was favoured with another audience, to which no
legal objection could be offered, but she declared that
she could no longer respect Mohammed as a prophet.
The fair penitent then left the house of the Turk, and
returned to her Jewish husband.

In the course of the last eight years, there have been
only four cases of Austrian subjects swearing by the
Koran.  The consul mentioned that he never offers any
obstacle to a change of religion, when it proceeds from
conviction, but that the convert to Islamism does not
cease to be an Austrian subject.  This fact prevents
some from apostatizing.

We cannot but be struck with the phenomenon of so
many Jewish converts to Christianity, and chiefly to
Protestantism, in the holiest city in the world, and with
the apparently important results of missionary labour,
but this impression is very much weakened if we

examine, from a religious and moral stand-point, the character of the sheep which have been brought within the fold by the shepherds. Even if I had been in a position to do so, it was not my design to investigate and to make myself acquainted with the means employed by the mission to induce the Jews to be baptized. But there is not the shadow of a doubt, at least at Jerusalem, that these holy fishers of men use a golden net, and every one who chooses to inquire about the matter will receive this reply.*

The Latins, also, only begin to support those who become Catholics after their conversion. The Protestants give earnest money, and demoralise families. When a father sternly rebukes his children, it is not unusual for them to reply with the insolent threat, " I will go to the Mission."

One day when I was walking with my host through the bazaar, I was addressed by a man, who asked me to make him a present of 3,000 piastres, which he owed to the mission; in this way I should save him, his wife, and six children from being baptized. This man had stolen 2,500 piastres, and as the Jews refused to intercede for the thief, out of revenge, he went to the Mission, and thus this noble Rhodian, certainly no Colossus of the faith, became a convert to Protestantism. This may serve as an example of the morals and

* The author, being a Jew, can scarcely be entitled to the character of an impartial witness regarding the operations of a Society, the avowed object of which is the conversion of his co-religionists.—T.

principles of those who, in the unalterable opinion of the Jews in the Holy Land, are converted into "idolaters" by the mission. It is notorious that many Jews go to Jerusalem for the express purpose of being baptized, because their baptism there is attended with greater advantage to themselves. It also frequently happens that these religious travellers receive baptism in the different cities which they visit on the way, probably as a preparatory process for their being re-baptized at Jerusalem.

The following witticism from the lips of a Jew may be given as an illustration of Jewish-Polish humour, and of the operations of the Missionary Society :—" Baptism was the only good business we had, and who has spoiled it ? The Jews themselves, by underselling one another."

If we could only close our eyes to the object which the mission has in view—but we cannot close our eyes to that which is immoral and bad—we should readily admit that it has conferred many material advantages on the Jews, and done much to promote civilization in the highest sense of the term. The mission has a well-managed hospital, with 36 beds, prepared for the poor of every creed ; a sewing-school, which affords employment to from 80 to 100 women ; a house of industry with 6 pupils, Polish boys, who are taught to be joiners and turners ; and an agricultural establishment, which employs 100 men. I often met these men in the evening, returning from their labour in a field, which the Missionary Society had bought. Many who are shy of receiving alms directly from the mission are employed here, chiefly to afford them a certain advantage, and thus attach them to the Society from gratitude. At all events, they are obliged to listen to a missionary sermon every evening. The sum received for a day's labour beneath the glare of the Syrian sun is only 4 piastres, and yet there are crowds who are anxious to earn it. I regard this fact as an additional proof that the mechanics and labourers, though very much oppressed, are by far the most respectable part of the Jewish population of Jerusalem, and that they are willing to use their hands even at the most painful kinds of labour.

The success of the mission is partly owing to the Jews themselves. While the conversion of a Jew to Christianity causes a painful sensation and excites surprise in a German or Austrian community, the same event is regarded with considerable indifference by the Jews at Jerusalem. It may be that they have grown indifferent owing to the frequency of the event, or that they are quite willing to make a present of the proselytes, who are usually not remarkable for their high moral principle, to the Society. The family of a convert, though grieved at first, are soon reconciled to the change, and the family ties are not dissolved; he visits them, he eats with them, he is still called "Reb," and addressed by his Jewish name. The family knows that, in most cases, his inward convictions have remained unchanged, and I have heard them say, " He will soon come back, after he has helped himself." Then there is great joy.

Cases of conversion to Judaism are very rare at Jerusalem. It is a duty positively enjoined on the Rabbis by the Talmud to hold back and to place obstacles in the way of every one who wishes to become a Jew. Rabbi Schamai forbids the Jews to attempt proselytizing, as the odious King Herod proceeded from the Idumeans, who were converted by force. I only made the acquaintance of two Jews in Jerusalem, who had been originally Christians; while I heard the names of a considerable number of Jews, who allowed themselves to be baptized, and afterwards returned to Judaism.

With some difficulty I at length prevailed on the Chacham Baschi to assemble the presidents of the different communities to decide regarding the proposed institution. The decisive meeting was held on the 2nd of July, and after a long and stormy discussion, it was resolved by a majority of 18 to 6 that the institution should be opened.

This resolution was a victory of the Sepharedim over the Aschkenasim, whose oppression had become more and more intolerable. Both parties appeared to be astonished; the Sepharedim at themselves, as they suddenly became conscious of their superior power, and felt themselves delivered from the moral oppression, which the foreigners, whom at first they had tolerated, had for a long time exercised over them in their native land. The Aschkenasim, on the other hand, were astonished at the boldness of an act of independence, of which, for many years, they had believed their indolent Oriental co-religionists incapable. At the same time, the establishment of the institution was a matter of sincere congratulation among the Sepharedim, who were deeply ashamed that they, the inhabitants of a city which the Jews deem to be the holiest on earth, should be without one. A short time before, also, after the proclamation of the "Hat Humayoum," the Chacham Baschi of the Turkish empire at Constantinople, had sent a circular to all the different Rabbis and communities, recommending them to open schools, and to provide for the religious and secular education of their youth. The chief congregation at Jerusalem, in consequence of the debt with which they were burdened, could never have complied with this recommendation, and it was quite a godsend to them to be unexpectedly provided from a distance with the means of being probably the first community in the large Turkish empire, that could carry out the wise intentions of the government.

Above all, the minority was obliged to yield to the moral influence of the majority. The Aschkenasim, being foreigners, could no longer disturb the Turkish subjects in the discharge of their civil duties. The majority, also, escaped from the humiliating thraldom of those who were hospitably received and protected, who are scarcely subject to any law, and who are grasping and tyrannical, like runaway slaves, that have become masters. They could not, and I here allude particularly to the Peruschim, bear this sudden act of independence on the part of the Sepharedim and their own defeat, and they therefore began to plot secretly against the execution of the solemn decision of a public assembly.

As I was not yet accustomed to the weakening influence of the climate, I felt all the more fatigued after the excitement and labours of the previous day. My medical friend advised me to wait a few days, till men's minds had become somewhat tranquillized, and, having met with some pleasant travelling companions, I undertook a trip to Jericho, to Jordan, to the Dead Sea, to the monastery of S. Saba, to Hebron, Bethlehem, and to Rachel's tomb. By hard riding I managed to accomplish the journey in four days, and instead of introducing it here as an episode, I shall give an account of it afterwards.

I arrived safely at Jerusalem again on the evening of Friday, the 6th of July, and was cordially welcomed by my friend, who was beginning to be anxious about my return, as the Sabbath was so close at hand. One of the Sepharedim, who brought me the key to Rachel's tomb, informed me that during my absence insulting placards had been stuck on the corners of the streets. I knew who were the worthless and ignorant authors of these insulting publications, which I read with the same curiosity and interest as if they had been a daily paper. But when one of them insulted my dead mother, the model of every virtue, in shocking terms, my self-restraint gave way, and I was deeply agitated. I seized my stick and passed through the gate, feeling as if all the horrors, that have ever found an appropriate home in this city, were dogging my heels.

As I passed over the dry bed of the brook Kidron, and ascended the Mount of Olives, I thought of that pathetic passage in the Book of Samuel, " And all the country wept with a loud voice, and the king passed over the brook Kidron; he went up by the ascent of Mount Olivet, and wept as he went up and had his head covered."

I slowly ascended the Mount of Olives, and reached the summit in half an hour. Before me lay the city of David. Deep down below, on the other side of the valley of Cedron, by which it is separated from the rocky mount with its ancient olives, rises the city of Zion, with its thousands of cupolas, battlements and terraces. None of the rooms in Jerusalem are flat-roofed. All of them are over-arched with cupolas, so that every house has as many cupolas as apartments, all of which are one story high. From the number of these cupolas, the city, which is situated on the sloping ridge of the hill, and shaped like an oblong pentagon, has an imposing appearance. The stones of which it is built have a light grey tinge, as the sun strikes upon them. As the eye wanders over this ocean of stone, it is attracted by two mountain waves, the cupolas of the Church of the Sepulchre. In the middle of this sea of cupolas rises a rocky island, shaped like an oblong square; on this platform stand two dark-grey, glittering mosques. It is Mount Moriah, with the mosques of ·Omar and Aksam. The narrow platform, on which the temple of Solomon stood, lies before us. A few large, dark cypresses tower from the midst of half-fallen arches, close to some ruinous buildings, and five palm-trees, all that Jerusalem contains, bend their leaves

like fans over the hot roofs.   Like captive gazelles, they
bear no fruit in Jerusalem.   The whole city is crowned
by Mount Zion.   Parti-coloured banners are fluttering
on five different buildings.   These are the flags of
Austria, France, England, Spain, and Prussia, hoisted
to-day because it is Sunday.   We do not hear the
sound of the bells, the hum of commerce does not reach
so high; a deep silence reigns over the city.   Its
environs, up to its picturesquely indented walls, are
naked, desolate, and full of sepulchres.   We do not see
a man or a beast.   It seems as if the pestilence were
raging within these walls, and the vultures and hyenas
were watching for the dead who have none to bury them.

Far away to the right rises a green hill, the Ramah
of the prophet, who is buried there, and, at a still
greater distance, glittering in the rays of the sun like
a lake of molten silver, lies the Dead Sea.   A dark
green, narrow stripe, visible only to the keenest eye,
marks the course of the Jordan, and behind it rise the
mountains of Moab, shutting out the desert from our
view.

On the top of the Mount of Olives is the little hamlet of Jebel Tur, in the centre of which stands a small
cupolaed building, supported on pillars, known as the
Chapel of the Ascension.   A monkish legend points to
a shapeless mark on the rock as the footprint of Christ
at his ascension, following the narrative of the Evange-
list Luke, according to which Christ parted with his disciples at Bethany and disappeared.   I ascended the
minaret of the little mosque, which is built close to the

chapel, in order to drink in with the eye and the soul the indelible impression of a scene, the actors on which, for the last three thousand years, have afforded abundant food for the intellect and the imagination.

We pass over those pious legends, which mark the locality of every word and of every deed; we make no allusion to those ingenious topographical researches, which lead to discoveries, soon to be displaced by others; * we are satisfied to gaze upon the great scene, while the thought passes through the mind :—" These are the still unshaken mountains, these are the actual valleys and gorges, this is the brook Kidron, that the pool of Siloah; this is the spot, unchanged by the lapse of time, where the spiritual destiny of man was decided in the most ancient and in more recent times for thousands of years."

I happened to be at Jerusalem during the feast of weeks. The communities of Palestine, whose knowledge of astronomy can scarcely be held superior to that of their brethren in Europe, have such confidence in their calculation of time, that they observe only one feast day, as in the time of the temple. I was therefore not a little surprised, when I was about to attend the usual service on the second day of the feast of weeks, to find that it was a working day among the Jews of Jerusalem. Foreign Jews who happen to be there, do not fail to observe two days, as at home.

The synagogue was not adorned with branches and

* M. de Saulcy is a fair specimen of this class of discoverers, or rather of inventors.—T.

flowers, as is usual with us, nor was the floor strewn
with fragrant rushes.  But at the opening of the Ark
of the Covenant, they sung a poem of the great Spanish
Hebrew poet, Ibn Esra, founded on the sublime song,
" Go forth, ye daughters of Zion, and behold King
Solomon with the crown wherewith his mother crowned
him in the day of his espousals, and in the day of the
gladness of his heart."

The singing of the Sepharedim is closely allied to
that of the Arabs; it is more rhythmical than melo-
dious, shrill rather than soft, and closely bordering on
snuffling.  On the whole, their singing is not quite so
disagreeable to the well-cultivated ear of a European
as what is called Polish singing, but it is certainly not
provocative of piety.  No doubt habit may have a
great deal to do in the matter.

One beautiful custom in the synagogues of Jerusalem is, that the priestly benediction is pronounced not
merely on high feast days as with us, it is offered up
daily, but at nine o'clock P.M., at the place where the
Jews weep over the destruction of the temple.

The morning-prayer is repeated four times every
morning on week days, in the chief Sepharedisch synagogue, " de las Stambulis," so that every one, even
after the commencement of the labour of the day, may
take part in it.

The summons to morning-prayer is a peculiar
custom.  When the oldest Rabbi in the institution
Beth-el, in which the Talmud is studied the whole night,
observes the first dawn of early morn, he despatches a

messenger to the roof of the institution, which commands an extensive view towards the East. There he announces in a loud voice, like the muezzin of the Mohammedans from the minarets, that it is the hour for prayer. The commencement of the Sabbath is announced to the Sepharedim by the cry " ascender," " light up," and immediately thousands of windows are illuminated, and from the synagogue is heard the fervent salutation, " Lecho Daudi, likras kalo ! "

My attention was directed to a large ruinous house, which seemed to me suitable, after some repairs, for the institution. According to Oriental customs, the negociations with the landlord were carried on for a considerable time. He required several days, and then several hours, before he could decide. At length we took a lease of the house for three years, for 6,000 piastres, and the wealthy proprietor, in true Turkish fashion, demanded a " backschiesch," or *pourboire*, after the bargain was completed. We gave him 150 piastres, with which he appeared to be satisfied.

After the lease had been written out, in Arabic, at the Austrian Consulate, it was signed, and copies retained by both parties. A document was afterwards drawn up, conveying to me the right of " chasaka." It is a great matter to have the right of " chasaka" over a house at Jerusalem, and a decided advantage for the Jews. No Jew can hire a house, on which another has the right of " chasaka," and thus the poor are protected from having their houses taken over their heads by the rich, and also from having the rent raised by

the landlords, most of whom are Mohammedans. The
" chasaka" may be sold—nay, it is even hereditary
and often fetches several thousand piastres.

I now entered on a new field of activity. The house
had to be cleaned, improved and whitewashed, the
doors to be taught to shut, the windows to be provided
with glass, and the whole to be freshly painted.
Tables, benches, and writing-desks had to be prepared
for the school-room; and thus, I suddenly passed from
the circle of the Rabbis into that of the workmen and
handcraftsmen.

I cannot conceal the fact that my entrance into their
society was far more pleasant and agreeable to me. I
saw sleek-looking men, who had, indeed, been brought
here by their longing after the Holy Land, but who
were pious and honest, good-humoured and capable of
providing for all their wants, and who, while dissatisfied with the government of the Rabbis, do not fail
devoutly to observe all the precepts of religion, which
the latter esteem to be holy.

They form in every way a respectable and important
part of the Jewish population of Jerusalem. I did
not require to employ Mohammedans or Christians for
any kind of labour; the Jews could do all that I
required.

Some brief statistics regarding the Jewish workmen
may be here introduced. While I was at Jerusalem
there were 1 mason, 2 stone-cutters, 12 joiners, 1 locksmith, 2 blacksmiths, 6 tinsmiths, 5 watchmakers, 1
knife-grinder, 2 lapidaries, 5 silver and gold smiths, 5

bookbinders, 6 lace-makers, 20 or 24 tailors, 15 shoe-ma-
kers, 2 dyers, 5 barbers, 10 bakers, 3 sugar-bakers, 30
or 40 distillers of brandy (all Poles and Russians) or
manufacturers of wine. These latter buy the grapes
produced at Hebron. Among the other kinds of employment at Jerusalem may be mentioned 40 *melam-
dim*, 5 writers, 2 musicians, 12 merchants, 20 shop-
keepers, 3 agents of exchange, and 10 or 12 hawkers.

The Aschkenasim are admitted to be the best workmen; they have learned their different trades in Europe;
they are, also, more numerous than the Sepharedim.
If we count the whole number of those who are thus
employed, we find that they amount to 239 persons, so
that only the twenty-fourth part of the whole popula-
lation is engaged in any kind of industrial labour; and
5,461 persons, including men, women, and children,
spend their lives in idleness, without earning anything
for their support.

It is deeply to be regretted that many Jewish workmen, who come to Jerusalem with the honest intention
of making their own bread, soon abandon their different
trades, which no doubt are more exhausting in a hot
climate, and live on alms. For example, about sixteen
years ago, a tailor, dressed in the European fashion,
made his way from Amsterdam to Jerusalem: the last
production of his needle was a Polish suit, made a
short time before his arrival. He at once renounced his
trade, and, following in the footsteps of his tailoring
countryman, the Prophet John of Leyden, he became
a president, and of course wealthy. A tailor from

Bavaria, who had previously tried to make his fortune in America, and at length succeeded by a marriage at Jerusalem, had to give up his trade, because his aristocratic spouse at Jerusalem told him roundly, " I do not sit," *i. e.* I will not live, "with a tailor," and they now both live very comfortably on alms.　When such ideas are prevalent, we need not be surprised that the industrial school, which, like all the other improvements introduced by Mr. Albert Cohen at Jerusalem, though founded with the best intentions, was not at first accompanied with much success.　A fresh impetus has been given to it recently through the active and intelligent management of Dr. Neumann.

The idleness of the parents produces its natural effect on the children, the feeling of honour, even when excited, is soon blunted by the universal receipt of alms.　In Jerusalem alone, where every word of the Bible is regarded as sacred, the command of the Bible, "In the sweat of thy face shalt thou eat bread," is practically ignored.

Lastly, the strength requisite for labour is destroyed by their early marriages.

When I visited the Trades' school, where the pupils are taught to translate the Bible, I found the Aschkenasisch and Sepharedisch boys separated from one another, and occupying two different rooms.　They were thirty in number, and three of them were pointed out to me by their teacher, Mr. Schiffman from Prague, as bridegrooms who were on the eve of being married.

I found the girls' school, which was founded at the

same time, and in which instruction is given in reading
Hebrew, in prayer and embroidery, in a languishing
condition. This institution, which was at once practically conceived and generously endowed, had a
splendid commencement, but soon ceased to function.
I found three girls in one room and five in another.
Three other rooms were empty. The girls were sitting
there doing nothing. The female teacher explained
that there was a marriage to-day, and the children had
run out; also that it was their dinner hour, and they
had gone home. It was 4 o'clock P.M., and of course
could not be their dinner hour. The benches of the
schoolroom were so covered with dust that it was
evident that no pupils could have sat on them for a
long time; the black boards were lying on the ground
half broken. Nor was the appearance of the industrial
school for girls, founded by Sir Moses Montefiore, in a
house for the rent of which for three years 18,000
piastres are expended, besides other 8,000 for repairs
and contingencies, at all more encouraging.

In one schoolroom I counted twenty-one children,
some of whom were sewing, but most of them were
sleeping, apparently in imitation of the example of their
teacher, whom I found in another room stretched out
on a carpet with six girls by her side asleep. My
guides, Messrs. Fränkel and Neumann, pointed out to
me some brides of from eight to ten years of age, who
were proudly conscious of their position. There are
five teachers connected with this school. The sleeper
was the only one we saw. In one room were lying six

or seven hundred pieces of cotton cloth, manufactured
by the girls, and intended for the poor.

We must give the parents credit for sending their
children to school, but they have their own reasons
for doing so. All institutions founded by Europeans
for the purpose of promoting education and civilisation
are not regarded by them as benefits in any sense of
the term, but rather as a sort of amusement, to which
some of their rich co-religionists in Europe treat themselves. But then they must pay for their amusement,
more especially as they erect themselves into a sort of
father confessors, and interfere with the religious
convictions of others. No one in the different communities seems to esteem it an honour to further or super-
intend these institutions for promoting piety among the
whole community. And even when a Rabbi is induced
to accept office, he discharges its duties remissly
enough, without any moral purpose, without any
higher aim than—backschiesch.

What pain these nobleminded men must have felt,
when they visited Jerusalem soon after I left, and saw
the state of these institutions!—trees which, though
planted by pious hands, and in the true spirit of civilisation, have never been able to strike their roots
into the stony soil of the Holy Land. Through sympathy with them, I was filled with anger and sorrow.
Moreover, I could not banish the thought from my own
mind, that I had come here to expend my time and
energies on a dangerous and disagreeable work, that
perhaps would be attended with no better success.

And the question ever arose in my mind, how these schools could exist here without opposition on the part of the Jewish population, especially schools for girls, the education of whom is considered in the East to be perfectly unnecessary, as even their appearance beyond the bounds of the family circle is directly opposed to Oriental ideas.

" You now see quite clearly," said one of my guides, " that an opposition from abroad has been artfully and wickedly organized against you. Besides, there were other causes at work, which operated in favour of the establishment of these schools. Mr. Albert Cohen arrived suddenly and unexpectedly, and before the Jewish population had time to deliberate; this energetic man, by his enthusiasm and eloquence, carried the minds of all along with him, in which he was aided by the universally popular name of Rothschild. His hands were full of gold, which he generously distributed. All other thoughts were vanquished by the benefits immediately secured. This was, also, the case with Montefiore ; and yet when this benefactor of the Holy Land, this strictly orthodox man, on the occasion of his third visit, was planning institutions, and had no more money to throw away, they excommunicated him, and certainly not for the reason assigned—because he had entered the mosque of Omar, which is built on the site of the temple of the All-holy."

An institution for advancing money as loans was also founded by Mr. Albert Cohen, and endowed by the Rothschild family with 100,000 piastres. Mr. Isack

Alteras, one of the Sepharedim and an Austrian subject, being entrusted with the management of it, lent
40,000 piastres to the presidents of the Sepharedim.
All of them regarded the money not as a means of
benefiting others by advancing loans without interest,
but as a means of benefiting themselves by lending it
out at usury.   One-half of the money thus advanced
with the best intentions was lost, notwithstanding repeated efforts on the part of the Austrian Consul to
recover it.

As a contrast to the melancholy picture presented in
the previous pages, we shall here give some account of
another institution—the hospital founded by the Rothschild family, which has been fraught with the richest
blessings, and calls forth our admiration.

The house is situated on the summit of one of the
declivities of Mount Zion.   The visitor first enters a
large airy court, surrounded by four walls, so that it
forms a large square.   Along the walls are doors leading
to the sick-rooms, to the apothecary's shop, to the
kitchen, and to the servants' apartments.

The object of the different rooms is written on the
white-washed walls, over every door, in blue Hebrew
characters.   All the rooms have glass windows; the
frames, the bedsteads, and the different articles of furniture are painted a bright green, so that the whole
establishment, remarkable for its cleanliness and orderly
arrangements, produces a very favourable impression.
The different beds, eighteen in number, are called
after the benefactors of Palestine, whose names are

written in Hebrew characters, over the heads of the patients.

In the year 1856, 542 patients were received into the hospital, of whom 505 were cured, 18 were still under treatment, and 19 dead. Four per cent. cannot but be regarded as a very low rate of mortality. 267 of the patients were from Turkey, 144 from Russia, 16 from Poland, 33 from Moldavia, 37 from Austria and Germany, 24 from France and Algiers, and the remaining 21 belonged to Italy, England, the United States, Morocco, Abyssinia, and Persia.

None but Israelites are admitted, but in the ambulances, which I sometimes met at an early hour in the morning, might also be seen Christians and Mohammedans, who likewise received advice and medicine gratuitously. 30,135 prescriptions were served at the apothecary's shop in one year. The expense for medicines used in the hospital amounted to 758 francs; the ambulance cost 2,020 francs; the expenses 4,401 francs, the management 5,088 francs. The support of the whole establishment, light, water, &c., cost 14,541 francs—certainly not a large sum, considering the relief which it affords to the suffering poor.

It appears, from recent information, that the Rothschild family has expended other 300,000 francs on the enlargement and improvement of the hospital, but the money necessary for the support of additional patients is still wanting. It is to be hoped that our co-religionists in all lands will not delay sending their contributions to aid in the promotion and completion of this truly philanthropic work—a work which is a permanent benefit to the Jews in Jerusalem, and a permanent memorial of those who have called it into being, or may afterwards aid in promoting its usefulness.

Sir Moses Montefiore bought a large piece of ground, which slopes down toward the valley of Jehoshaphat and looks toward Mount Zion, for the purpose of erecting a hospital. The purchase of this site met with much opposition, because 1,000l. seemed too much, though the broken stones on the ground alone were worth that sum, and because it is situated outside the walls of the city. The superior healthiness of the locality is questionable, as the neighbouring burying-ground of the Turks, who inter their dead at a depth of only two feet, is surrounded by anything but a pure atmosphere. The situation also is attended with many inconveniences; the gates are strictly closed at sunset; a person taken suddenly ill at night cannot be conveyed to the hospital; for the same reason the relatives of a dying person cannot be admitted to see him at night. But even during the day it must be difficult for a patient to get to the bottom of the steep declivity before the Jaffa gate in the glowing heat of the sun, which he must do before reaching the hospital. Besides, houses outside the city walls are not always quite safe from the attacks of the roving Bedouins, and when there is any reason to dread a sudden attack, or the introduction of the plague, the city is shut up, which renders access to a hospital situated outside the walls impossible. The foundation-stone was laid by Sir Moses Montefiore in 1855, and the extensive site is enclosed by a massive wall. Round it lie the luxuriant pleasure-grounds of the Greek monastery. Dr. Frankel shewed me a lithographed plan of the intended hospital by the English architects, Wyatt, Papworth, and Thomas Allason. The wards and arrangements are nobly conceived, and the front so imposing that the building looks more like a mediæval castle than a hospital. A builder was expected from England to execute the work.

Dr. Neumann kindly called on me one evening, as he often did, to take me out for a walk. Passing through the bazaar, we ascended a street that leads to the Jaffa gate. Before reaching it, we observed on the right shops which frequently reminded us of those of a small provincial town. A bookbinder's, the printing establishment of the Missionary Society, a Nuremberg warehouse, a tailor's shop with a sign, the only one that we saw in Jerusalem, and so on. On the left is a large open space with an ancient building believed to be the tower of David, from the battlements of which he looked down and saw the beautiful Bath-sheba bathing. Passing a long train of camels waiting to be relieved of their burdens, we see, hard by the gate, the large house occupied by the Latin patriarch, and the patriarch himself—a tall figure with a long black beard, and a black *talare*—walking up and down on the roof, enjoying the coolness of the evening breeze.

We pass through the lofty vestibule of the gate, and

find ourselves in the open country. Here, at the foot of the steep declivity, a group of leprous women are begging in a piteous tone. We drop down a few pieces of money for them, as all are careful not to touch them. Descending, we reach the valley, and climbing up a small, steep, rocky eminence, we find on its summit a beautiful plantation of olives and vines, the property of the Greek monastery. The fresh green sward is variegated with pomegranate trees covered with red blossom. In the midst of this luxuriant verdure, which in itself is a sufficient refutation of the superstitious belief that the soil of Jerusalem is cursed and can produce nothing, is a large terrace enclosed with low walls. In the centre is a cistern, in the background a vineyard. The landlord is always ready to supply his visitors with coffee and the narghilé. A small motley circle of the inhabitants of Jerusalem assembles here every evening to enjoy the cool breeze. Boys are busily engaged in play; their parents sit and look on in solemn silence.

But when the sun begins to set, and to light up the mountains of Moab, the Mussulmans start to their feet, and each one retiring apart engages in prayer. This feeling of nearness to God, altogether independent of fixed places of worship, on every spot on earth and without the intermediation of a praying or chanting priest, seemed to me a beautiful expression of the belief in the omnipresence of God, and of our childlike confidence that He will directly hear our prayers.

Towards evening, after the heat of the day is over, a cool refreshing breeze begins to blow on this hill and to shake the young plantations, the almond and the olive trees, the pomegranates and the vines. It looks as if the mount was waving thousands of green banners in honour of the victory which has been won by the cultivation of the soil. After it has seized these outposts, it will not stand still, but advance, up and down the valleys. However much the Latins in their jealousy may complain of the Greeks continually increasing their landed property, there is reason to desire that a still larger part of the soil were in their possession. It holds specially true here, that wherever capital and labour are employed, the naked rocky soil is converted into a garden.

I always took refuge on this terrace, when worn out with the toils and cares of the day, and was always sorry to be obliged to return to the town before seven o'clock. The Turkish Government treats the town as a fortress, and the Military Commandant delivers up the keys of the city to the Pasha at the hour we have just mentioned. Every one that is late must spend the night in the open air, which it is not always safe to do.

There is always a lively scene near the gate before it is closed. Riders rush over the stony path on lean horses, covered with parti-coloured mountings; solitary camels, loaded with their burdens, advance with phlegmatic tread; men may be seen driving donkeys before them, or seated behind the burdens on their backs. A group of veiled women, dressed in white, and glittering in the red rays of the setting sun, starts up in the valley; priests in black talares, French "dames de Zion," Polish and Sepharedisch Jews, labourers and effendis, are all approaching the gate at such a pace as to enable them to reach it in time, and yet linger till the last moment in the open air. The sentinels are sitting in the lofty, dark vestibule, or shouting to those at a distance to accelerate their pace.

On this occasion we leave the hill sooner than usual, cross the valley and return to the Jaffa gate. We do not enter, but turning to the right, we walk along the wall of the city, till we reach the gate of Zion, within which we intend to pay a visit.

One of my most pleasant reminiscences of Jerusalem is connected with that friendly, kind, and highly respectable man, Don Jose Perez. He paid me a visit, soon after my arrival at Jerusalem, for the purpose of inviting me to see his property on Mount Zion, which he has earned by his labour as a husbandman, and sent me some excellent potatoes, the produce of his skill as an agriculturist, and a valuable present in Jerusalem. Think of potatoes on Mount Zion!

After walking for about twenty minutes, with the valley of Hermon below on our right, we reached the gate of Zion, passed through its lofty portal, and descending, crossed over some desolate heaps of ruins, till we came to the small gate of a garden, enclosed with a wall. Don Perez gave us the most friendly welcome. I saluted him with the words, "I am delighted to find myself in the house of an heir to the property of King David." As he would not accept the hand which I held out to him, because his own was dirty with digging in the soil, I grasped it warmly: "It is a pleasure to me to press a hand hardened with honest toil."

He led us through garden-beds, carefully kept, to a plain stone house, which stands on the uneven summit of the hill. Cucumbers and melons, flowers and potatoes, were blossoming and bearing fruit, and one of the only five palm-trees that are to be seen in Jerusalem was towering over the depths below. It rose like King Saul, "from his shoulders and upward he was higher than any of the people." Don Perez broke off some of the leaves of the palm-tree, and gathered some of the flowers in his garden, and gave them to me as a *souvenir* of Mount Zion, and also a bottle of valuable oil, which he had pressed from a rhycnius planted by himself, as a gift "for the noble foundress of a school in Jerusalem." He lamented that the Jews were not placed in a position to enable them to cultivate the soil of the Holy Land, which would reward them a hundred fold. "Why," he asked, "does Europe send sum after sum to be swallowed up in an abyss? The land might become again as it was, before the Lord destroyed Sodom and Gomorrah, even as the garden of the Lord, like the land of Egypt, as thou comest unto Zoar."

One part of his garden is surrounded by the wall of the city, near which there is a deep hollow, covered with gigantic cactuses. We walked along the wall, to which we ascended by steps behind the embrasure. Don Perez directed our attention to an opening far down below, in the rock beneath the wall, where, according to a Jewish tradition, Nachmanides Rambam held divine service, when he came to Jerusalem.

The sun had set beyond the Jordan and the mountains of Moab, from which Moses the teacher saw the promised land, which he was not permitted to enter, and where, according to tradition, he died in consequence of a kiss from God. The ridges of the mountains, as they were illuminated by the golden rays of the setting sun, cast their gigantic shadows over the surrounding country.

A fresh breeze began to blow; we left the parapet of the wall, and came to the miserable abodes of the lepers. The Arabs call them Biut el Masakin, the abodes of the unfortunate. These poor creatures spend their loathsome and miserable lives in sixteen ruinous hovels, roughly built of stones and mortar, and covered with dry twigs and stones. From sixty to seventy lepers, Don Perez told me, languish here and are dead even before they die. This hamlet is certainly the only one in the whole of the Mohammedan countries in the east where both races live together. There are no Jews, but there are some Christians among them. A scheik rules over these unfortunate creatures, whose children are healthy and active, till they are about seven years of age. The appearance of the adults is revolting in the extreme; but the description of this loathsome disease should be confined to works on medicine.

After a few days, I repeated my visit to Don Perez,

in company with a Russian Jew, Reb Mosche Schnitzer
(carver), so called because he carves the most beautiful
objects in wood, or chisels them out of marble and sand-
stone, or makes them of asphalt from the Dead Sea,
suchas basins, cups, or bas-reliefs of the places which the
Jews regard as sacred.   He brought this art, in which
he is self-taught, and which his young son has learned,
from his native home.   He received a prize at the
great Exhibition at London, and the foundation stone
of the *Votivkirche* at Vienna was cut by Reb Mosche
Schnitzer, after a design by Ehdlicher, the architect.
But the skill of this member of the community of the
Pharisees is not confined to chiselling foundation-stones
for churches and synagogues; he manufactures also the
only *Bal schem*, *i.e.* workers of miracles in Jerusalem—
mysterious amulets against sickness, or for the benefit of
barren women, which find their way to Bagdad and
Bombay, to the ancient Mizraim (Egypt) and Algiers,
and are esteemed precious, and held in the highest
repute by the superstitious.

I brought him with me, after having obtained the
kind permission of Don Perez, to break a stone on
Zion, which was to be prepared by his chisel for the
foundation-stone for the new temple which is being
erected at Vienna.    The wonderful old man went
knocking with his hammer here and there on the projecting pieces of rock, and singing *sotto voce* strange
melodies.    Were they incantations, or were they pious
prayers?    At length, after the sound which followed
one of the strokes of his hammer, he said, "That is a

fine stone; have it dug out, Mereno!" Mereno is the
title of honour awarded to a theologian or to a doctor
of medicine.

I soon had the masons at work, and, with the aid of
the conjuror, a beautiful block of limestone was soon
excavated, which he cut, in the most workman-like
style, into a box, shaped like a sarcophagus, after a
design by Mr. Endlicher. I had the following verses
from the Psalms cut out on the sides in raised gold
letters:—

" Out of Zion, the perfection of beauty, God hath
shined," and, "For thy servants take pleasure in her
stones, and favour the dust thereof."

The ends were marked with the year, the name of
the holy city, and of the place from which the stone
was taken. The upper part was covered with bas-
reliefs of the arms of David, and of clusters of grapes,
the symbol of fruitfulness.

Don Perez asked me to procure for him vines from
Hungary, and different seeds of vegetables and flowers
unknown in Palestine, as he wished to try to rear
them on Zion, and to introduce them into the country.
After my return, I sent him a rich supply of all that
he requested. Madam von Herz Lämel showed her
appreciation of the fragrant oil and flowers from Mount
Zion by sending him a beautiful silver goblet. But it
was not to be the destiny of this amiable and excellent
man ever to fill it with the warm blood of Tokai. The
valley of Jehoshaphat had received him into its bosom
before our gifts reached Jerusalem.

I was invited to a marriage ceremony, and went to the synagogue of Zion, where the Chacham Baschi and his Besdin, and the bridegroom surrounded by his male relations, were assembled for prayer, before marching in solemn procession to the house of the bride. The Chacham Baschi wore a wide white robe, and a white turban, while the rest of the Chachams appeared in coloured clothes and bluish grey turbans.

On our way to the bridal abode, we met a troop of women in white dresses, with long white veils covering the head. The procession was closed by a girl—a mere child—dressed in the same way; her eyes were closed, and she was led by two women. Drums and fifes intermingled their shrill and hollow sounds. The child was a bride, and was thus solemnly conducted to the bath, before being led to her husband. We allowed the procession to precede us. The Chachams were especially careful to avoid being touched by any part of the women's dresses.

Having arrived at the house where the marriage was to be celebrated, we ascended a narrow stone staircase to a small terrace, where a large drum and a clarionet were murdering a duet in the most barbarous manner. In the room, women in white dresses were pressing close to one another, in silence, like doves in a storm; their children were playing around them. In the next room, over the entrance to which a coloured silk curtain, borrowed from the synagogue, was suspended, another curtain was extended in the form of a tent, with coarse tinsel fluttering around its borders. Beneath this

marriage canopy stood the bride; she wore a richly
embroidered dress, covered with gold lace. The pattern
represented a *corbeille* of flowers, while glittering spangles of different colours were substituted for diamonds;
over this dress she wore a silk caftan, red as a poppy,
and also adorned with gold. No wreath encircled her
loose hair, as the brides of Jerusalem are forbidden to
wear them, as an expression of sorrow for the destruction of the holy city. She kept her eyes firmly closed,
as etiquette required that she should not open them
before reaching the bridal chamber. The child's hands
were pressed to her waist, to represent the girdle, soon
to be unloosed. I call the bride a child, for she was
only twelve years old, and looked like any other child
of the same age in the West. On her right stood the
bridegroom, a boy of fourteen years; he wore a white
woollen caftan, and a bluish grey turban, like a Chacham, for, as I was told, he was studying the Talmud,
and it was hoped that he would continue his studies
till he became a learned Rabbi. While he was repeat-
ing the usual forms of marriage, he placed a gold ring
on the bride's finger; then both were covered with a
white cassock, as a sign that they now belonged to one
another, while all the spectators said, "simon tow," *i.e.*,
may it be a good sign.

After this, an embossed paper, covered with ornamental writing in different colours, was unfolded; it
contained the "Kesuba," the marriage contract, which
was read aloud. The women brought in a silver dish,
on which lay two live fishes, which they placed on the

floor. This was the symbol of fruitfulness, and the bride, still conducted by two women, advanced slowly and like a statue, and stepped thrice across it, while the spectators, each time, solemnly repeated the words of the Bible, "Be fruitful, and multiply." When the bridegroom, after this, stepped across the fishes, he did so in the midst of laughter and general hilarity.

The impression produced on my mind by the whole ceremony was a painful one; the bridal pair looked like two puppets, with which their seniors were playing at marriage. The rigid repose of the bride, all of whose movements, as she was led forward and backward by the women, seemed to be mechanical, her closed eyes and silent lips, all tended to strengthen the belief that I was gazing at a marionette.

On the same day I was invited to a marriage feast; but as I only wished to see another stage of the ceremonies, I did not go before 8 o'clock, P. M. My host accompanied me. We entered on the Almeidan into the only house with two stories in Jerusalem. On a small terrace, on the first story, young girls were sitting round a pan of charcoal, cooking coffee, striking tambourines with bells, and singing an Arab song; all were smoking, and the water in their pipes was gurgling.

We passed this strange group, and ascended by a staircase to a rather large square room. Along the walls were the usual divans, the men were seated on the right, along with the bridegroom; on the opposite side sat the women with the bride. She wore a bright red satin dress, a brown silk jacket, embroidered with gold, and a turban, from which a white veil descended over her shoulders. She wore also a necklace of pearls, and a long gold chain round her neck, while her arms and hands were adorned with bracelets and rings. The men and the women, with the exception of the bridegroom, were all smoking; some of them used narghilés, others chibouques. All stood up to salute us as we entered. After we had taken our seats, and lighted the chibouques, with which we were at once supplied, the bride advanced to me and my companion, and, after applying her hand to her heart, her forehead, and her mouth, respectfully kissed our hands.

The room was only imperfectly lighted, and we sat, for the most part in silence, drinking coffee and enveloped in clouds of blue smoke. It looked as if the guests had met on some mournful occasion. At length the men asked where the girls were, and why they did not come and dance. They were summoned, and Sultane—a name which corresponds with the Latin *regina* and the Hebrew *malke*—entered. She was a girl of about ten years of age, and wore a coloured chintz dress, fastened at the waist with a woollen girdle, and a silk jacket open in front. Her smoothly flowing hair was interwoven with dark blue silk thread, like a loose cue, and adorned with tinsel: her complexion was dark, her lips red, her eyes sparkling. She moved in a circle, dancing and singing, while the men clapped their hands. Then she applied, by turns, her right hand and her left hand to her forehead, like a soldier saluting, and stretched her arms straight out, after which she drew them back like a bow, and again put her hands to her forehead. Sometimes she only placed her arms on her waist, advancing and retreating with a quick step, or took hold of her dress and bent and bowed, as we do when dancing a minuet. There was something stiff and angular in all her movements, the features of the dancer were entirely destitute of expression, and the whole performance looked like a marionette mimicking a dancer.

Several girls followed; they never formed a group, but all danced separately. In the East the men do not dance, it is beneath their dignity; still there are some professional dancers, but, like our jugglers, they are not in much repute.

The company, at times, expressed aloud their admiration of the dancers, in which, of course, as a matter of courtesy, I warmly joined. The monotony of this dance, performed by all without the smallest deviation from the established forms, and the absence of all intellectual or other enjoyment at this ascetic ceremony, soon brought on an attack of *ennui* from which I was glad to escape. We rose to take our departure. The bride again kissed our hands. All the guests rose from their seats.

All was dark without, except the stars, which are larger and brighter than in the West. No one in the streets, no sound, save here and there the barking of dogs disturbed by some one returning home. We were obliged to take a circuitous path; the nearest way was through the bazaar, but it is closed at sunset. We entered a narrow street, in one of the houses of which we observed a light. Five Turks in white dresses were sitting cross-legged in the hall, smoking. A Bedouin in a brownish yellow cloak was squatting on the ground opposite to them and reading a letter; a young Abyssinian slave was kneeling, and holding the stump of a candle to enable him to see. The figures, with their shadows sometimes reflected by the light on the black, sooty walls, and sometimes concealed, formed a fine picturesque group. I entered with my companion, who knows every one at Jerusalem. We found ourselves in the house of an effendi, a friend of Montefiore's. He was having a letter, which he had just received from Abd-el-Kadr, read to his friends. We met with a friendly reception, and were entertained with coffee and chibouques. When I mentioned that I had visited the valiant Emir at Damascus, and conversed with him, I had to give the effendi a description of the appearance and dress, the language and manners, of the "lion of the wilderness."

# CHAPTER III.

THE Oriental Jews do not recognize the law of monogamy laid down by Rabbi Gerschon in the twelfth century, and among them a man is allowed to marry two wives, but only in two cases—when his wife has no children, or has only girls. The wife cannot resist the will of the husband, but she has the right to refuse to receive the second wife into the house. In this case, the husband, if he still persists in having another wife, must provide a separate establishment for her. As this involves considerable expense, polygamy is not so common, even among the Mohammedans, whose wives are invested with the same right, as is believed in the west.

There are six cases of double marriage in Jerusalem. In the year 1856 there were 16 cases of divorce, 6 among the Aschkenasim and 10 among the Sepharedim.

I had expressed a desire, if any death should occur, to be present at the funeral, and to take part in the last honours shown to the deceased. It so happened, that in company with my host I visited an elderly Rabbi, who had been suffering from fever for some days. He lay on a carpet, which was spread out in a corner of the dimly-lighted room, and could not specify the exact nature of his sufferings—only he felt languid and feverish. After prescribing for the patient, I promised to return to see him in the morning, on which he replied, " Ere morning I shall stand before God." When we had left the house, Dr. Fränkel said to me,— " The patient is right; fever in Jerusalem often kills rapidly. On my first arrival here, I often found myself in a very painful position in consequence of this fact."

On the following day I was actually invited to the

Rabbi's funeral. The street before the house of mourn-ing was crowded with men. It was with difficulty that I forced my way into the court of the house, where the wife and daughter of the deceased were sitting on the ground, surrounded by about twenty women. All were dressed in white, and ever and anon, after a pause, raised a strange, howling cry, which sounded like a huzza, while they passionately beat their breasts, their foreheads, and their cheeks.

The dead body, dressed in white, was extended on the floor of the room. A wax taper was burning at its head and another at its feet, in order that the soul, which must tarry by the body till the first clod of earth is cast upon it, may be able to do penance by contem-plating the tenement in which it has so often sinned. A considerable number of men were seated in a circle on the floor, and listening to a speaker who praised the virtues of the deceased; they sometimes interrupted him with passionate bursts of weeping. After this the body was carefully washed.

The number of men crowded into the small room, and the heat of the sun—it was 2 o'clock P.M.—obliged me to go out and wait for the funeral procession in front of the house. Here was heard the cry of the servant of the synagogue, "Bitul melacha," "Cease from work," and all the shops were closed, for "a prince in Israel" was dead. Loud dirges and violent cries of passionate grief proceeded from the house.

The body, covered with a coloured carpet, was now carried to the door of the house. Here some men were holding two poles, which were bound together with iron hooks, so that the bier resembled a wooden ladder with iron steps. The body was placed on the bier, which was then deposited on the ground. A speaker, after a white robe with fringes had been spread over the body, again raised his voice and spoke in praise of the deceased, while his discourse was often interrupted by the tears and wailings of the numerous crowd.

At the conclusion of this second discourse, the men raised the bier, which all followed in irregular procession. The bearers, who were relieved in turn from the crowd, sung the psalm, " He that dwelleth in the secret place of the Most High, shall abide under the shadow of the Almighty." A fearful shout of grief, which, as before, sounded like a wild huzza, arose from the roof of the house. I looked up, and saw on the roof female figures covered with long white veils. They were mourners, and as they stretched out their hands toward heaven, they looked like the dead risen from their graves in their white winding-sheets, and chanting a death-song in wild, unearthly chorus. The sun shed his brilliant rays over all these scenes and groups, and gave greater prominence to these skeleton-like figures.

The procession again halted near the chief synagogue; the bier was placed on the ground and another funeral discourse delivered. The procession then passed through the gate of Zion, as usual, when, after another eulogy on the deceased, most of the people returned to the city. We descended the steep declivity to the valley of Jehoshaphat. The bier was again laid down at

Absalom's tomb, and we seated ourselves in a circle on the ground to listen to a fifth funeral discourse on the text, " Let the whole house of Israel bewail the burning which the Lord hath kindled." The peroration was grounded on the words, " It is appointed unto all men to die."

When the body was deposited in the grave, we repeated the Jewish Confession of Faith.

The deceased breathed his last at two o'clock, and was buried two hours and a-half after his death. There is, at least, this advantage in being buried without a coffin, and covered with earth, that it saves one from the fearful possibility of awakening in a vault from which there is no means of escape. Mohammedans and Christians in the East shew the same haste in burying their dead.

It is a merry funeral, if we may be allowed the expression, when torn prayer-books, loose leaves of the Holy Scriptures and the Talmud, or pieces of the thora, written on parchment, which it is unlawful to convert to profane purposes or to destroy, are buried in the ground. The pious collect them and place them in a niche in the wall of the synagogue of Zion, intended for that purpose. When it is full, the contents are borne by the Rabbi, in the midst of singing and the sound of the drum and the fife, in solemn procession to the valley of Jehoshaphat, and buried in a grave at the foot of Absalom's tomb.

A thora roll, buried in this way, was found some years ago by a priest, and carried to Rome as a valu-

able archæological discovery,* but the eyes of the
learned were opened by a simple Rabbi, acquainted
with this custom.

The house was now finished, and ready for the opening of the institution, but meanwhile an event of an
unpleasant nature had occurred. Water in Jerusalem
is a valuable article, especially during the summer
months, when a large portion of that contained in the
cisterns is already consumed, and it is still a considerable time before the rainy season sets in. I was informed that a relation of the proprietor was in the habit
of conveying water during the night from the cistern of
the house to another close at hand; and that he was
assisted in this honourable undertaking by two of the
Aschkenasim. This was really the case, and for the
future I had the key of the house brought to me every
evening.

I found the greatest difficulty in securing a properly
qualified teacher for the institution. It was evident
that he must be a man strictly observant of all the
ordinances of religion, and, at the same time, possessed
of intelligence, a capacity for teaching, a fair education
at least, and some talent for management. There is
not in Jerusalem, where the Jews do nothing else but
study the Talmud, any one possessed of such attainments as that the Jewish communities in Germany
would entrust their children to his care. The native
Jews do not extend their studies further, and I was
assured that there is not among them a talmudist or

* Mr. Van de Velde alludes to this as an important discovery.—T.

pilpulist of any reputation. With the exception of the medical men and Mr. Joseph Schwarz, the Jews at Jerusalem are utterly ignorant of physical science, of geography and history, even of the history of their own nation before and after the destruction of the city.

The Jews who immigrate to Jerusalem usually possess a certain knowledge of the Talmud and a more enlarged experience; but here, if they do not give themselves up entirely to idleness, they do not extend their studies; they are satisfied with retaining that knowledge of the Talmud which they already possessed. They do not impart this knowledge to their children, and as we have already seen, the latter are not provided with any school, where they can obtain the same education as their parents, who, from their previous residence in Europe, are superior to them in knowledge of the world and general information. Their children or grandchildren have scarcely even a superficial acquaintance with science or history, or even with the more ordinary branches of reading and writing. Thus they naturally degenerate in intellect, in the same way as their physical vigour is destroyed through their early marriages.

We chose, if the term may be allowed in such a case, Mr. Mosche Perez, a young Chacham, connected with the Sepharedim community, and acquainted with the Hebrew, Arabic, and Spanish languages, who had just returned from a mission to Babylon and Bagdad, and who had thus acquired some knowledge of the world, in addition to his attainments as a talmudist. He was specially recommended by the Chacham Baschi, and was universally respected for his piety. His wife was capable of managing a household, and acting the part of a mother to the children, who were to be boarded in the institution. A pious Sepharedi was chosen to give instruction in the elementary branches.

It appeared that twenty pupils could be admitted, and a day had to be fixed for receiving them. The opening of the school was postponed by the Chachams to a later day, because in the passage of the thora, which was to be read the ensuing week, there was an account of the gainsaying of Korah, which might easily have been represented as a bad omen. The small synagogue of the institution had to be removed from the first to the second floor, because it is forbidden to walk over the ark where the *thora* is kept.

After this, whenever I appeared in the streets of Jerusalem, I was addressed by strange figures and groups. They were chiefly women, carrying children in their arms, or leading them by the hand. They addressed me in insinuating language, or described their wants and their misery in the hope of inducing me to receive their half naked neglected children into the institution.

" Receive my child into the institution, and the Lord will bless thee with children." " Thine entrance into the future world will be sweet and fragrant to thee." " Thou wilt eat with the pious of the fish leviathan." " Thy memory will be blessed. ' " See how naked we must stand before God and man. ' " We have nothing to keep the Sabbath." "The water in our cistern is dried up." "We have no tent to dwell beneath." Even when I entered the synagogue, they pressed round me, and entreated me to receive their children. Being summoned before the thora, I was requested by the clerk not to forget his children; and when leaving, the same request was made by many of the poorer members of the congregation.

On the day of admission, at the earliest dawn, the house was literally besieged by old people, men, women, and children; it was with difficulty that I could make my way through the people lying or squatting in the narrow lane. "Blessed be thy coming, O man of the west." "Be not angry with us on account of those who cause thee sorrow." "Do not make us atone for the sins of the ungrateful."

I was deeply moved at seeing so many poor creatures weeping, entreating, crying, and praying. There could not be a clearer proof that the outcry made by the fanatical zealots, who call themselves the leaders of the communities, did not express the feeling of the people at large, and that the poor in Jerusalem were languishing in deep misery, in spiritual oppression, in hunger and despondency. I felt myself reconciled to my task, and elevated with joy; I only regretted that all could not share in the advantages of the noble institution.

With the approval of the committee, especially of the medical men, who know all the families and their circumstances, twelve children, the offspring of Austrian subjects, seven of Turkish subjects, and one child belonging to a French subject, were admitted.

As many entreated that their children might at least be admitted for instruction, twenty boys were received as day scholars, as we could not afford to supply them with board and clothing. We gave the preference to orphans, and to children not under five, or above nine years of age. Notwithstanding the admission of the day-scholars, to prevent the school from being over-crowded, we were obliged to refuse fifty children, and to put them off to the next term of admission, at the end of three years. But it also happened that we were obliged to reject many children, whose wealthy parents wished to rob the poor of this benefit, or to receive payment for giving up their children. It was with deep sorrow that we rejected one poor orphan boy, whose foster-mother insisted on being paid for allowing him to be clothed, fed, and taught in the institution. A Karaitish Jew also begged that his son should be admitted, and when we were obliged to refuse him, he said with sorrow, "The Christians would not do this, and yet we are the only true pillars of Mosaic Judaism, and the most ancient Jewish inhabitants of Jerusalem."

The Russian-Polish Jews now ceased from all open opposition to the institution. But it was known, that letters denouncing it had been sent to London, Amsterdam, and Altona. The chief community felt themselves under the necessity of writing to these different places at the same time, in order to give an account of the real circumstances of the case; as there was really some danger that their contributions might be stopped. At the same time, also, a hypocritical Aschkenasi from Vienna, to whose denunciations we have already alluded, wrote a letter to the Rabbis of London, begging that they would anathematize the institution!

All was busy as a bee-hive in the house which we had hired for the institution. There was nothing but hammering, planing, white-washing, painting, and hurrying to and fro. On account of the oppressive heat, the workmen wore nothing but shirts and linen trousers, and small caps on their heads. According to our ideas, it seemed as if they were busy doing nothing, so gently and slowly did the work proceed. They began late, and left off early, under the pretence that they could not neglect divine service. On Friday, they ceased to work about noon, in order to prepare themselves for the services of the Sabbath. In Jerusalem, the workmen leave it to their employers to provide them with all the different articles which they require. I thus became acquainted with the bazaar, the art of commerce, the market price of different articles, and the customs of the people.

The city is intersected sometimes by straight, sometimes by sloping streets and lanes, which cross one another from the one gate to the other. Some of them are arched over; the upper part of the arches form streets, with houses on both sides. Recent researches have discovered in one of these arches, which extend even to the wall where the temple stood, the remains of a bridge, which connected the western part of the city with the temple.

These numerous streets, unpaved and dirty, as all streets are in Jerusalem, are named after the goods which are sold, or the trades which are practised in them. Thus, there is the grocers' bazaar, the goldsmiths', the meal and corn bazaar, the butter and oil bazaar, &c. On both sides of these bazaar streets are stalls, about two feet from the ground, which are not unlike those at German annual fairs. The merchants and workmen are seated on these stalls. The traveller, accustomed to the appearance and manners of workmen in Europe, cannot fail to be struck with the amusing contrast presented by the same class in this city; he sees, for example, a venerable, patriarchal looking Mussulman, with a long white beard, and a white turban bound round his head, but nothing on his breast, his neck, or his legs, sitting cross-legged, and if he is a locksmith, phlegmatically swinging his hammer; or, if a saddler, cutting out his leather; or, if a cobbler, patching shoes. Meanwhile, he "drinks" from a red tube, twisted like a snake, the smoke of tobacco, cooled by passing through water, and makes it pass through his nose in two white jets.

The goods in the stalls are not arranged in an attractive manner so as to strike the eye by their colours, as in Europe. They are all carefully rolled up in paper, and only displayed when a customer approaches the stall. He is often surprised at the rich display of beautiful and valuable goods. The Mohammedan merchant, who sits quietly at his ease and never thinks of addressing or attracting the passengers, invites his customer to a seat, hands him the pipe from his own mouth, and treats him also to coffee. The customer is justified in offering, at most, half the sum which the merchant asks. Jews, Christians, Mohammedans are all at one in this respect. If the merchant has no customers, he sleeps, or smokes, or reads the Koran,—bending his body backward and forward like the Jews—or he writes, —holding the sheet of paper in his left hand, or on his knee, and dipping his pen made of a reed into a silver or brass inkstand, which is soldered to a hollow tube for holding the pens, and stuck in his girdle.

Manufactured goods are chiefly from England, France, and Switzerland; Austria is represented by lucifer matches; Bohemia and Hebron by glass-ware, mirrors, and rings; silks and woollens are obtained from Damascus; Jerusalem itself only manufactures two articles, pottery-ware, especially unvarnished clay pipes, and the article which of all others seems to be used the least—soap. It is a saying of Liebig, that that people is the most moral which uses the most soap. Jerusalem has ten soap manufactories: most of the workmen employed in them are Christians. The soap is made up in round cakes, or balls, or half balls, and is of a yellowish white colour. It is usually stamped with the crescent, the Mount of Olives, the church of the sepulchre, or Rachel's tomb. The more valuable kind is perfumed with musk and ambergris.

The dealers in vegetables and fruit are principally

women—women with yellow olive complexions, with the corners of their eyes painted, the lips of a bluish colour, the nails and the palms of the hands dyed yellow, the forehead and the chin covered with blue tattooing. They are dressed in wide blue woollen or linen robes, open in front and leaving the breast exposed, with long, wide, open sleeves, which, when the arms hang at ease, reach as far as the ankles. The feet of the Bedouins are naked, and their whole bodies covered with an enamel of filth, such as in Europe would scarcely be deemed ornamental. The blue or white cloth descending from the forehead over the shoulders and reaching to the heels, is used as a veil, and drawn sometimes with the right hand, sometimes with the left, but not too carefully, over the face, whenever a man approaches on either side. Close rows of silver coins are strung obliquely over the temples and the forehead; on their arms are silver bracelets, and numerous rings on their fingers, and sometimes a ring may be seen glittering in their noses.

They carry their children on their shoulders in a white woollen cloth, the strings attached to the four corners of which are fastened to their foreheads in such a way that their arms are left perfectly free. Women, also, are often to be seen with their little children riding on their shoulders and clinging with both hands to their heads.

There is a lively movement among the stalls, especially in the morning, and the unwary passenger is often in danger of being pushed or knocked down. Men mounted on horses or donkeys are riding through the bazaar. Loaded asses, sheep and goats, are forcing their way through the crowd; dogs, the inevitable concomitants of Turkish towns, are sleeping in the bazaar, and start up with a howl when they are trodden on. The camel, renowned in eastern story, or a train of camels loaded with wood or other articles, pass between the buyers and sellers.

Equally striking and picturesque are the groups of men in their strange costumes; the Mohammedan walks with dignity in his flowing robes, the Bedouin, in his white and brown striped cloak, glances as if he were in search of plunder; the Polish Jew, dressed in a black silk caftan, hurries after him. The soberly-clad Prussian deaconesses pass with down-cast eyes; a closely veiled Mohammedan female, lazy and shapeless, shuffles past in yellow slippers, attended by a black or brown female slave, carrying her child or a basket of fruit. A Franciscan, with a broad-flapped hat and a cord round his body, is gazing at an unveiled female—she is a Jewess. A Greek priest, with a beautiful beard and long flowing locks, is walking as cheerfully by the side of a dervish, with a round yellow cap, as if they were both of the same faith. A Mussulman, with a green turban, the proof of his descent from the prophet, is looking at both. These men with black flowing robes, lofty figures, and noble features, wearing high-peaked caps, are from Persia. A man in a state of nudity—a revolting sight to the eye of a European, but which here gives no offence to either sex—advances; he is a so-called saint, who, with all his poverty, will take his place at the table of any family, even at that of the Pasha, without anyone daring to say him nay. Beside him may be seen the richly-dressed scheik, the elegant effendi, the inhabitants of Lebanon armed to the teeth, and groups of Turkish soldiers.

All the languages of the earth—but who would venture to describe that Babel of singing, gurgling, snuffling, shrieking, and shouting. In truth the ear is even more astounded than the eye. The effect is much the same as if one suddenly found himself a spectator of one of the scenes described in the Arabian Nights; but the illusion is soon dispelled by the advance of some European gentleman in a frock coat and a round hat, or of a lady in a dress similar to those which are to be seen daily on the *Graben* of Vienna or the Boulevards of Paris. The costume of our saloons never appeared to me so utterly devoid of taste as in the streets, the cities, and the valleys of the East.

When I was tired with walking and gazing, I used to enter one of the twenty coffee-houses at Jerusalem. Divans furnished with cushions extend along the walls. The guest sits cross-legged, or lies extended at his ease, and inhales the fragrance of the tobacco of Persia, from a narghilé filled with water and rose-leaves. He sips excellent coffee and cooling sherbet. Music and fairy tales, and all the delights which the youthful imagination associates with Mohammedan life are here united, and the soul sinks into a state of calm dreamy enjoyment.

All this sounds very beautiful in the poetical descriptions of our modern travellers, but how different is the reality! The coffee-house in Jerusalem, as almost everywhere in the East, is neither more nor less than a kitchen, with the door opening into the street and the walls blackened with smoke. Along the walls are wooden benches, with cushions covered with calico, which may certainly have once been clean. In the corner nearest to the entrance, water is boiling in a copper kettle. The master, without being ordered, brings a narghilé to the guest, and prepares the coffee in his presence. It is roughly ground in a small copper vessel, boiling water is poured over it, and when it begins to boil it is quickly poured into a porcelain cup, which stands in a metal saucer, and handed to the guest with the usual courteous application of the hand to the breast and the forehead. He is supplied with sugar only when he asks for it. The coffee is boiling hot, with a clear brown foam on the surface, so that it looks like chocolate, and has a strong fragrant taste. A cup of this noble beverage costs five paras ($\frac{1}{2}$d.) Sometimes two or three musicians may be seen seated in the coffee-house, striking a tambourine with bells, and a guitar, blowing a shrill pipe, and singing an unmelodious Arab song. A story-teller usually treats his audience to some passage from the history of the crusades, not at all reflecting honour on the warriors of Christendom, or reads a fairy tale from a book, or recites it from memory. A young boy, dressed as a girl, dances one of those lascivious dances,

which we shall afterwards have occasion to describe.
In the evening, the dirty room is filled with smoke, the
floor slippery with expectorations, in the midst of which
the tubes of the narghilés are writhing like snakes in a
swamp. It is lighted with a few lamps, attached to a
lustre of roughly-painted wood, which usually consists
of a few rods glued together. In the background of
one of these coffee-houses there is always a place where
the guest's horse or donkey is stalled and fed while he
is surrendering himself to that sensual, dreamy *dolce
far niente*, the *beau ideal* of Mohammedan bliss. This
arrangement is quite in keeping with Mohammed's
paradise, where men and beasts dwell together, and
enjoy the same happiness.

Having rested for a little, we mingle again with the
noisy crowd in the bazaar. A strange procession
advances; we see men marching with measured tread,
to the shrill music of a clarionet and the hollow sound of
a *tom tom*, and clapping their hands; boys carrying different objects of peculiar shape, strangely-painted flower-
stocks, a chibouque with a mouth-piece of green-glass,
wooden slippers inlaid with mother-of-pearl, a female
dress, and a round glass, and, last of all, a roughly-
painted wooden box. These articles form all the wealth
of an Arabian bride, and are being conveyed to the
abode of her husband. Occasionally, the sound of the
clarionet is interrupted by a song, which is rather
snuffled through the nose than sung with the lips, and
the subject of which is the happiness of the bridegroom,
and the haughty beauty of the bride.

A man has stopped at the same moment with us to witness the procession. His face is brown, his body half naked, and he carries two gourd bottles at his girdle. In his right hand he holds a stick, the head of which is an iron crescent, with the points turned downward. A beautifully-carved staff, the end of which is shaped into a spoon, is resting on his shoulders. We recognise in him a Mohammedan pilgrim from India.

In walking through the bazaar, we can scarcely advance a step without being addressed by beggars, who hold a plate as a sign of their profession. Men and women of all sects, with the single exception of the Jews, are importunate in demanding alms. Sometimes on the right hand, and sometimes on the left, but especially at the corners of streets, the passenger is addressed as "Chawadschah," "Lord," or "Hadsch," "Pilgrim," but we would not advise him, if he is to remain long at Jerusalem, to give alms on the street. If you relieve his wants to-day, the beggar thinks that he has a right to your charity to-morrow.

The Russian-Polish Jews did not give up their active opposition to the institution, which was now ready to be opened. On the 15th of June, a meeting, presided over by a Polish Rabbi, was held in the Churba; it resolved to visit the institution with a "Jszur," *i.e.* to protest against it, and to read the protest on the following sabbath in the synagogues.

On the following day, which happened to be a Friday, some young married boys tried to excite the fanaticism of the crowd at the temple wall, by telling them that the institution was about to be anathematized; and one Jossele Becker, a countryman of mine, from Galicia, notorious for his ignorance, began to sound the alarm on a "Schofar," or ram's horn. The women especially began to howl and to weep, and their children took part in the chorus.

I was suddenly woke up at night; shouts, proceeding at first from a distance, gradually approached, till I could hear them beneath my window. I could clearly distinguish these words : " Up, up ! come, sing 'Eiches,' songs of lamentation, religion is in danger ! Up, come, ye faithful ones of Zion, up ! " Such were the shouts raised in the bright starry night, and which gradually retreated, till at length they died away in the distance. I raised my head, and listened, but all was silent, and it seemed almost as if it had been a wild dream. I struck a light and was still awake, when the Bet-tel—the summons to morning prayer—sounded from the terrace.

In the morning, the "Jszur" was read in some of the small synagogues, but in others it was prohibited from being read by Messrs. Joseph Schwarz and Nissim Back, and our readers will easily understand that no attempt was made to read it in the synagogues of the Sepharedim. The Austrian Consul now felt himself insulted, as his authority had been directly set at nought. When he examined the presidents, they declared that they could not prevent the assembly ; they themselves had not attended it, and they left it to the Consul to punish those who had been guilty of participating in the recent riot. The Consul, though he

knew officially that their assertions were not true,
left the presidents this loophole of escape, and condemned five of the rioters to three days' imprisonment;
two of them, one of whom was the blower of the *schofar*,
were confined in the prison at the consulate, the other
three, though one of them was a rayah*—and imprisonment there is a much more severe punishment—were
confined at the seraglio. While the prison at the consulate is bright and clean, so that confinement in it
seems rather a reward than a punishment when we consider the miserable hovels which many of the prisoners
occupy, the prison at the seraglio is narrow, dirty, and
specially disagreeable to the Jews, because they are
obliged to remain in the society of their despised des-
pisers, the Mohammedans.

I must here mention a humane trait in the conduct
of the Turkish Government which they have borrowed
from the European consuls at Jerusalem. At the time
when Count Pizzamano, the first Austrian Consul at
Jerusalem, was sent there, he felt himself under the
necessity of arresting a Jew, who was suspected of
having poisoned another from motives of jealousy.
After remaining quietly a prisoner during several days,
he all at once disappeared. The Consul found himself
in a very embarrassing position, and threatened to make
the warders of the prison responsible for his escape.
The oldest cavass, who happened to be engaged in
some business at a distance from the consulate, when he
was called to account for his unpardonable negligence,

* A Turkish subject.—T.

answered with perfect composure: " What, sir, do you not know that this is the Jewish sabbath? There can be no doubt but he has gone to his family, and after 'they have smelt the frankincense' (*i.e.* when the sabbath is over), he will come back again." And so it really happened; the man charged with this heavy crime actually yielded himself up to the hands of justice on the evening of the same day. Every Jew, even when he is sentenced to several weeks' imprisonment at Jerusalem, is set at liberty on Friday evening, both by the Turkish Government and the consular authorities, that he may be enabled piously and devoutly to observe the day of rest in the bosom of his family.

One afternoon I wished to know how long it took to walk round the whole of the city, and, accompanied by several companions, I passed through the Damascus gate. Turning to the right, we saw the beautiful wall of the city, jagged like the living rock on which it is built, and of which it seems to be merely a continuation. After walking for ten minutes over stony rough ground, planted with olive trees, we turned to the left, in the direction of the tombs of the kings. We passed through a low entrance into a vault hewn out of the rock, and filled with rubbish, which has a beautiful portal, and was divided into three equal parts by the four columns with which it was adorned. Clusters of grapes and wreaths are skilfully cut out on the archi-trave. The Jews in Jerusalem believe that the wreaths are twisted bread, and that the vault is the tomb of the wealthy Kalba Zebua. They have followed the ex-

ample of those fanciful discoverers of sacred places—
the monks, and exercised their ingenuity in naming
memorials of the past, which they cannot understand,
after illustrious individuals. But in general industrious
topographists, and even such investigators as Robinson,
do not pay sufficient attention to the remarks and
passing allusions contained in the talmud; which,
while they may not always lead to any discovery, at
least, deserve to be known.

The tombs of the children of David, or of the kings of
Israel, were on Mount Zion; four of them were buried
outside the city; but there is no author or historical
record extant, which proves that the so-called tombs of
the kings are really such. The description given by
Pausanias and Flavius Josephus leads rather to the
conclusion that Helena, Queen of Adiabene, a convert
to Judaism, who died at Jerusalem, is buried here.

Passing through the vestibule, which is behind the
portal just described, we entered the chamber of the
tombs by a low opening. The passage is so full of
stones and rubbish that we were obliged to creep
through on our knees; the walls and the roof are
smoothly polished. Three different passages lead from
this chamber to others, where perpendicular niches for
the reception of sarcophagi are cut out. We descended
from one of these chambers, by some steps, into a
smaller vault, which is provided with large niches, in
which marble sarcophagi must formerly have stood.
The stone doors, which were cut out of the rock and
moved on pins adapted to holes above and below, have

all disappeared. The last one, we were told by our
Jewish guide, was carried off to Paris seven years ago,
by a Vandalic Jewish pilgrim.

A short walk over stony ground, also planted with
olives, brought us to the prison of Jeremiah, as it is
called. After we had knocked for a little, a small low
door was opened. On entering, we found ourselves in
a pretty little flower-garden, and came to a lofty,
almost circular grotto, with a natural dome for its
roof, about thirty feet high, supported by two massive
columns of rock. The grotto is forty feet in diameter;
it is pretty well lighted through a lofty, natural entrance
from the garden, which contains some Mohammedan
sepulchres. The Mohammedans come here to offer up
prayer; it is a pleasant and pretty room, with walls of
rock. On leaving, we gave the young guardian what
we thought a handsome backschiesch, but he did not
regard it in that light, and called us dogs. Our guide
told us that we might esteem ourselves fortunate in not
having been pelted with stones.

We continued our walk along the city wall, and saw
below on our left the Valley of Jehoshaphat, with the
sepulchres situated on the opposite heights. Passing
the Sion gate, where there is a small Mohammedan
burying-ground and an ancient pond, we saw the deep,
dry bed of Kidron. On the opposite side of the
valley were the tombs, which have passed for centuries
as those of the prophet Jeremiah and Absalom, but
which really are Roman buildings of a more recent
date. Near them, but reaching higher up, as far as the

village of Siluan, are the graves of the Jews, covered
with flat stones. This part of the side of the hill, when
seen from a distance, looks as if it were paved with
broad greyish-white stones. The Mount of Olives
with its three summits towers over the valley and the
graves on the other side.

When we looked in the direction of the city wall,
which was always on our right, and passed the Sion
gate, we saw the valley of Hinnom deep down below,
and we sometimes found in the wall near the former
site of the temple, huge stones 22 feet long, which, notwithstanding the destruction of the city at different
times, unquestionably occupy the place where the
stonecutter placed them many thousand years ago.
One shapeless block, $7\frac{1}{2}$ feet thick, was pointed out to
us in a corner. We were told that it would not fit in at
the building of Solomon's temple, and was therefore
rejected by the builder. This was the only stone that
resisted the worm " Chiloson," which the sage required
only to place on the stones in order to cut them
asunder, as no iron, of which the sword is made, was
allowed to be used in the peaceful work of building the
temple. Many of these large blocks are cut at the
edge, like the square stones in the western wall of the
temple.

A fragment of a pillar which projects horizontally
from the wall, and is three feet in length, is pointed out
as the one astride which the prophet Mohammed is to
sit on the day of resurrection and judge the souls of
men. We are indebted for the following to another

Mohammedan legend :—Mohammed will examine whether Christ has judged righteous judgment, and will then give him his sister in marriage, as a sign of their everlasting alliance. Towards the close of the 15th century a false prophet appeared, placed himself on the pillar in presence of the Arab tribes that were attached to him, and began a discourse. He lost his balance, fell down, and was killed.

We now began to ascend, and reached the Jaffa gate. We passed it, and crossing some stony ground planted with olive trees, we came to the Damascus gate, from which we had started. Our walk round the city took an hour and a quarter, without including the time that we spent at the tombs of the kings and the prophet's prison. During the whole of this time we did not meet a single man or beast. All was silent, as in a solitary neglected burying-ground. Jerusalem is little else, and yet there are memories connected with her graves which the world will not willingly let die.

Our attention was directed to a troop of gipsies encamped at the Damascus gate. I was surprised at meeting here these brown *pariahs* of the earth, as I had done twenty years before in St. Peter's Church at Rome. Men, women, and children began to beg aloud in the Turkish language. The warm climate was favourable to their limited *toilettes*. Their only article of dress, a long striped blanket, rather gave prominence to their figures than concealed them. The children were perfectly naked. One man, busy in mending a patch, did not even look up; another, to my great surprise, was playing on the violin the rebel Rakoczi's long-forgotten air.

I threw a few small pieces of silver to the beggars, and one of the women cried, " White money, white man ! May God give you as many white sons as you have given me white coins, and no daughters to bring you disgrace."

The day fixed for opening the institution had now arrived. The house which we had hired for it was gaily adorned with red and white flags, in honour of our guests. The school-room was adorned with the Austrian colours, and with a portrait of his Imperial Majesty, the Emperor of Austria, which was presented by the foundress. Opposite to it was placed the portrait of her deceased father, Simon von Lämel. Along the walls was ranged a series of representations of animals and plants, and biblical scenes, intended for the instruction of the pupils.

The restless, idle zealots contrived to give me considerable annoyance to the last. The night before the ceremony of inauguration I was woke up and informed that the report had been spread by the Russian Jews that there was a crucifix in the institution. I imagined that a crucifix might have been wantonly thrown into it, or painted on the walls. I hastened to the house, but I could discover nothing, till my attention was directed to the fact that the Grand Cross of the Emperor's own Order was painted on his breast. I contrived with some difficulty to scrape off the points of the cross with a knife; in the same way I managed to remove the

carving of a silver lamb, part of the arms of Simon von
Lämel, which were introduced beneath his picture, as a
graven image is not allowed in a synagogue. At the
inauguration of the institution, which was honoured by
the presence of the European consuls and the *élite* of
society at Jerusalem, an address was delivered, pointing out the advantages of education to the Jewish
youth at the present day; and the Turkish National
Hymn, translated into Hebrew, was sung by the
choir.

This truly elevating solemnity, the like of which
could scarcely ever have occurred in Jerusalem before,
produced a peculiarly sad and affecting impression, from
the sublime scene on which it was represented. The
consuls who were present offered me their sincere con-
gratulations on the success of my mission, and expressed
a desire that I should convey to the benevolent
foundress their feelings of gratitude. The assembly
was then entertained in Oriental fashion with refreshments in the refectory of the institution, which was
tastefully adorned; at the same time an abundant
supply of bread was distributed among the poor of
Jerusalem, and the splendid gifts, sent chiefly from
Vienna for the institution, were exhibited.

These are painful pictures, which we have exhibited;
their effect is all the more striking, as we have placed
them alone, without regard to the equally miserable
circumstances of the Mohammedans and Christians.
A faithful picture of the social and moral condition of
the inhabitants of Jerusalem must excite grief, and

indignation, and sympathy in every heart. We have not painted these scenes, and groups, and figures for the purpose of awakening these sentiments in our readers; our object has been to prepare their minds for the all-important question—how can this state of things be remedied?

There is something infinitely moving and poetically beautiful in the description of the object of a Jew's journey written on his passport: "In order to die at Jerusalem." What strength of faith, what joy in sorrow and self-denial are expressed in these few pathetic words! How powerful must be the influence of that uncontrollable longing, which induces a man to snap asunder all the ties of home, of family, and of daily associations, and to leave the land of his birth for another distant land, that he may live poor and despised amid the mighty memories of his glorious ancestors, dream of the splendour of the temple, and the light of the cherubim, amid heaps of ruins, weep over the graves of kings, of judges, and of prophets, and then "die at Jerusalem."

He is surrounded with a sort of halo, when contrasted with the Mohammedan or Christian pilgrim, who travels from distant lands to Jerusalem, who is surrounded with all the comforts and enjoyments which money can procure, and who returns after a few months to the happy circle of his own family, enriched with a treasure of glorious reminiscences. On the other hand, how worthy of our admiration is the tottering old man, the weary hunted Jew, who, unprovided

with money, has to encounter all the difficulties and
privations of a long journey, who renounces all hope of
ever returning, and whose only ambition is that his
dust may be mingled with that of his fathers in the
valley of Jehoshaphat.

The Jews have sometimes been compared to the
monks who offer up prayer beside that sepulchre which
the Christians esteem to be most sacred, and who are
supplied with money from all parts of the world.   The
comparison is not just.   The monks, in humble piety,
give themselves up to prayer and self-denial, but they
also work.   They have the cure of souls, they baptize,
they comfort, and take their stand by the bedside of
the dying, even when struck down by pestilence, as is
often the case; they are teachers, physicians, apothe-
caries, bookbinders, mechanics, and servants to the
pilgrims.   They are (I here allude to the Franciscans)
outposts left behind by the Frankish kings, six centuries
ago.   This order can shew more martyrs on account
of the holy sepulchre than all the orders of Christendom together.   We have obtained too deep an
insight into their moral decay to appear as their
panegyrists, but truth has its rights, and the merit of a
noble life of self-sacrifice should be recognised.   And
above all, it should not be forgotten that the monks are
single men without families, who come here, and die
here—alone.

Most of the Jews have wives and children, or at
least they are young enough to indulge the hope of
enjoying these blessings.   The children, as we have

seen, receive no instruction, and marry so young that they are enfeebled in mind and body, and little adapted for training their own children, who become still more effeminate. Of course no longing for the Holy Land has brought them here ; it is rather a contemptuous feeling for their native place, the daily sight of which has produced a feeling of *ennui*, or at least it is not surrounded by that enchantment which distance lends to the view. Destitute of knowledge and of that poetical feeling, which always attracted their ancestors and their forefathers to this place, they are nothing else but idle vagabonds, in whom every sentiment of honour has been extinguished by the reception of alms. Enfeebled in intellect and physical energy, and sunk in the deepest poverty, they are yet continually on the increase, and it is impossible to foretell the result of this state of things.

What other power, save the anarchical government of Turkey, would permit this in the city which, after Mecca, they esteem to be the most sacred on earth, or in the other cities of Palestine, Safet and Tiberias? The United States of America ask the immigrant to the new world if he is provided with a certain sum of money, or can name any person who will undertake to support him, if he should become incapable of labour. If the immigrant fails to give satisfaction on these points, or if he is disabled in body, he is rejected without mercy by the freest country in the world.

" There are treaties that secure free immigration."

Good ! we are favourable to freedom of travelling in

the fullest sense of the term.    But the governments of
Europe must put a stop to this.    None would wish to
prevent the aged man or woman, tottering on the brink
of the grave, from enjoying the melancholy satisfaction
of dying at Jerusalem.    None would wish to stretch
forth a cold hand, and to arrest the mysterious impulses
of godly piety, or of sincere desire.    But when whole
families, whose children and descendants are inevitably
exposed to moral and physical decay, and who are
themselves sunk in the deepest poverty, and are yet
averse to labour, travel to the Holy Land for the sake
of alms, it appears to us that Government, as the
guardian of the people, should at least try to warn and
dissuade them.    This is really done in the case of those
who emigrate to America.    There should be a law passed,
that, for the future, every Jew who emigrates to
Jerusalem, shall shew that he is possessed of a certain
fixed sum, or that he is a mechanic or a husbandman.

As the means of communication have become easier,
the number of immigrants to Jerusalem has proportion-
ally increased, while the contributions for their
support, we are bound to say, have diminished.    There
are two different causes, then, that have tended to
increase their misery : alms flow there more sparingly,
while the number of immigrants is on the increase.
Most of the latter are from Russia and Poland, and
their removal to Palestine has much the same effect on
their manners as that which is produced in the character of Europeans when they emigrate to America.
The Russian or Polish Jew passes at a bound from the

servitude of his native country to the anarchical liberty
of a Turkish Pashawlic. Thus, in the case of most of
them at least,[1] there are social as well as religious
motives—a certain undefined poetical enthusiasm and a
decided aversion to labour, which attract them to the
Holy Land. Here, unless they commit some crime,
and even that will disappear before the magic word
" backschiesch," they are perfectly free. In fact, they
have more liberty than is consistent with their previous
habits, and hence they become overbearing and violent,
as men who have been slaves always are on regaining
their liberty. But they do not suspect that they have
only escaped from the knout to subject themselves to
the still more painful lash of poverty. And poverty
is seldom the parent of the social virtues.

Such are the men who swell the ranks of Judaism in
Palestine ;—such are the watchmen of Zion !—the men
who weep beneath the palm trees in Jerusalem !

Emigration from Jerusalem, on the other hand, is so
limited that it is scarcely perceptible. Old men, of
course, never leave the Holy City, and men who see
every appearance of sanctity disappear soon after their
arrival, whose religious feelings are shocked by the
universal immorality and hypocrisy, and whose health is
injured by the climate and their new mode of existence,
are prevented from returning by the want of means, and
by a feeling of shame. I have heard them utter
many a sigh—many an ardent desire that they could
return to their homes in Europe. Young men, again,
are so bound to the soil through their early marriages,

that, ignorant as they are, they neither have nor can have the courage to gain a livelihood in Europe. In recent times there is only one case of a rich man, who settled in Jerusalem, and left it. Soon after the Polish revolution, Mr. S. L., a contractor from Moghilev, in Russia, came to Jerusalem with thirty followers and three millions of piastres, or 300,000 silver florins, with the intention of settling there permanently. After two years, the pious man was undeceived, and turned his back on Jerusalem in indignation. The expression he used on leaving has become proverbial. " He that will enjoy 'aulom haze,' the pleasures of this world, must live in Moldavia; he that wishes to renounce these, and to obtain 'aulom habo,' the happiness of the other world, must live in Russia. But let him that wishes to have neither *aulom haze* nor *aulom habo* live at Jerusalem."

The same divisions and hostile feelings exist among the different communities at Jerusalem as are perceptible among the Christian sects. This is the worst lesson that the Jews could have borrowed from the Christians, whom they affect to despise. In consequence of these deplorable divisions, and the efforts made by each community to obtain a superiority over the rest, and the selfishness of one small circle, which leads them to consult only their own interests, nothing has been done for the general welfare of the Jewish population. If it had been the intention of the Jews to draw down on themselves the contempt of the Mohammedans and Christians, who, as they are sunk in the same misery, have certainly no right to despise them, they could not have adopted more effectual measures for securing this result. It would be very difficult to effect a reunion between the Oriental and the European Jews. Difference of language, of religious views, of manners and customs, tends always to keep them asunder. It might be possible, however, to re-unite the Aschkenasim, and this must be a preliminary step, before the condition of the Jews can be improved. We are fully aware of the difficulties which such an undertaking would have to encounter, in consequence of their quarrels about the distribution of alms, and the hostile feelings of nationality that exist among Russians, Poles, Galicians, Bohemians, Hungarians, Germans, and natives of all the principal countries of Europe.

It may be mentioned as characteristic of the Jews in Jerusalem, and I am indebted for this information to one whose veracity is beyond a doubt, that the political movements or insurrections that occur in their native countries produce no effect upon them. They have all gladly renounced their fatherland, and its future fate is to them a matter of complete indifference.

Where shall we find a hand strong enough to grasp the reins and to direct the movements of this hard-mouthed brute ? In the first place, the representatives of the different European Powers must give up their mutual jealousies, and cause their united influence to be felt ; and, above all, there must be a real government, instead of the decaying empire which now casts its sinking shade over this gloomy scene. Their union

would also be attended with the best effects, in a moral
point of view, because they would form only one community, which would admit or reject every immigrant
on his arrival, according to the merits of the case, and
introduce improvements for the benefit of all.    Something like public spirit would be awakened, and each
individual member would profit by the change.    The
different institutions, which are now small because they
are divided, would attain a higher degree of usefulness,
schools would be founded, and a more equitable division
of alms introduced.

We have already shown that the presidents of the
different communities receive their appointments in
Europe.    They may do whatever they choose, so long
as those who nominated them in the distant West are
satisfied with them.    No member of the community
dares to complain of an act of injustice, however glaring
it may be, or if a poor man ventures to say a word, he
is reminded of his offence at the next distribution of
*chaluka*.    Notwithstanding this danger, the feeling of
indignation is so general, that many would venture to
speak were it not that the presidents have them in their
power in another way.    The contributions of alms
scarcely ever arrive regularly.    The poor are starving,
and when their temporary wants are relieved they consider it an act of humanity.    The presidents profit by
such opportunities, and show their magnanimity by
advancing from the treasury of the community, so far as
it will permit, a certain sum for the relief of their
wants ; but soon after they inform them that the

treasury is empty, and that money can only be obtained at a high rate of interest. At length the money arrives from Europe, but the loan has to be deducted with interest. The sum owed by the poor is almost equal to their share in the alms ; they are obliged, therefore, to borrow again, and thus they can never escape from the chains which the presidents have forged for them, and which they wear in silent indignation.

In no city in the world are there so many anonymous letters written as in Jerusalem. All of them complain bitterly of the injustice and cruelty of the presidents. There are palpable reasons why the poor should not bring forward their charges publicly, and an appeal to those who have nominated the presidents in other countries would lead to nothing. If a union of the different communities cannot be speedily effected, they should reclaim their natural right to elect their own presidents, and choose men who enjoy their confidence, who are responsible for their conduct, and who are bound to resign their office after a certain number of years. But then, the question occurs, whether presidents elected in Jerusalem would enjoy the confidence of those who collect the alms in Europe, and entrust them to them for distribution. Surely a public explanation of the circumstances of the case will be sufficient to effect this, and we are convinced that all charitable persons will contribute as before, when they know that the poor are really benefited by their charity. Charitable contributions might be sent through the governments of the different countries to their consuls, who might be held responsible for the distribution of them, and might distribute the money with the concurrence of the presidents of the different communities. This plan was partially adopted a few years ago. The money sent from Galicia for the benefit of Austrian subjects is paid by the consul, with the full approval of the community. Latterly, Mr. Horwitz, the Rabbi of Vienna, adopted the same plan, and Mr. Eisenstädter of Unguar, and Mr. Hartstein, of Ujhely, have also forwarded their contributions through Mr. Horwitz, to be distributed in the same way.

The Austrian Consul announces at his office the amount of money received immediately after its arrival, and this is a great advantage for the poor, and a decided step in advance, as formerly the presidents never informed the communities how much money they received. Another practical improvement has been introduced; the money is always remitted in gold, and the exaction of an agio, often incredibly high, is prevented. A short time ago, in consequence of a rapid change in the currency, the poor lost the fourth part of a contribution of 40,000 piastres.

If this plan were generally adopted, the money would really be distributed among the poor according to their several necessities. It certainly would not be favourably received by the Presidents and the Rabbis, but it would be highly acceptable to the mass of the people. We advise all, who send alms to Jerusalem, to remit them in gold through their consuls, to be distributed with the concurrence of the presidents, at least until the plan, which we are about to propose in the following pages, has been adopted.

We have already described the ceremony of a Jewish marriage at Jerusalem, and we have no doubt but the reader has felt the same moral repugnance as ourselves at seeing two children converted into married people.

As the ignorance and immorality that prevail in the East are caused chiefly by polygamy and too early marriages, and as the views and opinions of a whole nation are always represented in its individual members, some excuse may be found for the Jews, if their conduct in this matter cannot be altogether justified. It is surprising that the Mohammedans, whose prophet married Aïscha when she was nine years of age, do not marry so early as the native Christians. By the canons of the church, a girl ten years of age is allowed to marry ; the present Latin patriarch will not allow the marriage to be consummated till she is fourteen. Among the Christians, as well as the Mohammedans, the girl is bought from her parents. The latter, when they have several girls, are anxious to sell their daughters as soon as possible, in order to increase their wealth. The lowest price is a thousand piastres ; this money is received for " education and maintenance," and though this custom seems quite right in the eyes of a Mohammedan, it appears to us simply the purchase of a female slave for a certain sum. But the Jews, who give a dowry with their daughters, outstrip the Mohammedans and the Christians in their early marriages. While a Jewish girl at Jerusalem is not allowed to marry before her twelfth year, yet this prohibition can easily be set aside by the families betaking themselves for a few days to the little village of Tur, on the Mount of Olives, and having their children married there. Perhaps our readers may wish to know how the Aschkenasim act in this matter. It is well known that they contract very early marriages in Galicia, Poland, and Russia, in order to escape from military service. The same pretence does not exist in the Holy Land, and such marriages cannot be excused among the European immigrants, as among the Orientals, on the ground of premature development. On this subject, I cannot do better than quote the words of Dr. Tobler, who has given so much valuable information regarding the topography of Jerusalem, and the moral and social condition of its inhabitants.

" Before the children have reached the years of puberty, or their physical frames are at all developed, they are united in wedlock. Before they have reached their full maturity, their vigour is already exhausted. The mothers bring forth in sorrow, and almost at the expense of their lives, miserable little creatures, two-thirds of whom die after a few days or weeks. I have seldom met with a family blessed with many children ; on the contrary, these early marriages are often without children. If the Rabbis of Jerusalem had the least desire that the Jewish population should increase in numbers and vigour, they would take steps to prevent this crying evil, they would, as a matter of course, devise some prudent measures, and put a moderate restraint on these early marriages. The madness of the Jews in worshipping the golden calf was nothing to their folly in this matter; their early marriages do them far more harm than the London Mission—which rarely even catches a diseased sheep that has wandered from the fold—or even a hundred London Missions; they become the victims of this sensual, ignorant, and corrupt system, and death ensues in a hundred different forms. The merest trifle calls forth the anger of the priest-hood, and the thunder of excommunication, but not a single voice is raised against this fearful evil."

We have nothing to add to the words of this highly-respected physician. But, as we believe that the Rabbis will do nothing to check the ignorance and baseness of the parents, we hold that permission to marry should be made dependent on the consent of the representatives of the different European Powers, as is done at home; and in order to know their age, a register of births and deaths should be kept at the offices of the different consuls; and this measure would have the additional advantage of furnishing us with those statistics, which at present do not exist. If it involved any restraint on personal liberty, we should be the last persons in the world to advocate it, but Jerusalem is altogether an exceptional case. At present it would be a decided advantage, and it could be laid aside when a healthier tone of feeling and more enlightened views rendered it no longer necessary.

In an earlier part of this work, we have directed special attention to the fruitfulness of the soil around

Jerusalem, and in Palestine generally ; the only difference is that it is presented to the eye in a different form from what we see in European countries, blessed with water. Industry and skill are the magic wands which here, as elsewhere, call forth rich and abundant harvests. Fields and gardens still germinate and bring forth fruit as in the days of the Bible; even the stony hills and rocks, which during the long reign of barbarism were left uncultivated, are covered with mulberry trees and vineyards planted by the Greeks.

No traveller, unless he trusts in legends instead of using his eyes, will assert that the soil of Palestine has been cursed and unfruitful for 1858 years. No doubt it is so to the Jews; they neither plant, nor plough, nor reap. They are too indolent, and too little accustomed to the hot climate to be fit for cultivating the soil, if that can be called cultivation which would excite the laughter of a German farmer. A race, in short, that is always degenerating more and more in consequence of the system of early marriages, is too weak to perform that species of labour which men consider to be the most satisfactory of all, even when they do not enjoy the pleasure of cultivating their own ground.

In the village Der el Kamar, on the inhospitable heights of Lebanon, there is an entire Jewish community engaged in agriculture and in rearing cattle. None but Jews are employed on Sir Moses Montefiore's plantations of citrons and pomegranates at Jaffa. But all this is out of Jerusalem ; here we saw only one man, who had bought and cultivated a corner of Mount

Zion, which amply repaid him for his labour. Mr. Meschulam, an English Jew, who has now been baptized, bought a few years ago "the enclosed garden of Solomon," as it is called, near Bethlehem, and raises the finest fruit, and such excellent vegetables as were never known in Jerusalem before. At first he suffered from the hostile feeling shewn toward him by the Mohammedans, but now that he is under the protection of the English Consul, he is left unmolested, and his labours are richly rewarded. At Jerusalem the Jews only labour in the field purchased by the mission in the way we have already shewn. But who is to teach the people, who is to incite them to labour? The teachers? They do not labour themselves. The Rabbis? It is their interest that the present state of things should continue, that the cry for bread should reach to every land, and that all the Jews in the earth should shew their sympathy by sending alms, without suspecting that, by doing so, they are demoralizing their co-religionists in the place which they esteem to be most holy.

Give them work that they may learn to work; buy them lands, which they may possess here though they cannot do so at home, that they may earn their bread as God has appointed, in the sweat of their brow, that they may become a noble community instead of a colony of beggars, and that they may sanctify the name of the Lord.

# CHAPTER IV.

KING DAVID is venerated as a prophet by the Mohammedans as well as the Christians, and the tomb of the
royal bard is considered by the former to be quite as

sacred as the mosque of Omar, if not more so. I received permission from the Pasha, as an extraordinary act of favour, to enter the tomb. In modern times this favour has not been accorded to any but the Duke and Duchess of Brabant, the Archduke Ferdinand Maximilian, and myself. No Jew has ever entered the place, but it did not strike me that the Jews at Jerusalem have the same longing to enter this tomb, as in the case of the sepulchres of the patriarchs at Hebron. This may arise partly from the circumstance, that in the Book of Kings, it is simply said:—" And David was gathered to his fathers, and was buried in the city of David" without any further particulars.

Benjamin of Tudela, the legend-relating Jewish pilgrim, of the 12th century, gives the following story regarding the tomb of David:—" The tombs of the family of David and of the kings who reigned after him were unknown. Fifteen years ago the wall of a church on Mount Zion fell down. The patriarch ordered it to be rebuilt, and stones to be taken from the Zion wall for that purpose. Twenty labourers were employed in the work. Two of them, who were intimate friends, continued to labour after the rest had withdrawn. They came to a stone, which they had great difficulty in removing, and saw the mouth of a cave, into which they descended, in the hope of finding treasure. They entered a long, narrow passage, at the end of which stood a marble palace, the columns of which were adorned with gold and silver. On entering, they saw a table in the middle, with a crown and sceptre of gold lying on it. And this was

David's tomb, and on the left was the tomb of Solomon, and then the tombs of all the kings. There were also chests there, but locked, so that no one knew what they contained. When they were about to advance farther, such a violent tempest assailed them that they fell down insensible, and remained in that condition till towards evening. Then a spirit called to them, 'Men, depart from this place.' They rose in terror, groped their way out again, and went to tell the patriarch all that had befallen them.

"The patriarch informed Rabbi Abraham Hachoszid, who was known by the Arabian name of Al-Constantino, and who was one of those whose lives are spent in lamenting the fall of Jerusalem, of this singular affair, and asked his opinion. The latter answered : ' These are the tombs of the house of David and of the kings that have reigned after him.' Next morning the patriarch sent for the two men, but they were still overpowered with terror, and answered : ' God will allow no one to proceed.' On this the patriarch ordered the place to be walled up, so that it has remained concealed to the present day. Rabbi Abraham Hachoszid," concludes our Jewish pilgrim, " related the circumstance to me himself."

The armed cavasses of the pasha and the consul conducted me to the Zion gate, or as it is called by the Mohammedans, " The gate of the Prophet David." Notice of my intended visit had been previously sent to the scheik of the tomb by the pasha. We entered an open gateway about fifty yards from the gate, on the left of which lay a broken column covered with filth. We then found ourselves in a dirty court, where children and dogs were chasing one another, and entered the scheik's apartment. He was a tall, noble-looking old man, of eighty years of age; his long beard was whiter than his white flowing robe, or his white turban. Four of his friends were assembled around him. He provided me with a pipe, coffee, and *eau sucré*, flavoured with rose leaves. After the usual forms of politeness had been exchanged, the scheik asked me,—" You come from the land of the Sultan njemsza?" It is a singular circumstance that the Emperor of Austria is known over the whole of the East as the " German" emperor, and that this anachronism is always kept up by the use of the Slavic word " njemsza." When I told the scheik that I was from the country of the German Sultan, he asked his name. I told him it was Francis Joseph. For a moment he was silent, as if buried in thought ; then he said : " It is written in the Koran, ' I have set Joseph in the land of Mizraim to interpret dreams.' Your Sultan interprets the dreams and thoughts of the nations with our Sultan; the One God will bless the rulers of the believers and of the unbelievers ; and as they are friends, we shall also be the same. I am your humble servant."

He applied his right hand to his heart, his forehead, and his mouth, and I saluted him in the same way. Two of his servants, one of whom wore a red turban— the only one I saw at Jerusalem, were now ready to conduct me to the holy tomb.

Having taken off our shoes, we entered a church with three arches, two of which are pointed and supported by open columns in the centre of the building. A third column is half enclosed in the wall, and shows that the church was formerly longer, and was divided by a wall, in the upper part of which is a window, from which we afterwards looked down. There are three windows on the right of the entrance, which, in accordance with the barbarous architecture of a later date, are of different sizes. In the wall, opposite to the entrance, is a wooden partition of a reddish brown colour, which conceals a niche. You reach this niche by means of a broken column, which is used as a step.

In a corner, to the left of the entrance, is a stone baldachin shaped like a cupola, supported by a column and pointed arches; there is a staircase beneath it which ascends to a dark room, which is separated from the mosque by wooden lattice-work. Its roof, which is rather low, is supported by a heavy square column; the walls are painted grey and covered with passages from the Koran; the floor is covered with green and yellow carpets of little value. A rather low door to the left of the entrance opens into a room which is only imperfectly lighted through the open door. In the wall opposite to the entrance there is a long sarcophagus of stone, concealed from view by a heavy silk curtain. On drawing this aside, the sarcophagus announces in Arabic letters of gold, " This is the tomb of King David."

The Mohammedans threw themselves on the beau-

tiful carpet, and, touching the ground with their foreheads, began to pray. One of them, observing that
I gave no outward manifestation of respect, asked,
" Do you not venerate this prophet ? " It would have
been a bold act, and quite unintelligible to the pious
Mussulman to have told him, that to the Jews their
king—to borrow the language of Scripture—is nothing
more than the beautiful singer of Israel, and that,
personally, I did not consider him to have possessed
the spirit of prophecy, in a higher sense, than any other
poet possessed of genius and imagination.

On ascending again to the church, where, according
to the legend, Christ celebrated his last supper, we
were surrounded by a troup of inquisitive children—
boys and girls, white, brown, and black. All of
them entreated for backschiesch, with which I readily
supplied them. In the diagonal of the Moorish cupola
of stone, beneath which we again stood, is a small door,
with six stone steps leading to it. Our guide invited
us to accompany him from the church to the terrace, so
as to allow the ladies time to retire from the apartments behind this entrance. After a little, four
females, covered with white veils, passed us. They
were not so closely veiled, but that we could see their
black eyes sparkling through the opening. We again
entered, and ascended by the steps to an ante-
chamber, with a pointed arch half concealed. We
passed from it into a room, with bare, whitewashed
walls, with windows protected by wooden lattices, with
a dirty broad divan extending along the walls, and

over it niches with latticed doors, used as wardrobes. This was the harem of the watchman of Zion.

On our return to the church, we ascended by a staircase in the court to a broad terrace, which commands a beautiful view of the whole city. Straw mats were spread before a niche in the wall, for the use of the Mussulmans when engaged in prayer. A narrow staircase led into a hall, where there is also a sarcophagus in the wall, which has recently been whitewashed, and is covered with a canopy of green cotton. In the arch above, we deciphered thirteen names, written in Hebrew letters with a pencil ; probably, the whitewashing had been entrusted to a Jewish mason. From this room we could see the church below, through the window, to which we have already alluded. Another window on the opposite side commanded a view of part of the city beyond the Zion gate.

On returning to the court, we put on our shoes, and passed through a majestic lofty hall with pointed arches, into the open air. Here I dismissed all my armed followers, except the cavass Mussa. I now found myself in the Christian burying-ground, which is divided into separate divisions, for the use of the different sects, whom even death cannot unite. I read many of the inscriptions on the flat tombstones, which lay strewn around me like so many white leaves torn from a book, written by the hand of death. They told of pilgrims from every part of the world, and praised their lot in having been permitted to die in this place.

It was now evening, and the sun sank behind the mountains of Moab, around the summits of which there played a golden violet light, such as Moses saw when the glory of the Lord passed before him on Mount Sinai.

## JEWISH LEGENDS CONNECTED WITH KING DAVID'S TOMB.

In ancient times, a Pasha of Jerusalem once visited the tomb of King David, or "Nebi Daud—the Prophet David," as the Mussulmans call it, on Mount Zion. In order to see better, he stooped down and bent over the mouth of the vault. While in this position, his dagger, which was set with pearls and diamonds, fell from his girdle. He at once ordered search to be made for it, and, accordingly, a Mussulman was let down by a rope.

After a few minutes, he was drawn up again—lifeless. On this another Mussulman descended, and, after a few minutes, was also drawn up lifeless. A third and a fourth met with the same fate.

Then the Pasha swore that he would have his dagger, though the recovery of it should cost the lives of the entire population of Jerusalem. On this the cadi said to the Pasha :—" My lord, let not so many of the true believers become the victims of thine anger! But if thou wilt give ear to thy servant, send to the Chacham Baschi for a Jew to search for thy dagger. If he refuses, threaten him with the destruction of all the Jews. But my own private opinion is, that the dagger will be recovered, for the Jews stand well with Nebi Daud, and have great influence with him."

The Pasha approved of this proposal, and sent an order to the Head Rabbi of Jerusalem to provide a Jew to fetch his dagger from King David's tomb. The godly Rabbi was very much shocked at being ordered to desecrate the sacred tombs of the Kings by commanding any one to enter them. He begged with tears for a respite of three days, which was granted.

On his return home, he assembled the whole community, and ordered them to fast for three days. Each day, attended by the men and the children, he marched from the city in the direction of Bethlehem, to recount at the grave of Rachel, the pious wife of the patriarch, the fate that impended over her children, and to weep over it. This was done for three successive days; all fasted, prayed, and wept.

On the fourth day, the Rabbi said to the community: " One must die for all, and enter the tomb of the kings. Which of you will go?" All were silent. "Then it must be decided by lot." The lot fell upon one of the servants of the synagogue, a man of distinguished piety. " I am the servant of God," he said, and prepared his soul to meet death by bathing, and by immersing himself three times in water. After this, he bade adieu to his relations, and to the weeping community, and then went up to Mount Zion, to the vault where the kings of Judah were buried.

The Pasha already awaited him with his armed followers, and the poor Jew was lowered into the vault.

The Pasha applied his ear to the mouth of the tomb to listen; the hearts of all the Jews who had accompanied him were trembling with expectation, when, after a few minutes, there was a hollow cry, "Up! up!" The rope was drawn; first appeared the glittering blade of the dagger, then a hand grasping the hilt, which was set with pearls and diamonds, then the face of the Jew, pale as death, till at length his whole body emerged from the vault, and the astonished and delighted Pasha recovered his dagger.

From that time, the Pasha held the Jews in great honour, on account of the special protection which Nebi Daud extended to them.

The community held a jubilee; in every house might be heard the sound of feasting, accompanied with the music of drums and cymbals. But the poor family of the servant of the synagogue was the happiest of all; they were loaded with meat and drink, with presents of gold and silver.

Everyone wished to hear a description of the interior of the tombs of the kings; but he kept his own counsel, and confided his secret to none but the Chacham Baschi. When surrounded with darkness, he suddenly saw the figure of an old man, radiant with light, who gave him the dagger without saying a word.

### THE PIOUS WASHERWOMAN.

Once upon a time, there lived in Jerusalem a pious and virtuous woman; her husband and her children had long been sleeping in the Valley of Jehoshaphat, and she had no relations remaining on the earth. She waited quietly and patiently till she also should be carried through the Zion gate to the valley of the resurrection, and spent her time in prayer and in the strict observance of all the religious duties imposed on her sex. But as she was poor, she was obliged to work, and gained a scanty subsistence by washing for the rich. Among others, the scheik of the tomb of Nebi Daud on Zion gave her his linen to wash.

One day, when she had brought him his linen beautifully got up as usual, and he was alone with her in the court of the mosque, he said :—

"You are an honest woman, and I am disposed to reward your virtue. Would you not like to enter the interior of the tomb of David, which no one of your faith has ever seen?"

When she answered :—

"I should esteem such a favour the highest happiness."

He said :—

"Then follow me."

He walked before her till they came to a subterraneous door, which he opened, and ordered her to enter. Scarcely had she crossed the threshold, when he suddenly shut the door behind her, and left her in darkness. Then he hastened to the Cadi, and told him that a Jewish woman had stolen into the tomb of Nebi Daud, which was considered a heinous crime. As soon as he discovered this, he at once shut her in, that she might be delivered up to the punishment which her offence merited. The Cadi exclaimed, in anger :—

"By the life of the Prophet, she shall be burned alive."

Meanwhile, the poor pious woman saw that she had been betrayed by the scheik, and that her life was in danger. She threw herself on the ground, wept aloud, and entreated God, for David's sake, to rescue her from the fate which impended over her.

All at once, there stood before her a venerable old man, and though she had not seen him advance from any particular quarter, she did not feel at all astonished. It seemed quite natural, too, that he should be visible in the darkness which surrounded her. She could only see his outline in a dim, imperfect light, which did not extend beyond his figure. He took the woman by the hand—and even this act excited no repugnance on her part—and led her through a long, dark, subterraneous passage, till he reached the open air, at a heap of rubbish, near the synagogue of Zion; he then said to her: "Go to your house, begin at once to wash the linen which you have there, and do not show in any way that this has happened to you." The pious woman wished to thank her deliverer, but he had disappeared.

Meanwhile the cadi, the mufti, and the effendis of the city had hastened to Zion, for the purpose of seizing the criminal, and sacrificing her to Moloch. The subterraneous chamber was opened, and strictly searched; but no one could be found in it. The cadi angrily asked the scheik, " Are you making fools of us?" The scheik swore by the life of the prophet that he had told the truth, and gave the name of the washerwoman. The cadi immediately despatched some of his servants to the woman's house. They found her busily employed at her daily labour, and without stopping for a moment, she asked what they wanted with her.

"Have you not been out to-day?" the men asked.

She answered in a querulous tone :—

"Been out? I have been working since daybreak, trying to finish my linen, and to return it in the evening. Look, what a large heap of dirty linen still remains. These are hard times, and I earn but little, especially during the heat of the day. I have no time to go out, or to stand gossiping with you. Been out, indeed!"

When the messengers returned, and told how they had found the woman busy at her work, the scheik's report was pronounced by all to be a falsehood, which he had invented in order to make sport of the venerable cadi. There happened to be some dry olive branches lying about, with which a fire was speedily kindled. The cadi ordered the scheik to be seized and cast into the flames.

The pious washerwoman now got all the linen belonging to the community, as everyone was anxious to get her to talk about this singular affair. But she only rated them for their curiosity, and kept her own counsel. It was only when on her deathbed that she related her wonderful adventure. She bequeathed the property which she had earned by her industry to the community at Jerusalem, on condition that the prayer *kadisch* should be offered up at her grave, on the anniversary of her death, by a pious Rabbi. And this is done even to the present day.

ARABIAN LEGENDS.

King David, as we have seen, is regarded as sacred by the Mohammedans, and known as Nebi—*i.e.*, the prophet David, for God says of him in the Koran: "We have appointed him caliph of the earth; we bestow on him wisdom and the gift of eloquence, that he may judge men in righteousness. We give him dominion over the mountains from the rising to the setting sun, and also over the flocks of birds." There is a Mohammedan legend connected with this passage to the effect that when the body of the deceased king was being conveyed in solemn pomp to its final repose, a large eagle appeared above the procession, and spread out its wings. It hovered over the procession, till the body was laid in the tomb, when it slowly disappeared.

The Historian Hafis Ibn Aszakir introduces many of King David's sayings, which have been handed down by tradition, and of which the most original is :— "A stupid speaker produces no more effect than a mourner at the head of a corpse."

We are indebted to Mohammedan legends for the following traits in King David's character and circumstances connected with his life. After the treachery of which he had been guilty towards Uriah, the king was seized with the bitterest remorse. For forty days and forty nights he lay in the dust and wept. Two rivulets gushed from his eyes, and flowed from the terrace of the royal palace into the garden, where they were lost. The weeping willow and the incense tree sprang up upon the spot.

The Lord of the heavenly host sent down an archangel to him, who announced that his repentance was accepted. But David continued to weep, and asked :—

"How shall the Lord judge on the day of judgment between me and Uriah ?"

The archangel could not solve this question, and promised to ask the Lord. The Lord said :—

"I will indemnify Uriah on the day of judgment ; but my servant David must be reconciled to Uriah."

David went to Uriah's tomb, and throwing himself on his face, he cried into the tomb :—

"Uriah ! I have done thee a great wrong. Wilt thou forgive me ?" When a hollow voice answered :—

"Yes, my lord and king." The king continued :—

"Uriah ! I lusted after thy wife, and exposed thee to certain death on the field of battle through a treacherous letter. Dost thou pardon me in the tomb ?"

But the tomb was silent, and there was no reply.

The Lord sent the archangel to the tomb, who promised that it should be made up to Uriah a thousand-fold in Paradise, and then at length he forgave the king.

David had the art of bending iron soft in his hand,

and made shirts of mail such as were previously unknown. He used to sell them, and supplied his table
with the proceeds. A travelling angel had taught
him the art, and submitted to him that every king
should learn another art besides that of government, by
which he might earn his bread if his people should
expel him from the throne.

King David never omitted, on leaving his fortress, to
shut the door of his bedroom, and was very much
shocked when he returned one Sabbath, and observed
that he had forgotten to do so.

And actually a stranger of singular appearance had
stolen into his chamber. The king asked in anger,
"Who art thou, who thus dares to enter a king's
chamber, without being announced?"

"I am one," replied the stranger, "who have no
dread of kings, and whom bolt or curtain cannot shut
out."

The King said sadly, "Then thou art death," lay
down quietly on his bed, and gave up the ghost.

Mr. Endlicher came for me a little after sunrise,
attended by an armed escort; we mounted our horses,
and rode rapidly in the direction of the heaps of ashes,
which are situated about a quarter of a league from the
city, and are supposed to be the remains of the ancient
sacrifices offered in the temple.

These heaps of ashes are of a bluish grey colour,
and some of them are 40 feet high. There is a tradition, which cannot be relied on, that these are the heaps
of ashes formed by the burnt sacrifices offered in the

temple of Solomon, while most men are inclined to believe that they are the refuse of the potash used in the soap manufactories at Jerusalem. Mr. Finn was the first who directed public attention to them, and a quantity of the ashes was sent to Munich, and analyzed by Liebig. The latter gave it as his opinion that the ashes had really proceeded from the burnt offerings, as they were composed chiefly of animal substances, without any mixture of vegetable matter, and small pieces of bone and teeth were found in them.

We rode over stony ground, such as is to be seen everywhere in the vicinity of Jerusalem, and through scattered plantations of olive-trees. After passing the tombs of the judges, we found ourselves in a perfectly barren district, through which we rode for two leagues, till we reached a small village, which is situated in the midst of a beautiful plantation of fig-trees, pomegranates, olives and vines.

Behind it we ascended the steep eminence, 500 feet high, of Ramathaim Zophim, towards which Saul, the man of God, came, when he was searching for his father's asses. Recent researches prove, beyond a doubt, that this hill is the Ramah of the prophet Samuel, and that the modern village of Roba is the city of the prophet. Here also has been recognized the far-seeing Mizpeh, which means a watch-tower, where the tribes of Israel often assembled to be judged by Samuel, and to offer sacrifice to the Lord. We shall, in this instance, follow the threefold tradition of the Jews, the Mohammedans, and the Christians, without allowing a doubt to enter our mind; at all events, we are standing on holy ground.

Having reached the summit, we found ourselves before a ruined mosque, which is built on the foundation of a Latin monastery shaped like a cross, probably on the ruins of the monastery of St. Samuel, which existed here at the period of the Crusades. Thus this mountain, like many a minister of the present day, learned, according to circumstances, to be the representative of opposing systems, and to lend its shoulder to the founders of three religions: Moses, Christ, and Mohammed.

The ruins of ancient buildings hewn out of the rock are scattered around. Among these, three tanks can still be recognised. We dismounted from our horses; a little girl, ten years of age, with beautiful features, fastened their bridles together, in order to lead them to drink, and held them during our stay. We entered the desolate-looking stone building. We ascended a staircase, and found ourselves in a hall, which had open windows on three sides. There is a splendid view in every direction; the horizon extends beyond Jerusalem and the Mount of Olives; the Dead Sea glimmers in the distance; the towering forms of the mountains beyond the Jordan are clearly visible. Nearer at hand is the monastery of St. John in the Wilderness, the ancient Engedi. In another direction may be seen the level sea coast with its scattered villages, the lofty tower of Ramleh and Jaffa. By the aid of a telescope we could also see the white gleam of the Mediterranean.

A sublime feeling of solitude and repose reigned over the whole of this extensive landscape.

We lay down on the straw mats on the terrace, to rest ourselves after our ride and our exposure to the heat, which, even at this early hour, was oppressive, and partook of a slight meal, consisting of bread, eggs, cheese, and wine, which we had brought with us. Suddenly a noisy caravan approached, and halted beside us. It consisted of thirteen Jews, dressed in the Oriental costume. The most distinguished man amongst them was Mr. Isaac Russo, from the Dardanelles, a stately old man, with a white beard. After leading a chequered life as a dragoman, he had come to Jerusalem to die. He was accompanied by twelve of his friends; they were travelling to Hebron, Zafet, and Tiberias, and, at the end of their pilgrimage, they would bid adieu to their friend for ever, and return to their homes. But he would remain, and be buried in the valley of Jehoshaphat "after a hundred years."

The pilgrims began to intone the morning prayer, and the sound of our ancient and sacred language was again heard on these beautiful heights and among the rocks and ravines of the Holy Land, the same as it was thousands of years ago. Each one then offered up a prayer through the chorister, in behalf of some dead person highly esteemed.

After prayers, we descended by a staircase to a large square place enclosed with walls, which is now only partially covered by an arched roof, which has fallen in. We passed from this hall, which is filled with stones and starving rats, through a rude latticed wooden partition, and found ourselves before the prophet's coffin. Each of us lighted a lamp, which a servant of the synagogue had brought from Jerusalem, in honour of the holy place. We saw a long sarcophagus with a piece of dirty woollen cloth suspended over it, and copper *ezchajim*, trees of life, at the four corners. We lifted up the cloth, and saw a whitewashed stone chest, slightly arched above, which certainly did not seem to be of any great antiquity. There is a hole in the centre of this room, like that in a cellar, which leads to the real tomb. With the aid of our lamps we descended, but we could not discover a single object in the empty vault. The muezzim of the mosque led us into a side room and shewed us an entrance blocked up with stones, which he said led, by a narrow descent, to the iron door of the vault, which has never been opened.

We again ascended by the stair to the hall, which commands such an extensive view, where we were entertained with chibouques and coffee. I asked the muezzim if many pilgrims came here. "Not many," he answered, "and more Jews and Mohammedans than Christians."

We took leave of the pilgrims, mounted our horses, and rode rapidly along the green path at the foot of the hill, till the nature of the ground obliged us to proceed at a slower pace. After an hour we again reached the tombs of the judges.

In a pleasant wooded valley, the Wady Beit Hanina,

along a small eminence, where the small watercourse slopes down in the direction of the Mediterranean, there are a number of sepulchres with handsome portals. We descended into some of them, and found them divided into separate chambers, in which are niches for the reception of the dead. We passed through one of these portals into an entrançe-hall, in which four low narrow doors lead into side chambers, which contain seventy niches. This has led to the belief that these are the tombs of the Sanhedrim. The Jews honour them as the tombs of the judges, and esteem them to be sacred. They never pass without descending into one of them to offer up a prayer.

One morning, at 6 o'clock, in company with Mr. Endlicher, I rode through the Zion gate, and descended the steep hill to the fountain of Siloah. On reaching the valley, which is planted with olive, fig, and carob trees, with oleanders and vines, we turned round and had a splendid view of that part of the city which was over against us. It looked like one of the noble fortresses of the middle ages, defended and adorned with lofty walls, battlements, and towers, built on the summit of a rock, and apparently impregnable.

In the valley, men and women were busily engaged in field labour. Some of the latter were carefully collecting the dung of the cattle, which are frequently driven here to pasture and drink, into small heaps, which they enclosed with circles of stones, to prevent it from being scattered again. They remained unveiled, probably because they did not wish their labour to be

interrupted, and did not take the least notice of us.
The little valley had quite a lively appearance. Cows,
goats, and sheep were enjoying the pasture. The
fountain, called by the Arabs Ejub, the fountain of
Job, is enclosed with large stones. Colossal blocks of
stone and a large water-trough may be seen close to a
broken arch. Here we found an old man, who supplied
us with water by lowering a leaky leather vessel, shaped
like a bag. The use of a water-wheel, or any similar
convenience, has been quite unknown in Syria and
Palestine for thousands of years.

The tepid water had a peculiar flavour; it does not
taste of salt, except when it attains a greater
elevation.

The little tank, which is close at hand, and enclosed
with a wall, is reached by some steps, which descend
below. It was only half full of water, which was
covered with green slime. It is 53 feet long, and 18
feet broad, and is the pool or fountain of Siloah, of
which the Koran says, " Zemzen and Siloah are the
two fountains of paradise."

We came to another fountain on the rocky rising
ground. We mounted, by sixteen broad steps, to a
small level space, from which we descended by eight
steps to the place where the fountain flows from an
ancient slit in the rock. The learned Rabbi Schwarz
proved, from different authors, that it is the fountain of Gihon, and identical with the fountain of
Siloah, from which the pool of Siloah is fed through a
channel, hewn out in the rock. Robinson, with much

difficulty and self-denial, succeeded in crawling through this channel, and found it 1,750 feet in length. He also observed a phenomenon resembling the ebb and flow of the tide, which has not yet been explained.

We sat for a long time in the cool pleasant shade of the vault of rock. Memories of past ages floated through our minds. I was suddenly reminded of another grotto in another valley, as solitary and silent as this, close to one of the world's great cities—a grotto where I had sat twenty years ago, and in which Numa received the inspirations of the nymph Egeria. I thought of Jerusalem and Rome, which have twice been brought into close contact with one another in the course of the world's history, in ancient days, as the conquered and the conqueror, through Titus, " the villain," as the Jews still call him, and, at a later period, through Golgotha and the Vatican. What historical events shall the pilgrim ponder over a thousand years after this?

We mounted our horses, and rode from Siloah through the valley of Jehoshaphat. We ascended through the graves, and arrived at Bethany in half an hour. It consists of about twenty miserable houses, in the walls of which may occasionally be seen ancient stones, with rounded edges. These houses are scattered along the stony heights. A sunburnt girl, with large black eyes, about twelve years of age, came up. She held my horse till I returned from examining the sepulchre of Lazarus, which monkish tradition places here. We descended, by twenty-six steps, to a considerable depth, with the aid of some wax-candles, which we had brought along with us. Not a single trace is to be found of the church, which once stood here, or of the convent, which Queen Melisinde erected here for black nuns.

All was silent and desolate. None of the inhabitants, who are famous for their skill in straw-plaiting, appeared either to gratify their curiosity, or, what is still more remarkable, to beg for backschiesch. None but the girl, who held my horse, asked for it, and nothing could induce her to part with any of the silver coins, which were strung round her forehead as an ornament. The glittering, white frontlet had at each end a dollar stamped with a half-length figure of the beautiful German Empress, Maria Theresa, which reminded me of home. We mounted our horses, and rode up the Mount of Olives, where we again enjoyed the beautiful view of Jerusalem. The guardian of the mosque entertained us with lemonade, chibouques, and coffee, as we lay comfortably extended on straw-mats of a mosaic pattern—a specimen of the fine arts from Bethany.

After recovering from our fatigue, we rode down to the garden of Gethsemane. The gardener—an Italian Franciscan—opened a small iron door, and we entered the garden, which is shaped like an oblong, and enclosed with white walls. The elegantly-arranged flower-beds, in which roses, gillyflowers, and carnations, surrounded by borders of rosemary, were blooming, were shaded by a large cypress, and by eight olive-trees, which, though full of cracks, would scarcely have been pronounced by any botanist to be eighteen hundred years of age. An arbour of light lattice-work leans against the wall nearest to the city. We enjoyed the coolness of the arbour, which is overgrown with the tendrils of the vines. Surely their juice is better entitled to the name of Lacrima Christi than the wine which the hermit on Vesuvius once gave us under that name. We were allowed to pluck a small twig from one of the olives, and to break off a very small piece of the bark. In the days of the pilgrims, this was strictly prohibited, and we were indebted for this extraordinary favour to Mr. Endlicher, who knew the gardener. We were delighted with our visit to this pretty little garden; it was one of the few happy hours that we spent at Jerusalem.

Who can visit Jerusalem without desiring to see the Church of the Sepulchre? But the Jewish pilgrim, however much interested he may be in this building as an object of history or of art, must not venture to enter the place, which Christendom esteems so sacred. This fanaticism is, to say the least, imprudent. In no place are Christians more anxious for the conversion of the Jews than in Jerusalem. But so long as they exclude them by force from the Church of the Sepulchre, as is done at present, the less hope can be indulged of their conversion; or is there a shrewd suspicion, that if the Jews were admitted, there would be fewer converts?

It is evidently a strange inconsistency, of which the Christians are apparently unconscious, that the Mohammedan, who, from the very nature of his religion, is the implacable enemy of Christianity, walks without hindrance through this church, while the Jew is forbidden even to approach the entrance or the streets in the immediate neighbourhood. Moreover, this prohibition is uncalled for, as the Jew in Jerusalem, animated by the same spirit of fanaticism, looks upon a church as an unclean place, which, unless compelled by necessity, he is careful to avoid.

I had to enter the church at an early hour in the morning, when there are scarcely any visitors; the Austrian Consul's Mohammedan cavass accompanied me. I was obliged to wait at the entrance, which is beautifully paved, while the cavass went to get the door—before which several poor creatures were begging —opened for our admission. I was alone, and had an opportunity of leisurely examining the façade, which is very beautiful, though not quite consistent with the unities of art. An odour, peculiar to such establishments, proceeded from a tannery built in the immediate neighbourhood of the church. Two men came out of the building, and, regardless of the place, emptied a tub full of the lees used in tanning. After I had waited for a long time, the cavass returned, and the lofty portal was opened. Thus I am the first Jew who has entered this place during the last fifteen centuries, and I am thus in a position to describe it.

It is singular, that when we stand before some

mighty monument of the past, especially when it is consecrated by religion and history, and when the imagination has formed noble conceptions of it, while yet unseen, there is always a cold sensation of disenchantment. Such was my feeling on seeing the cupola of St. Peter's at Rome; the Acropolis at Athens; and the Pyramids in the desert. The imagination had invested the roof and gables with a grandeur, a splendour, and an atmosphere of holiness, such as the arches, however bold, and the lofty columns do not actually possess. The clever descriptions of the Church of the Sepulchre, which I had previously read, produced a far more powerful effect on my imagination than the building itself.

I do not like to see Shakespeare's tragedies—written domes—represented on the stage. The scenes and figures are compressed and diminished by the *coulisses* and the boxes. But, in reading them, the action proceeds uninterrupted by the assistants shifting the scenes, and the wide world forms the background. The everlasting mountains are the *coulisses*, the lofty clouds, illuminated by the sun, the boxes ; the royal apartment and the wild ravine have a majesty, a splendour, a freshness, and a dread reality, when viewed with the eye of the imagination, such as no stage-painter, however skilful, can ever produce.

The songs of Tasso, the verses of Klopstock, composed in honour of the world-renowned sepulchre, are still sounding in my ears like the solemn peal of an organ. I still listen to the transports of Chateaubriand,

and the pietistic phrases of Lamartine, which only excite disgust, called forth by a sepulchre, to obtain possession of which the Crusaders did not consider the sacrifice of a hundred thousand lives too high a price. And have we ourselves not lived to see a disastrous and fruitless war occasioned by these holy places? Such were the thoughts that passed through my mind as I, the adherent of another faith, crossed the threshold of the Church of the Holy Sepulchre, mingled at the same time with those feelings of reverence and of awe, which a building so important in the world's history and so interesting as a work of art could not fail to excite.

It is not my intention to give a historical or artistic description of the Church of the Sepulchre, which has been done thousands of times before. Nor shall I even write down those thoughts which were immediately suggested to the mind of a Jew in this church, as they could scarcely be realized or understood by the general reader. I shall confine myself to a mere sketch of the outlines of the church, and of the appearance it presented to my view.

On passing through the lofty portal, my attention was directed to a beautiful marble slab, on which the body of Jesus Christ is said to have been anointed by Joseph of Arimathea. Still advancing, I found myself beneath the boldly-arched cupola of the church, which is supported by sixteen noble columns, and contains two lofty galleries. The rotunda, with its marble floor of Mosaic work in different colours, is about seventy feet in diameter. The cupola, like that of the

Pantheon at Rome, is open in the centre, so that you can see the sky through it; but you can also do this at many other places, where the copper has been eaten away with rust, or been intentionally destroyed by the Greeks. They wish to make the building indispensably necessary, to keep it in repair at their own expense, and thus to enhance their claim to the possession of the church. The only way of ascending to the cupola is by the terrace, which belongs to the Greeks, and it so happens that it is most damaged on this side, while the north side—the one exposed to the storms—is almost uninjured. The birds which Venus yoked to her team were twittering through the openings, possibly to remind us that the heathen Romans here erected a temple to this goddess in derision of the Christians. The one sect will not allow the other to repair the roof of the cupola, because each is afraid that, if the other should do so, it would have a better right to the possession of the church.

"We hope," said my Italian guide, by way of explanation, "that the great Sultan will furnish a new roof for the cupola."

This appears to us the proper place to correct an error common to Christian pilgrims, which is frequently repeated in conversation and in their writings. They believe that the Mohammedans are in possession of the holiest place in Christendom. But it is not so. The Turkish Government does not claim to exercise any authority over this property of the Christians. This fact is indisputable. The matter stands thus :—Three

Mohammedan families have for centuries been invested with the feudal right, so to speak, of acting as janitors at the church. To prevent disorder, one of these families retains possession of the key, and shares with the two others the small fee of 60 paras, which they receive for opening the door. When the great door is opened, the fee is 70 piastres, or 100 piastres for the right of entering the church at any hour during the day.

I must confess that this arrangement appeared to me a wicked parody on the keeper of the gates of heaven. When I expressed my surprise to a Catholic priest at Jerusalem, I received this striking answer : " God be praised that such is the case. If it were otherwise, every one who wishes to support the dignity and services of religion would pray for the present arrangement. As the Trojan war broke out on account of St. Helena, to whom we are indebted for the discovery of the holy cross, and who is buried here (I am not responsible for the worthy abbé's strange anachronisms) in like manner a contest would soon arise among the Christian sects for the possession of the key. Such a contest would bring religion into contempt, and probably be attended with bloodshed. And, in fine, the church itself is best protected against the fanaticism of the Mohammedans, when the janitor happens to be a Mohammedan."

We had now reached an open marble chapel, which stands in the rotunda, and is over-arched by the cupola. I entered a place lighted by fifty silver lamps, suspended on silver chains. Beneath this brilliant light is a stone, which the legend points out as the one on which the angel sat, when he announced that Christ was no longer to be found in the sepulchre. Opposite to the entrance of the chapel is a small opening, so low that I had to bend before I could pass through it. I found myself in a dark narrow place, which contains a marble trough six feet long. This is the tomb of Christ.

The fertile invention of legends and traditions connected with this place has proved a very fortunate idea, as it has had the effect of attracting pilgrims from a distance.

Judging them by pure psychological principles, the monks cannot be regarded as altogether a useless race, inasmuch as they give a visible representation of those objects which pious pilgrims long to behold. Plain men, full of child-like simplicity, who require to be influenced from without, are thus incited to the fervour of ardent devotion.

I once stood in a splendid under-world. White alabaster stalactites, reflecting the red light of our torches, had something of the effect of enchantment. We soon entered a place, which our guide told us was the dome. We ascended some steps to a sparkling throne of ice ; then we passed through rows of columns, and stood before some altars, over which were suspended white baldachins, which borrowed a reddish tinge from our torches, and we saw the outlines of a gigantic organ. Such names were not strictly applicable to the different objects, but the imagination was easily excited by these names and resemblances, and could create from them, without an effort, a church, a palace, or an obelisk.

The church of the sepulchre may produce the same effect on pious Christian pilgrims. It may present to their minds a poetical representation of all the forms and groups of sacred history, and an illustration of the great events connected with the early history of Christianity, and may thus have the effect of a marble volume illuminated with gold and silver initials and arabesques. At all events, this place has been venerated as the sepulchre of Christ for fifteen centuries, and therefore may be regarded as a monument which, though it does not contain the dead, has been erected to his memory. As such it should be respected by all true believers, and ought never to be stained with the blood of hostile sects.

We bestow a smile of pity on the dancing or the howling dervishes, or on those who throw themselves beneath the feet of the Sultan's horse to be trampled to death.

How barbarous and grossly inconsistent with the character of Christ is the conduct of the Christians, who butcher one another at the sepulchre which they esteem most sacred, even at the tomb of Christ, in their struggle to light their tapers first, at the annual descent of the fire from heaven on Easter day, or on similar occasions. At the side of the chapel, is the opening through which the fire is extended to the expectant believers. " This miracle," my catholic guide explained, " only enables

these heretics to exact more money from the pilgrims."
I was touched with the sight of the small wooden
altar of the Copts, at the outer wall behind the chapel
of the sepulchre. It looked like the nest of a bird,
which had migrated from some far distant country, and
built a home for itself in the gilded roof of a marble
palace. This humble poverty struck me as being more
in keeping with the nature of the place, than the osten-
tation of the Armenian and Greek churches.

We then walked through the large labyrinthine
church, which really consists of several churches and
chapels, built sometimes on the same floor, and sometimes above and below one another. We visited the
prison of Christ, the place where he was mocked, and
where Mary waited while her son was being put to
death, the chapels of Longinus and of St. Helena, to
which we descended by thirty steps. Here the archduke Ferdinand Maximilian recently erected a marble
altar, on which there is a representation of St. Helena
holding the cross in her arms, on the spot where a
wooden altar formerly stood.

On entering the church of the Latins, which has
dark pews for the choristers, extending along the walls,
we were saluted by a peculiar odour from a neighbouring passage, the exact nature of which we shall not
describe. A circle in mosaic marks the spot where
Mary Magdalene mistook Christ for the gardener.
The picture over the altar, like all the pictures in the
church of the sepulchre, is perfectly worthless as a
work of art, and it is surprising that, while Christians

delight in adorning their churches with pictures, this church, which may be regarded as the property of the whole of Christendom, does not contain one real work of art. Is there no Giotto, no Cimabue, no Bellino, no Kranach, no pious painter left?

The Franciscan monk, whom I found here, conducted me with the greatest politeness to the sacristy, and drew from a wooden chest the heavy gold chain, the spurs, and the long heavy sword of Godfrey de Bouillon. I observed on the black iron hilt some traces of former gilding. I drew it from its modern sheath of red morocco, and solemnly saluted the spot where the sarcophagi of this chivalrous romantic hero and his brother Baldwin formerly stood in a dark passage. When the Greeks rebuilt the church, after it was burned to the ground in 1808, these sarcophagi, which were adorned with Latin inscriptions, and had been spared by the flames, were carried off. The report is general in Jerusalem, that they are still concealed in the Greek monastery, or that they were barbarously destroyed, and the ashes of the hero, to whose bravery the Christians are indebted for the possession of the tomb of their Saviour, scattered to the winds. On the spot where the sarcophagi formerly stood, are stone benches, covered with straw mats, intended for the use of visitors.

There is a small coffee-house at the end of this passage, where the visitor is offered a cup of Mocha with oriental courtesy. I felt very much disgusted at such a custom in a place like this.

The Franciscan then conducted us by a series of
steps to certain small cells, situated in crooked, angular
passages, where some of the monks of the Latin monastery are always engaged in watching, in doing penance,
or in fasting. They must remain in these cells for
three months, till they have been absolved by their
brethren. There is a stable, containing the horses of a
Mohammedan, built close to these cells, and the vapour,
with which they are all filled, is not at all agreeable to
a stranger. We withdrew as soon as possible.

On our return to the principal church, we again
ascended by flights of steps to a small church, the roof
of which is supported by a pillar, and which has an
altar on each side. This was Golgotha. All the rock
here is richly faced with marble; at one space a silver
plate is introduced into the marble. It represents, in
*alto-relievo*, the fissure in the rock, caused by the earthquake at the death of Christ.

Though learned researches have proved, beyond a
doubt, that this is not the place where Christ was put
to death, it is still esteemed to be so by the faithful,
and even thoughtful minds will look upon it as
symbolical of that event. It is for this reason that this
rock should never have been enclosed within the
building. It may be, however, that not a trace of it
would then have been left on the earth, as each of the
countless thousands of pilgrims who have visited it
would have carried off a small fragment as a relic.
But the impression and the poetical effect are lost.
The rock on which " that man," as the Talmud desig-

nates him—who is recognised by the deeper thinkers among the Jews as " the apostle of the Gentiles," and who is worshipped by millions of men as their Redeemer, was put to death—should never have been disfigured, concealed, and almost hidden from view in this way. This rock should have stood free in naked solitude, like that of Prometheus, " the godly sufferer," or should have towered aloft in the midst of the ocean, like that of the chain-forging Titan, of modern times — a pyramid in the desert of the world! If this rock were the real historical one, it would be an act, not of vandalism, but of magnanimity, to break down the gigantic arch of the church of the sepulchre, and to hurl its marble ruins down the sides of the hills on which Jerusalem is built.

My guide—if I may venture on the expression— hurted me through all these places. He was anxious to finish his task as soon as possible, and to receive his fee of five francs, and I was heartily tired of his monotonous explanations, recited from memory. The building produced no other impression on my mind than any large cabinet of curiosity would have done. I confess this with sorrow. All the earnest expectations and lofty sentiments which I had connected with it were disappointed by the objects presented to the intellect and the senses, and the pre-occupation of my mind with the undertaking in which I was so deeply interested, may have aided in producing this effect. Mussa, the cavass, afterwards informed me confidentially, that the guide, having observed that I did not show any of those signs of reverence which the Christians exhibit in presence of the holy places, asked him with much anxiety whether I was a Christian. " His mind was at ease," said Mussa, " when I told him that you were a mad Englishman, and that the English, while they profess Christianity after a sort, are a nation of heretics."

As we were leaving the entrance, we found the Mohammedan janitor sitting cross-legged on a carpet with some of his friends, drinking coffee, and blowing clouds of smoke, which entered the church. He also eats his dinner here, which is sent to him from the monastery.

I was addressed by two men before the church, who asked me if I would like to have a representation of some sacred object tattooed on my arm. The Holy Scriptures clearly forbid tattooing. " Ye shall not make any cuttings in your flesh for the dead, nor print any marks upon you; I am the Lord." In glaring opposition to this prohibition is the Mohammedan legend, which ascribes the invention of tattooing to King David. After he had been guilty of such treachery against Uriah, he was seized with the deepest remorse. In order to retain a painful remembrance of his crime, he scratched out, with a sharp iron stylus, on his legs and arms, the accusation against himself. Since that time it has been the custom in the east among pilgrims to Jerusalem and Mecca to tattoo the year of their pilgrimage, or a verse from the Koran, on some part of the body. This pious custom afterwards spread, and lovers burned out on their arms fiery hearts, or even complete portraits of their mistresses. The Bedouin women, even at the present day, tattoo their lips in blue, and sometimes impress indelible beauty-spots on their foreheads, their chins, and their cheeks. The crusaders introduced this custom into the west, where it is still observed among soldiers, wandering apprentices, and pilgrims to Jerusalem.

One day we were startled by the information that subterraneous chambers had been discovered. Our curiosity was excited in the highest degree, and we descended to the foundation of the Austrian hospital by means of ladders. We found ourselves in a grotto, in which we could stand erect, with columns hewn out of the rock, and still connected with it, two of which are quadrangular, while the other three resemble the petrified stems of trees. Two windows and a door were blocked up with stones. In the stone floor, near the walls, are round holes, cut out apparently for the reception of ropes, on observing which the Arabs at once pronounced the grotto to have been a stable for horses. It appeared to us rather to have been a den for wild beasts, where they were kept by some Roman emperor, before being introduced into the circus. Though we were very anxious that the excavations should be continued, we were not provided with the necessary funds, in consequence of which, discoveries which might have been of the deepest interest have been lost for centuries; this much, however, seemed to be certain, that these buildings were beneath the level of the *via dolorosa*, and thus proved that its claims to antiquity rest on a very uncertain foundation. Another grotto, nearer the Damascus gate, is higher, but smaller, and the floor is paved with a sort of mosaic of stones, an inch in diameter. Two pieces of beautiful white marble were lying on the floor; I carried one of them home with me, along with a fragment of mosaic, which Mr. Endlicher kindly gave me.

One day, I rode out to visit the Monastery of the Cross. After riding past an open Mohammedan burying-ground, over stony fields covered with olives of a greyish green tint, and through a valley on the left, we halted, after twenty minutes, before the Monastery of the Cross. Jerome relates that the ark of the covenant must have stood on one of the small hills close to the road along which we had passed. What period or circumstance is there which may not afford food for a bold imagination! The monastery stands on the spot where they felled the tree from which the cross of Christ was made.

It is difficult to describe this monastery. Large courts, open staircases above and below, large apartments, balconies, a belfry, halls with arched roofs and open terraces, all seem to have been built at random, without any fixed plan, and for that very reason have a peculiar effect on the imagination. No eye, save that of a skilful architect, could detect any fixed law in the erection of this modern Arab building.

We saw two schoolrooms, where boys are instructed

in the elementary branches of education, in religion, in geography, and languages; and were then conducted to the admirably-arranged and well-ventilated hall where the pupils sleep, and to the refectory, where the tables were spread with exemplary propriety with supper for the monks and the scholars.

## CHAPTER V.

A ·TALENTED and graceful Servian lady, resident in Vienna, whose own heart may have been labouring under some great sorrow, had one made of silver as a gift for the Church of the Sepulchre. She requested me to convey it to the Greek Monastery. My name was engraven on the heart as the pilgrim who was to bear it to the Holy Land, and as I was provided with a letter of introduction from the Greek Patriarch of Jerusalem, whose seat has been at Constantinople for many years, I felt the less difficulty about the visit, which I had put off till my mission was completed.

We were struck with the noble heads and handsome features of the priests, who received us in the most friendly manner; they knew that I was a Jew, but did not seem to consider that there was anything extraordinary in my being the bearer of such a gift, or of a beautifully-carved cross of linden wood, which a friend had requested me to get consecrated at the holy sepulchre. A priest was sent to the church of the sepulchre, which had to be opened expressly for that purpose, to fasten the heart to the altar, and to consecrate the cross.

Meanwhile, we were entertained with chibouques and coffee, with candied fruits, liqueurs, and fresh water. The representative of the patriarch gave me a receipt in Greek for the sacred heart, and had great difficulty in writing my name, as in truth he did not seem much accustomed to handling the pen. When acting on a hint from my companion, I offered a small sum in return for their kindness, in opening the church and consecrating the cross, it was declined with these words :—

" We are indebted to you for the gift which you have brought to us from a distant country. The name of the pious lady is not unknown to us, may God bless her and her distinguished father." We parted in the most friendly manner; about twelve priests escorted us to the gate.

Though I had no letters of introduction, I met with the same friendly reception at the monastery of the Armenians. It forms, with its extensive buildings, its courts, its terraces, its church, and its garden, almost a quarter of the city.

In the dwelling of the patriarch, who was present, we were entertained with the usual refreshments on silver dishes. The walls of the lofty and extensive apartment in which we sat were resplendent with painting and marble. We were particularly struck with a fountain, skilfully cut out in alabaster, and with a beautiful trellis of polished brass; the floor is covered with a mosaic of marble, painted in different colours. The paintings, however, are all worthless as works of art. Garlands of empty ostrich eggs, strung on cords of red silk, and suspended before an altar as ornaments, had a peculiar effect. A hospital, which forms part of the building, has just been completed. It forms a parallelogram on the first floor, and will afford accommodation for a hundred boys.

As the miserable little chapel of the Copts in the church of the sepulchre forms a touching contrast to the splendour of the whole building, so also the Abyssynian monastery can only be compared to an asylum for poverty, when contrasted with the palaces of the Greeks and the Armenians.

In a large court, one of the sides of which is enclosed by the church of the sepulchre, may be seen fragments of columns, some scattered on the ground, others standing erect, but broken through the middle. The joints of arches are visible in the walls, and the whole place has a ruinous appearance. It is shaded by some mulberry trees. In the middle of this court is a building which looks like a chapel, and on peeping through the window, I saw a low gloomy chamber, dimly lighted by a lamp, supposed to be the tomb of the Empress Helena. Along the walls are isolated rooms, the doors of which open into the court, and thus admit the light, for they have no windows. These are the cells of the black monks and the black nuns, who may be seen clothed in tatters, squatting on the filthy floor and smoking, or walking round the court, not merely resembling beggars, but actually begging. A nun, who veiled her old, black, shrivelled face more from habit than modesty, was grinding maize between two stones. I was struck by observing among these monks what I had never seen before—a black face with snow-white eyebrows, bleached by age, and a long white beard. I was invited by the monks, whose poverty would not altogether excuse the neglect of Eastern hospitality, to partake of the ripe mulberries, which were hanging on the trees. The monk who acted as our guide, expressed his gratitude for the small present which I gave him, by kissing my feet.

I formed a very favourable impression of the establishment of the Prussian deaconesses. On entering, I found sister Charlotte, for whom I had been entrusted with a message from the superintendent of the evangelical church at Vienna, sitting in a room in the court. She was suffering from fever, which unfitted her for more serious labour, and was amusing herself by arranging dried flowers, which had been gathered at places of historical celebrity. She kindly gave me some wreaths, arranged with an artistic sense of beauty, as a pilgrim's gift for friends, and at my special request plaited a crown of thorns for me.

Sister Rosette led us to the sick chambers, where there are five beds for men and four for women.

The sisters' special care is to provide the sick with attendance, medicine, and food. There were four girls in the school-room who are instructed by one of the sisters in the elements of religion, of natural history, and of geography, and also in English and German.

The Protestant minister, for whom Dr. Roser, the Prussian Consul, has just purchased a house for 13,000 dollars, in the name of his Government, was instructing one of the sisters from the Bible, in the library.

My conversation with the sisters and the minister, though very agreeable, contained nothing worthy of insertion in my note-book. They seemed to have a clear and intelligent conception of the duties of everyday life, and did not manifest, at least in their discourse with me, the smallest approach to pietism. The institution has been established on a broad and liberal basis;

and everything connected with it gave me the impression of admirable order and fragrant cleanliness.

Dr. Fränkel, who is employed as a physician in many Mohammedan families, procured me a favour which is always alluded to in the West with longing curiosity or a knowing smile—I mean, admission to a harem. As I have just returned from the harem, without having been exposed to any danger, or suffered any damage from the white, brown, and black wives and female slaves, or excited the jealousy of Turkish husbands, I shall describe this paradise of the Mussulmans, and disclose some of its mysteries.

Without being previously announced, we entered the house of the wealthy effendi Faëdi. We ascended from a narrow, dark entrance hall, by a series of steps, to an open terrace ; here the master of the house, who was walking up and down, received us with the greatest kindness, and invited us to accompany him into the women's apartments, on the next story.

On reaching the top of the stairs, we found ourselves standing before a small door, near which were lying several pairs of wooden sandals and yellow slippers, just as they had been laid aside by the women, so as not to dirty the carpets.

The lady of the house, who was not old, though she appeared to be so, was sitting with her four married daughters, one of whom, who had formerly lived at Nablous, and been left a widow, had returned to her early home. Dr. Fränkel met with the warmest reception, the same as a family friend in Europe would do ;

in fact they almost embraced him. Then we were requested to be seated on the divan.

The conversation was carried on in Arabic, and referred to ordinary subjects, in which I felt little interest. I had thus time to observe the scene and the actors. The room had four windows, which were furnished with narrow wooden lattices instead of shutters. They enabled you to see everything that passed on the street without according the same privilege to the passengers. Along the walls were broad divans, about a foot high, covered with coloured chintz; the floor was covered with a carpet. A niche in the wall, with a wooden door painted in different colours, was used as a wardrobe.

The ladies wore flowing striped robes, open in front, so that the breast could be seen through the bright rose-coloured, delicate veil. The head was covered with a *tarbusch*. The eyes, lips, and cheeks were painted; there was no particular expression in their features, which, though agreeable, had nothing very remarkable about them. The nails and the palms of the hands were painted yellow.

The ladies now and then drew their veils over their chins, and then dropped them again, so that this act seemed to be more the result of habit than of intention. In this matter, as in many others, the law of the Prophet has become obsolete in the East.

An Abyssinian female slave, young, and strikingly voluptuous in form, brought us lemonade, narghilés, and coffee, with the usual silent salutation. Her hair was somewhat crispy, and hung dishevelled over her dark, bronze-coloured face, while a peculiar light flashed from her bright, grey eyes. Her nose was short, and beautifully shaped; and her protruding lips and dark complexion, while they marked the race from which she sprung, imparted a peculiar brilliancy to her splendid white teeth. It may be that the master of the house noticed that my eye rested on this slave a little too long; at all events, he gave a knowing smile, and hearing that I wished to buy a black boy, he sent me a diplomatic note a few days after, to inquire if I would not prefer a black girl.

The widow was the liveliest of the party; there was no end to her jokes with the doctor, and, using him as her interpreter, she addressed to me the following questions :—

" How can you have a man like this, who never gets married again, for your friend ?   Have you a wife ? "

I answered in the affirmative, and then she asked :

" Have you only one ? "

" In the West we are not allowed to have two."

She said in a tone of real, sincere compassion : " Ye poor creatures !" and then in a more lively voice : " Do you know anything on earth more beautiful than a woman ? "

" Yes; four women ! such as your prophet allows every Mussulman to have."

The ladies laughed, and our host said : " You are a very knowing Frangi, and I am surprised at the extent of your scholarship; but in the West you labour under a

N

mistake regarding us. We have seldom more than one wife; but we can easily get quit of our wives when we are dissatisfied with them, and can always marry another."

The ladies listened with serious and deep attention to our host's remarks. In fact they always listened to him with the greatest respect whenever he spoke.

The lady of the house now asked me whether we guarded our wives strictly; and when I observed that with us every lady has her own and her husband's honour in her own keeping, and can only be said to be guarded in the sense of being under his protection, she replied:—" There can be no better proof of a husband's affection than his keeping a strict watch over his wife."

After remaining for an hour, we parted with mutual regret, and their invitation to call again became more pressing when the ladies learned that I was a physician. Following the beautiful custom of England, they gave us a hearty shake of the hand at parting, and accompanied us to the door of the room, while our host escorted us to the door of the house.

After this, we went to another house to visit a Mohammedan lady, who was suffering from fever. She was lying on the floor in the corner of a room, exactly similar to the one we have just described. In Mohammedan families the beds are prepared every evening and removed again in the morning.

The sick lady was fifteen years of age, and the mother of two children. There was something very graceful in the expression of her countenance. The fever gave a hectic flush to her cheeks, and, after complaining of acute pains in the liver, she cried several times in a tone of entreaty that reached the heart, "Make me well soon, for my husband's sake." A female slave had conducted us to the room where she lay, and probably owing to the great pain which she was suffering, she did not betray any uneasiness when she saw me, a perfect stranger, enter with the doctor. He introduced me as a brother physician, and she at once extended both her hands to allow me to feel her pulse.

The interior of the house of Effendi Mohammed Ali had a richer, and to me a perfectly novel appearance. Passing through a small gate into a dark, arched entrance-hall, where a horse and an ass were stabled, we ascended a few steps to a large court filled with mulberry trees covered with red blossoms, in which twelve black slaves of both sexes and of every age were engaged in light labour. The women were dressed in long robes, the men were half naked, and all were engaged in the liveliest conversation.

The women were washing vessels of brass, fire-pans, ewers, and narghilés, at the cistern; the men were cleaning pipe-stems, or carrying small bundles of wood ; the children were tumbling about in merry confusion.

The lady of the house was walking about among them, dressed in a picturesque costume, and smoking a paper cigarette. On our entrance, she covered her face with a thick black veil. She saluted the doctor, and expressed her regret that her husband was not at home. At the same time she invited him and his friend to make the house their own. Then she at once left the court, and retired to the women's apartments.

The doctor explained to me, that she had veiled herself and retreated thus rapidly, on account of my presence and the absence of her husband. He had attended her some years before, when she was delivered of twins, and since that time she has shown an amount of gratitude and esteem for her medical attendant such as is not always exhibited by ladies in the West under the same circumstances. He declared that his experience has led him to the conclusion that gratitude is one of the most striking features in the Mohammedan character.

Two handsome boys, seven years of age, now rushed from the apartment to which the lady had retreated, and ran up to the doctor, their faces beaming with joy. " Look now ; the mother sends her children to show her respect for me. Listen to the answer they will give me. Who am I, my dear children ?"

They shouted as if with one voice : "Thou art our second father."

They conducted us round the house. At the top of a staircase was a large room, with numerous latticed windows. The divans were adorned with bright red woollen cloth and fringes of gold ; the cushions were also covered with red cloth, inwrought with gold flowers. There was no lustre or mirror to be seen ; the frames of the windows, the cupboards in the walls, and the doors were of common wood, and no attempt had been made to paint them.

"Such is the boasted splendour of the East," said the doctor.

We crossed the terrace, and passed through arches, courts, and an indescribable chaos of building, to another side of the establishment, where another saloon, with adjoining chambers, had just been completed.

In the year 1855 a Jew happened to mention to the Scottish traveller, Douglas, that there is a small opening in the city wall before the Damascus gate, which leads to large, deep caverns, from which the stones used in the erection of the temple were quarried. Mr. Douglas contrived to visit them secretly along with a few friends, and gave a short account of his discovery in the London "Athenæum."

A short time before my arrival in Jerusalem, a scene occurred in connection with these caverns, which, though rather suspicious at first, had an amusing end. One day a considerable number of Jews, provided with ladders, ropes, crowbars and lanterns, were seized by the Turkish soldiers, and conducted to the residence of the pasha. As most of them were Aschkenasim, they were taken for Russian spies, who, as the Turkish-Russian war was still raging, wished to betray the city of Jerusalem into the possession of the Russians, by measuring the fortifications, and digging secret mines.

As most of them were subjects of Austria, or at least under her protection, the circumstance was brought under the notice of the Consul, who soon solved the difficulty. The report of the Scotchman's visit to the caverns before the Damascus gate had been circulated

among the Jews, and when they heard that they had
supplied the stones for the erection of the temple, they
could not resist the impulse, and imprudently went to
examine the caverns, without having obtained permission.

My curiosity was also excited, and Count Pizzamaho
who was himself anxious to see the caverns, made
known our wishes to the Pasha. Mr. Barrère, the
French Consul, and Mr. Endlicher, the architect, had
joined us.

Preceded by the cavasses, and followed by several
men carrying torches, ladders, and some bottles of wine
and cognac, we reached the Damascus gate at three
o'clock P.M. After crossing the heaps of rubbish, that
have been conveyed from the foundation of the Austrian
hospital, we found, about 50 yards in front of the gate
toward the right, a low and narrow opening in the
living rock, on which the city wall is built. After descending about a fathom, we found ourselves beneath
an extensive, low, vaulted roof, which forced us to bend
down as we advanced. The floor was covered with
rubbish, which varied in quantity according to the
depth of the caverns. The bones of animals, such as
hyenas or jackals might have left after their meals, lay
scattered around. At the end of this area we found
ourselves on the edge of a deep chasm, roofed by large
arches, which were supported by lofty, gigantic columns
of rock. Two men descended with torches, the red,
picturesque light of which was reflected from the
lofty cupola, and spread through the surrounding space.

We made our way through narrow passages, here and there over the narrowest rocky paths, through clefts, past grottoes and niches, over heaps of detached blocks of rock, beneath arcades and vaulted roofs supported by columns. At one place we heard the trickling of water, and, following the sound, we saw it dropping down. The water had a bitter taste, and softened the rock. I named the spring "The Jews' Tear."

On advancing farther, an inverted pyramid seemed to arrest our progress; it was only the partition wall, behind which we found other places, where colossal blocks of rock were cut out, which, in size at least, were similar to those which we had seen in the temple wall and elsewhere in Jerusalem.

Again we saw other places, where the outlines of similar blocks were marked out in the rock by a slight incision, and remained thus incomplete, in consequence of the work having been interrupted. We wandered with difficulty, sometimes ascending to a giddy height, at other times descending into a dark abyss, for two hours, through this subterraneous world, which was formerly known traditionally only to a very few individuals.

Our imaginations were excited, and we felt that we had a right to bestow a name on the new world, which we had discovered. A piece of rock in the roof, shaped like an acute-angled triangle, was called "David's Harp;" a long gallery of rock was named after Godfrey de Bouillon; a lofty wall and tower of rock was the prison of Richard Cœur de Lion; a grotto close to it, that of the minstrel Blondell. A piece of rock threatening to tumble down from one of the heights was the stone of Sisyphus; and a quadrangular space, with a niche at the bottom, was the church of Leopold the Glorious. Four domes were named by the consuls—the residence of Queen Victoria, the mosque of Abdul-Meschid, the palace of Francis Joseph, the mausoleum of Napoleon.

On our return to the entrance to this subterraneous world, we drank to the peace of Europe, the newspapers announcing which had just reached Jerusalem. Fiery toasts in a world of sepulchres, in the land of miracles, of vanquished kings and of silent prophets !

When we handed the bottles and the glasses to our attendants, who were partly Jews and partly Mohammedans, they drank the brandy and the wine with pleasure, and, as if animated by the noble sentiments to which we had given utterance, began to dash the glasses against the rocks, the fragments of which, as the light of our torches fell on them, sparkled like stars in a dark night.

A few days after this, I visited these caverns a second time, with Dr. Rosen, the learned Prussian Consul, whose thirst for knowledge had been excited by my account of our expedition. He hinted that we might have seen the " cavati sub terra montes," mentioned by Tacitus, and that passages connecting these caverns with the subterraneous places beneath the site of the temple might yet be discovered. A closer examination, conducted by such archæologists and topo-

*graphists as Robinson and Tobler, will, no doubt, disperse the darkness which rests, as yet, on these subterraneous places.

Mr. Endlicher promised to undertake new measurements, and to draw up a plan of these caverns, which we supposed to be ancient, long-forgotten quarries. We shall soon submit his labours, accompanied with explanatory notes, to the learned world.

My attention was directed by Mr. Finn, the British Consul, to the sepulchres in Aceldama, the field of blood, where the skulls of different races are arranged separately. Mindful of the task assigned to me by the Academy of Sciences at Vienna, which I had already tried to execute at Athens and on Mount Lebanon, I was very anxious to examine the sepulchres, and, if possible, to carry off some trophy to prove that I had visited this subterraneous world. Mr. Finn invited me one day to accompany him to the field of blood, but business prevented me from accepting the invitation. He afterwards kindly introduced me to Mr. Rogers, the English Vice-Consul at Khaifa, under whose guidance, attended by a cavass, I visited this interesting world of sepulchres.

We passed through the Jaffa Gate, and, advancing along the dry bed of the Kidron, we came to a steep perpendicular declivity, forty feet high, in the valley of Hinnom. It is full of sepulchres, consisting usually of one vault divided into several chambers. The most of the sepulchres are blocked up with stones and rubbish to such an extent, that you do not observe them till

you are close to them. At the entrance of one of
these sepulchres there is an inscription in Hebrew
characters, consisting of four lines; only five words of
which are legible. The first line begins with the word
למלכות, the second with שנת; in the middle of
the fourth line are the words למלכותש and a ש
which is not very legible. Rabbi Hillel, the picturesque
describer of Jerusalem, was misled by the last letter,
which is an S, to read Solomon, and thus to suppose that
the sepulchre was as old as the reign of the king. The
Hebrew words, taken in the order in which they stand,
signify "days," "year," "under the reign of the king
and lord." Unfortunately, the most important point of
all, the date, is lost. Some peculiar veins in the stone
of a neighbouring sepulchre have also been taken for
Jewish inscriptions. There are Greek inscriptions in
some of the others.*

A modern English author affects to have discovered
these sepulchres, which Edrisi mentions in the twelfth,
and Felix Fabri in the fifteenth century, as ancient
Jewish sepulchres. They seem to be the same as those
to which Benjamin of Tudela alludes. They have also
been supposed to be the sepulchres of pilgrims and
strangers, in which pious hermits, like the Mohammedan *marabus*, formerly lived.

I asked when we should reach Aceldama, or the field
of blood, bought for thirty pieces of silver, and learned

* Dr. Stanley must have been ignorant of the existence of these
inscriptions when he wrote his "Sinai and Palestine." At page
148 he says:—"Instead of the acres of inscriptions which cover
the tombs of Egypt, not a single letter has been found in any ancient
sepulchre of Palestine."—Tr.

to my surprise that this was it.   The limits of the field
of blood are not clearly defined, and it is only tradition
which points for centuries to a certain spot in the declivity of the hill as the original field.   A long arched building of stone, now in ruins, from which you can look
down into a deep place resembling a cellar, is the ancient
dead-house, through an opening in which the dead
bodies were lowered into the vault.

I remembered that twenty years ago I had already
stood on the Aceldama in the sacred field at Naples.
At the commencement of the thirteenth century,
quantities of this earth, which, it was piously believed,
destroyed dead bodies in twenty-four hours, were conveyed to Italy as ballast.

We had brought wax candles with us, to enable us
to examine the caverns more minutely; but we could
not light them before we reached the sepulchres, as we
had to crawl along on our hands and our feet.   At
the entrance of the vault, which was hewn out of the
rock, we saw low openings cut out on both sides of the
rock.   We entered, and found in all of them open
coffins, in which were skulls, and only a very few other
fragments of bones and small pieces of cloth, fast
crumbling to dust.   After we had entered each of the six
sepulchres, and had returned to the entrance vault, we
crept into an opening, which descends through the
floor, opposite to the entrance.   We here found hundreds of skulls lying in chaotic confusion.

Only a very small number of them seemed to have
belonged to the Caucasian race; most of them exhibited
the negro type; but this may have been merely the

result of accident, as in another vault we found the case reversed. There was nothing approaching to a symmetrical arrangement, such as I had heard of at Jerusalem, or as may be seen in the catacombs at Sedlec in Bohemia; there was not even a division of races. Perhaps there may have been such a division originally; but every visitor may have removed skulls from their places as we did, without restoring them to their former position. Several also rolled beneath our feet into another vault below. I carried off three of the skulls.

Another vault had an entrance, composed of three cut stones, which were adorned with two wreaths and twisted bread, like the sepulchre of Kalba Zebua. The entrance exhibited faint traces of blue and red paint.

Dr. Neumann, whose ample rotundity of person prevented him from gliding through the low and narrow openings as we did, was waiting for us at the entrance. The cavass carefully concealed the skulls in a bag, so as to prevent the robbery which we had committed for the benefit of science from being observed by any of the passengers we met. Our act would have been equally condemned by Jews, Christians, and Mohammedans, and we might even have been exposed to some danger.

It is surprising and remarkable how often the number forty occurs in the Holy Scriptures. The waters of the flood prevailed forty days and forty nights. Jacob presented Esau with forty gifts; both of them were forty years of age when they married. The people of

Israel sojourned forty years in the wilderness; Moses remained the same number of days on Mount Sinai. The men who were sent to spy the promised land returned after forty days. The land had peace forty years after the victory over Cushan-risha thaim, and after the victory which Deborah gained on Mount Tabor. Forty days Goliath stood mocking before the camp of Israel. King David, and Solomon, and the High Priest Eli reigned forty years. Jesus Christ was seen of the disciples forty days after his death, and forty stripes was the ancient Jewish punishment. Forty is the round number used in the Scriptures when the exact number is not known. It so happened that I remained exactly forty days in Jerusalem, and if I may also venture to speak in round numbers, received forty moral stabs in my soul. The most painful and sorrowful of all was the fortieth day which I spent in Jerusalem.

I stood on the place of the Holy of Holies in the temple of Jehovah.

Where is the man who has not longed to visit this spot? It alone is worthy of a pilgrimage to Jerusalem. The accomplishment of the ardent desire of hundreds of thousands was always prevented by the Mussulmans; but the Jewish pilgrim was also prevented by his own co-religionists. Since the time when the temple was reduced to ruins, and purification could no longer be effected through the ashes of the mystical red heifer, every Jew considers himself unclean. But, according to the Holy Scriptures, no unclean person must enter the temple, and the curse of extirpation adhered to every Jew who violated this command. Such was the law while the temple remained entire.

After its destruction, we find in the *Itinerarium Hierosolymitanam* of the year 333 after Christ, the following passage : " There is a stone there"—we shall afterwards see this stone on the site of the temple in the mosque of Omar—" to which the Jews come every year ; they anoint it, weeping and wailing, and rending their garments."

Rabbi Akiba, a martyr to the doctrine of the unity of God, ascended the Mount of the Temple with some friends. When they descended, and began to say : " Our temple, our glory, where our fathers once praised Thee, is burned to the ground, and all our splendour destroyed," a fox started up among the ruinous walls and rushed past them, and at this sight they all began to weep. But Rabbi Akiba laughed.

" How canst thou laugh, Rabbi," they asked, with surprise, " when thou seest the fulfilment of the prophecy : ' Because of the mountain of Zion, which is desolate, the foxes walk upon it ? ' "

And he answered : —

" The fulfilment of this prophecy is an earnest to me of the fulfilment of another, which says : ' I the Lord, will build up Zion, and enclose it with a wall of fire.' "

Mr. Rabbi Schwarz told me, that at the time of the Egyptian conquest of Syria, in 1833, the Mussulmans one morning found a young Israelite in the mosque, who had stolen into it the previous night, and madly broken the lamps and different utensils. He was soon discovered to be insane, but, notwithstanding this, he was cast into prison.

No Jew dared to appear in the streets, and the high council condemned the madman to be burned alive. This sentence required to be confirmed by Mehmed Ali. Instead of doing so, he surprised them all by giving the following decision :—

" Let the guardians of the *haram*, who have been so remiss in the discharge of their duty, be punished. The punishment of being burned alive can only be inflicted on the uncircumcised. The Jew should certainly not have entered the holy place, but, being circumcised, he cannot be burned."

It struck me that the pious Rabbi intended this circumstance as a warning to myself, for, as I often directed the conversation to this subject, he must have divined my secret intention.

My longing desire to see the site of the Temple was excited at a very early period, by reading descriptions of it and of the holy service. My imagination often dwelt on its sacred battlements and its desecrated ruins; it mastered me when I had the unexpected good fortune to be allowed to visit Jerusalem as a pilgrim ; it would not leave me at rest in the holy city, and when I had seen the view from the pasha's audience chamber, which looks into the court of the Temple, and witnessed the whole from the Mount of Olives, it broke forth into a passionate impulse, which I could no longer control. When I approached the vicinity of the haram every day, and saw the entrance to the Temple standing open, I always lingered near it, and it was with the greatest difficulty that I could restrain my almost irresistible impulse to enter, and thus expose myself to fatal danger.

A short time ago, the Archduke Ferdinand Maximilian and the Duke of Brabant were allowed to visit the site of the Temple. The Austrian Consul, who procured them admission, took advantage of this opportunity, and, as there was a great crowd assembled to see the princes, he allowed all who chose to accompany them. The Mohammedan population thus became accustomed to the sight of "Christian dogs" in the place, which, after Mecca, they esteem to be the holiest on earth, and as the scheik derived considerable profit from the visit, it was no longer difficult to obtain permission.

The very pious and strictly orthodox Sir Moses Montefiore, did not scruple to visit the mount of the Temple, and to force his way even to the holy of holies.

He was the first Jew, in the course of fifteen centuries at least, who stood in the place, where the high priest alone ventured to enter, and that only on the day of atonement.

It was a sabbath; I attended morning prayers at the synagogue of the institution, so as to be able to visit the site of the Temple at a later hour, when the Jews were assembled at the chief synagogue, and none of them visible in the streets. The Russian and Polish

Jews would only have been too glad to use this as a pretext for excommunicating me, and, as the chief community would have been grieved at this, I did not wish to give them an opportunity.

I had no scruples about my own personal purity or fitness for admission into the holy place, and I was certainly not disposed to deprive myself of a pleasure, which could never be forgotten, because some foolish talmudist has prohibited it.

It is one of the characteristics of Judaism that it renounces, nay even strictly prohibits, all stimulus to devotion through the medium of the senses. This is clearly proved by the Scriptures, by tradition, and by history. There is no memorial of the past, no picture, or peal of music to excite the pious feelings of the Jew, and to direct them heavenward. His divine service is marked by the strictest asceticism, which admits of no outward representation of the invisible God, of no sculptured figure in the attitude of prayer, pointing the way to eternity. How deeply rooted in the Jewish mind is that faith, which, like a perennial fountain, has poured forth its waters for thousands of years—waters often polluted and poisoned, but ever purified and healed again! And yet the Shemitic race are reproached for possessing a preponderating sharpness of intellect, which has certainly been ever whetted by social oppression at all times, and in all countries. The study of sacred and profane literature, which was always tolerated, nay, even commanded, could not fetter the wings of Jewish faith, as it soared aloft towards the One

Invisible ; persecution, shame, derision, death, could not destroy it. What more striking proof can there be that science, study, knowledge, are not opposed to pure faith or pious feeling?

I have no hesitation in expressing my belief that the most intelligent and sober-minded race in the world —the race of merchants, represented by Jews and Englishmen—are the most strictly observant of the precepts of religion. On the other hand, twenty years ago, I visited a land, where all scientific researches were prohibited, where the free development of the intellect was fettered, and I found that in that land religion and morality were extinct. And this same land, the government of which was most strict in enforcing the observance of all the outward forms of religion, was the very first, in which, during the late critical period, a political revolution broke out.

Delighted at having obtained the Pasha's ready consent, I betook myself to the harem at eight o'clock in the morning, attended by the cavass of the Austrian Consulate. We entered the guard-room of the Pasha's house, the walls of which were adorned with muskets, pistols, and sabres, and which, if it had been a little cleaner, would have had rather an imposing appearance. The officer of the guard invited me to a seat on the divan, which was covered with a torn carpet. I declined the chibouque and coffee which he offered to me, under the convenient pretext that it was the Sabbath, on which the Jews are not allowed to touch fire, or of course to taste anything that is newly cooked.

After waiting for a few minutes, I was joined by the scheik of the mosque, a tall, powerful man, armed with a long staff, the Pasha's cavass, several men, some of whom were armed, and a Syrian Christian, who acted as interpreter. The scheik invited me to follow him. We passed through a narrow, dark passage, from which we soon emerged into the full light of the site of the temple.

In order to convey to the reader a clearer conception of the whole, I shall not interrupt my narrative with any description of my own feelings.

The platform of Mount Moriah is about 1,000 feet in breadth, and 1,600 feet in length, and is enclosed on all sides by lofty massive walls, about fifteen feet high in the interior. Five entrances lead from the western side of the city, where the wailing place of the Jews is situated, up to the site of the temple.

On this side are Saracen buildings, balconies, turrets, arches, halls, in which there are some "medreschen," or Mohammedan schools, and places of abode for the dervishes, the servants of the mosque and pilgrims. On the open ground before them are two baths, over-arched by cupolas. On the eastern side rise the lofty walls of the Golden Gate, or the Gate of Mercy, as the Jews call it.

Higher up on this platform is a terrace, which is reached by a series of broad steps from every side. We ascended one of these stairs, which consisted of about fifteen steps, and had a pointed arched roof. This upper platform is 550 feet long and 450 feet broad, is inlaid with marble of different colours, and supports the judgment-seat of King David and the mosque of Omar. Before ascending the steps, I had to take off my shoes, which made walking over the wide stony space that lay between very unpleasant.

The judgment-seat, as the Mussulmans call it, is a cupola supported by lofty, slender marble columns, and inlaid with a species of marble of different colours. Beneath it is an oratory, arranged in such a way as to enable the pious Mussulman who enters to look toward Mecca.

The neighbouring mosque of Omar, erected in the seventh century of the Christian era, is shaped like an octagon, each side of which measures 67 feet. The light is admitted through fifty-six windows with pointed arches, which are furnished with bright, painted glass. The pilasters between the windows are inlaid with black, green, red, and white varnished tiles, while the lower part of the wall is adorned with marble of different colours. The glittering tin-roofed cupola is crowned with a ring that shines like gold. Perhaps it is intended to represent the full moon. The building, which you enter by four lofty gates looking toward the four points of the horizon, is surrounded with arched marble halls. On entering I found myself surrounded by a dim religious light. The brilliant light of the windows was softened by the boldly-arched dark cupola, which is supported by four heavy stone pillars and twelve Corinthian columns of marble.

Beneath this cupola is a huge, round block of stone,

with a covering of red damask suspended over it, and
a gilt iron railing enclosing it.   This is the *eben sch'tia*,
"the stone on which the ark of the covenant stood—
from which the world was created," as we are told in
the Talmud.   It is a block of limestone, similar to the
huge aerolite which fell on the area of the temple, and
is still lying there, and which caused the mosque to be
called Kubbet es Sukhrah—the cupola of the rock.   I
walked round the open circle between the gilt railing,
by which the huge block of stone is enclosed, and
a corridor, composed of eight stone pillars and sixteen
Corinthian columns of marble, which extends round
the whole building.   The scheik raised the heavy covering of red damask several times to allow me to see the
stone.

The walls of the mosque and the cupola, which is
skilfully constructed of beams of wood, are painted
gold and green, and adorned with arabesques and passages from the Koran.   We descended by a stone
staircase beneath the carpeted floor of the splendid
building, which, with all its decorations, is very dirty
and very much neglected.   We were now in "the
noble cavity of the Mussulmans," an extensive space
hewn out in the rock on which the mosque is built.
Here it was to be seen naked, undermined, and supported by beams of wood.   The place was about the
height of the human figure, but its circumference enclosed a considerable space.   On descending, the scheik
pointed out to me two niches used as oratories, where
David and Solomon used to watch and pray and un-

bosom the desires of their hearts before the Lord of the Universe.

When the scheik struck a metal plate inserted in the rocky bottom with his long staff, it gave a hollow sound, as if the floor had been undermined. Beneath this plate there is really a deep, empty space, which the Mussulmans call Birraruah, "the well of the souls," and believe to be the mouth of hell. It is frequented by all those who wish to hold mysterious converse with the dead. As the bold visitors were exposed to considerable danger from the attacks of evil spirits, the open mouth of the well was covered with the iron plate.

The Christians as well as the Mohammedans regard this rock as sacred. The former believed during the middle ages that it was the stone on which Jacob slept, when the angel descended to him from heaven, and on which the angel of death, who was sent to destroy the people on account of David's sin, stood. There is a legend also that this stone lay beneath the Holy of Holies in the temple, and that its interior still contains the ark of the covenant and the sacred vessels. The Mussulman regards it as inferior only to the stone at Mecca in sacredness; it is called "one of the stones of paradise," and is also supposed to be the one on which Abraham sat before he went to sacrifice his son. The scheik pointed out to me the prints of the fingers of Abraham's hand.

Leaving this mysterious place, we again ascended by a flight of stairs, to the platform of Moriah. Gigantic cypresses, many centuries old, here tower into the deep blue sky; a marble basin is shaded by some orange and olive-trees.

We now proceeded to the other mosque, which is situated on the south side of the area of the temple. This mosque is supposed to be an ancient Christian church, dedicated to the virgin; it is shaped like an oblong square, and has an imposing effect with its eight rows of marble columns, which support immense architraves overspanned by bold arches. The antiquary will attach far more importance to the vaults hewn out in the rock beneath and near to the church, which are supported by colossal pillars and square stones of immense size. The scheik explained to me that this was the under part of Solomon's temple. He broke off some fragments with a stone, and gave them to me as a *souvenir*. He also broke off some twigs from the cypresses, and presented them to me as "children of the sanctuary."

I now put on my shoes again, and walked round the site of the temple, attended by the scheik and his armed followers, who never left me for a moment. No one else was to be found on the large area, except a few workmen who were repairing the walls.

It was with a feeling of deep sorrow that I wandered over the quiet sunny spot. The walls were overlooked by the Mount of Olives with its stony ridges covered with greyish green olives, which looked like pilgrims, who had climbed up and remained standing, gazing at the mournful landscape and the city spread out below, and raising their branched arms aloft in the attitude of prayer.

All at once there arose a quarrel among my attendants, in consequence of one of them having asked for a backschiesch, while I had previously handed over to the scheik the whole of the sum which I had agreed to pay, to be divided among the rest. The interpreter would not condescend to explain to me the cause of the quarrel, but I had no difficulty in discovering that the scheik had kept the most of the money for himself. This was not the first time that I had seen Arabs quarrelling, otherwise I should have been afraid that there would have been blood spilt on the occasion, so violent were their gestures, while their eyes flashed with anger, and their voices were raised to the loudest pitch. And yet, in a few minutes, they were all following me or walking by my side on the most friendly terms.

As I continued my walk, I observed on the south side of the city wall, a sort of trench without any steps for descending. In one of its sides was a wide opening, which seemed to lead to a cavern. When I asked if it was possible to enter, the men answered in the affirmative, and encouraged me to make the attempt. I looked inquiringly at the Christian interpreter, who gave me a re-assuring answer. My attendants remained above, while I glided down one of the sides of the trench, which was about three fathoms in depth, sometimes planting my feet on the projecting stones, or in the openings in the wall, while I held on with my hands by the stones above. I then passed through the opening into a deep cavity, which descended far below the level of the site of the temple, and found myself surrounded with darkness. Gradually a faint light was visible, which enabled me to examine the place more closely. It was of considerable extent, and contained massive stone pillars, which supported large arches.

The whole place is full of stones and rubbish, often reaching to the very roof; it was with the greatest difficulty that I managed to advance a few yards, aided by the faint light, which entered through some holes in the side by which I entered, and which had to force its way through the heaps of rubbish which had accumulated before this subterraneous excavation.

This discovery filled me with the greatest surprise. The place reminded me of the thousands of subterraneous columns near the Almeidan at Constantinople. My only regret was that such investigators as Robinson and Tobler should not have been able to examine this place as well as the site of the temple, and to give the learned world the benefit of their talented researches. As I was quite unprepared and unprovided with instruments for making observations, I could do nothing more than impress a general picture of the whole on my memory. I was inclined to believe that this might be the "cavati sub terra montes" of Tacitus; the excavations beneath the site of the temple, to which Simon, the last warrior of Jerusalem, retired with his followers, when the city was besieged by Titus.

I was one of the last who entered the ever-remarkable site of the ancient temple of Jehovah; now that Kiamil Pasha is no longer governor of Jerusalem, admission is sternly refused by the Mussulman authorities.

# CHAPTER VI.

## LEGENDS CONNECTED WITH JERUSALEM.—THE
### LAST HIGH PRIEST.

ZION had fallen, and the work of destruction had been almost completed by the rude soldiers of Rome. The temple of the Lord had been destroyed, and the atmosphere, which had once been perfumed with the incense of the sanctuary, was now filled with clouds of smoke and dust. The priests of the Lord had shared the fate of their countrymen, all except the venerable old man who stood at their head. A special providence had seemed to watch over him and to guard his hoary head from the daggers of the Roman soldiery. But as he gazed on the noble columns of the temple, now broken and scattered around, and saw only heaps of ruins on the place where the glorious shechinah had once shone, and thought of his brethren, who had once aided him in the solemn services of the temple, his heart melted within him, and he felt that it was better to die and not to live. His eyes were heavy with sorrow, and his white beard was wet with tears. He passed through the desolate streets of the city. All was still and silent; it seemed abandoned of God and deserted by man. He reached the site of the temple, over which a dark cloud was still impending—the emblem of Jehovah's anger. He knelt down among the ruins, and raising his streaming eyes to heaven, thus spoke :—

"It is finished. Thou hast left Thy people and for ever. Thy temple is desecrated. The shechinah is extinguished, the altar hewn in pieces. The streets are slippery with the blood of Thy priests and Thy people. I alone am left, a minister without a people, a priest without a sacrifice. It is enough, my task is over, and now I kneel in Thy presence and restore to Thee with trembling the key of Thy temple."

He held aloft the key of the temple. For a moment all was still; there was no voice and no answer. Then all at once there was a rift in the dark cloud, a flash of light illuminated the heights of Moriah, and a hand of fire descended and seized the key. Next morning's sun saw the old man extended on his face amid the ruins of the temple. The last high priest of Jehovah was dead.

### THE FIRE IN THE ARK OF THE COVENANT.

It is customary in Jerusalem for the servant of the synagogue, after the *kidusch* or benediction is pronounced on Friday evening, to take the wine to his own house, and to carry it back again to the *hafdalah*, at the close of the Sabbath.

One Friday evening, the servant of the Talmud-thora synagogue, who was quietly sleeping in his bed, was suddenly awakened by a person whom he did not know. The stranger ordered him to hurry at once to the synagogue, as a blood-red fire was blazing in the *heichel*, the ark, where the thora rolls are kept, and threatening to destroy not only the synagogue, but also the whole congregation. The terror-struck servant rushed to the synagogue and opened the Ark of the Covenant, but could not perceive any traces of fire; he observed, however, in the faint light, that the bottle of wine, which he had placed there, after the benediction, had been removed from its place. This circumstance excited his suspicion.

He took out the bottle, and saw at once by the faint rays of the *ner thamid*, the everlasting light, that the bottle had been exchanged for another, and when he

poured out a little of the contents, he perceived at once
that it was filled with blood. He destroyed the bottle,
and placed another filled with white wine in the Ark,
closed the door of the synagogue, and again lay down
and slept.

Next morning, immediately after the commencement
of divine service, the Pasha of Jerusalem and the Bishop
of the Greek monastery, followed by a large number of
Mussulmans, Greeks, priests, and soldiers, made their
appearance in the synagogue. All the Jews were pale
with terror, except the servant of the synagogue; he
knew that the terrible fire in the *heichel* was fortunately
suppressed and extinguished.

The Pasha ordered his servants to search every hole
and corner of the synagogue, and when nothing was
found to excite suspicion, a Greek pointed to the
*heichel* and cried : " You must look there." The
servants opened the *heichel* and immediately found the
bottle beside the thora rolls. The Greek shouted :
" That is the blood of a Christian child, which they
have butchered for their sacred rites."

The Bishop took the bottle and said to the Head
Rabbi : " What does this glass bottle contain ? "

The Rabbi answered : " Wine, which we use in pro-
nouncing the blessing."

The Bishop took the silver cup, which stood in the
ark, and filled it from the bottle. It was a gold-coloured,
fragrant wine, such as is pressed from the grapes of
Hebron. He handed it to the Pasha and to all the
spectators, to convince them of this. After all had

examined the silver cup and satisfied themselves about its contents, the Bishop begged the Head Rabbi to forgive them for having interrupted the service; a liar, pointing to the Greek, had deceived them.

The Pasha drew his dagger from his girdle, intending to put the offender to death; but the Bishop restrained him with the words; " Do not defile a sanctuary that has been consecrated to the One God, the Father, with the blood of a traitor."

When they had left the synagogue, the Greek thought that he could save his life by penitently confessing that he had placed a bottle full of blood in the ark, and could not understand how it had been removed.

But the Pasha's anger was still more excited, and he struck him down with his dagger.

### RAIN.

About 150 years ago, the inhabitants of Jerusalem were in a state of great anxiety, because the autumn was already far advanced, and no cloud had yet appeared in the heavens, to indicate the approach of rain. They are dependent upon the autumn rains, not only for the fruitfulness of the soil, but, also, for the supply of water for the cisterns. When the cisterns are not sufficiently full, men and cattle are reduced in the summer months to the last extremity.

All the cisterns, and especially the terraces, from which the rain-water flows into them, were carefully cleaned. All were longing for the life-giving rain, and not a drop would descend from heaven. Jews, Mohammedans, and Christians spent their time in prayer, in fasting, and in forming processions to the tomb of Rachel, which is toward Bethlehem, to the tomb of Nebi Daud, and to the Church of the Sepulchre. The heavens remained closed, and their flood-gates would not open.

Then the Pasha sent to the Head Rabbi of Jerusalem, to the pious old Galanti, blessed be his name! and threatened to banish him and all the Jews from Jerusalem and Palestine, and to destroy their sanctuary, if it did not rain in three days; as the wicked nation of the Jews were alone the cause of the obduracy of heaven.

" You pride yourselves," he said, " on being the chosen people of God, and call Him your Father. Prove now, in the hour of your trouble, that He hears your prayer. Otherwise, by the life of the prophet, I will do as I have spoken."

The Jewish community was in despair. The head Rabbi ordered a three days' fast, and crowds of men, women, and children assembled before the wall of the temple, weeping and praying.

Towards sunset, on the third day, the Head Rabbi commanded the whole community to follow him in solemn procession to the tomb of Rabbi Schimon the Just, blessed be his memory! in order to implore for rain there. At the same time he ordered them to provide themselves with cloaks, mantles, and shoes, as their return from the tomb would be accompanied with violent floods of rain.

While all were astonished at this prediction, they did as they were commanded, and followed their pious Head Rabbi in solemn procession through Bab-el-Amud, the northern gate of the city. When the officer of the guard saw the procession dressed as if it were raining in floods, he could not restrain his laughter. When he was told of the pious Rabbi's prediction, so little in keeping with the cloudless sky, he flew into a violent passion, and struck the venerable Rabbi in the face. The old man looked him calmly and solemnly in the face, and proceeded with his followers, till they came to the valley of Jehoshaphat, to the tomb of Schimon the Just. The Rabbi knelt down on the spot where the head of the deceased lay, and the others knelt around him. Loud and solemn was the sound of their wailings and prayers; but the Rabbi—as was reported by those who knelt next to him—spoke inaudible words into the tomb. The words were so powerful, that their hearts trembled, even though they could not hear them.

All at once there arose a strong wind, so that the trees on the Mount of Olives shook their branches, and the blue, white heavens were overcast with clouds. Heavy drops of rain began to fall, but the Rabbi never ceased to speak ardent, inaudible words into the tomb, till torrents of rain descended from heaven, and all were obliged to wrap themselves in their cloaks and coverings.

The officer of the watch now hurried to the spot, threw himself at the Rabbi's feet, and humbly begged him to forgive the insult which he had offered him.

Then he raised him on his shoulders, and carried him to his residence.

The joy of Jerusalem was unbounded. In every house, for three days and nights, might be heard the sound of cymbals and kettle-drums, of singing and clapping the hands, and the Jews held feasts and enjoyed themselves three days and three nights without ceasing.

Mohammedans and Christians openly expressed their belief that they were indebted solely to the Jews for the rain, and acknowledged with shame that the prayers of the Jews had met with more acceptance from God than their own.

On the fourth day, the officer of the guard came to the Rabbi and requested to be admitted into the covenant of our fathers, and to wait on him as his servant.

### THREE CABALISTS.

Rabbi Schalom Scharebi, Rabbi Chajim del Rosa, and Rabbi Joseph David Azulai were men of deep piety and learning. They had mastered all the mysteries of the cabala, and they knew more about the things of earth and heaven than any other men, and they rejoiced in their knowledge and ceased not to study day and night. Their only source of sorrow was that the Jews were still languishing in the chains of slavery, and scattered over the whole earth, while the Messiah delayed His coming. On the eve of one of the festivals, they formed the violent resolve to force the Messiah to come by their strength of intellect and firmness of will.

They began to prepare themselves for this conspiracy

by fasting three days, which they continued to do through successive weeks, with only one day of an interval in each. They scourged one another's bodies, and when there was a fall of snow, such as occasionally happens in Jerusalem, they exposed themselves in the snow. During the whole of this period, they withdrew from all intercourse with their wives, and prayed and studied more than they had ever done before.

When they believed that their spirits had reached the necessary degree of purification, they arose at the hour when *chazos* is performed, and ascended the lofty terrace of the synagogue, and engaged apart in ardent, fervent prayer. Then they approached one another, and uttered the mysterious, mighty name of God, which they had never dared before to pronounce, and when it passed their lips, their hearts trembled, and their knees shook.

Then through the air came the solemn sound of the Bas kol, the voice of the Invisible: " If ye do not cease from your ardent thoughts, and your violent attempts at coercion, the world must be destroyed, as ye wish to accelerate that, the time fixed for which in the councils of God has not yet arrived."

All three fell on their faces, and listened, breathless, to hear what the voice would still say to them.

" One of you must withdraw from the holy city, as only three together can constrain the Messiah."

The three continued to listen, but there was no other voice or sound, and they rose up, pale as death, from the terrace, for they knew well what must be done.

Each one wrote his name on a piece of parchment, and placed it in a book. It was agreed that the one, whose name was drawn, should leave Jerusalem immediately.

On the same day, Joseph David Azulai prepared to depart, and no member of the community could understand why he left the city so suddenly, and all were very sorry for the pious Rabbi. He embarked at Jaffa for Leghorn, where he passed a life of great strictness, devoted chiefly to silent meditation, and, after his death, he enjoyed the reputation of a great cabalist.

Many years had elapsed since this occurrence, and, as Rabbi del Rosa lay on his death-bed, surrounded by his pupils, he said to them :—

" When I am dead, do not carry me from the house ; seize me by the legs, and drag me down stairs through the city, through the Zion Gate, and throw me into the ditch."

His pupils were seized with horror, and trembled before the dying man.

When the Rabbi was dead, and his body washed, and the wailing for the dead had begun, the corpse was placed on a bier, and borne on their shoulders to " the house appointed for all living," as they could not find it in their hearts to comply with the request of the dying man.

When they had set down the bier, the men of the village Siluam, which is situated above the burying-ground of the Jews, came up and began to abuse them, on account of some money which was due to them.

As the Jews were unarmed, they were obliged to flee, and the Fellachim, wishing to insult the dead body, seized it by the legs, dragged it over the tombstones, till the head was crushed, and then threw it into the ditch.

I could learn nothing regarding Rabbi Schalom Scharebi, and know not what death he died.

### THE HAND.

Towards sunset, three maidens sat on a terrace shaded by three mulberry trees, covered with red blossoms. The first bore the same name as Abishag, the beautiful Shunamite. Her cheeks were like a " piece of pomegranate within her locks." The second was called Sultana. Her eyes were blue, and might be called dove's eyes, like those of the Shulamite; " her hair was as a flock of goats, that appear from Mount Gilead." The third was called Miriam. Her lips were like " a thread of scarlet," and all three were fair to look upon.

These three maidens sat on the terrace, engaged in gay conversation, such as maidens delight in, and bound flowers among the gold ornaments on their temples, and among their hair, which fell down in numerous tresses over their necks, even to their waists.

At the same time three young scholars sat in the Jeschiba of a pious Rabbi at the foot of Mount Zion, deeply pondering on some difficult question of talmudistic lore, and striving to find the solution. But one of them only seemed to be thus engaged; his cheeks were pale and sunk with watching through successive nights, and both his friends had often seriously warned him to avoid all intercourse with the spirit-world. But he wished to have the mastery over spirits, and studied the cabala. His friends were too deeply engaged in their talmudistic researches to observe that he was thinking only of Abishag, whom he loved with an all-absorbing passion, which was not returned. As he dreamed of her charms, he felt himself so near to her, that in the delirium of passion, he resolved to force her to love him.

On this the three maidens on the terrace witnessed a singular occurrence. The sun was setting; and as they twined their arms round one another, and gazed on his dying rays, they sung the lovely passage of the sublime song : " I am the rose of Sharon and the lily of the valleys." Then they were encircled with a gleam of bright light, from which a small, white hand descended and seized the hand of Abishag, and a feeble voice pronounced the words of the marriage ceremony : " Hare at mekudeschet li." Then the pale, delicate hand rose like a white dove and disappeared.

The maidens had stopped short in their song, and looked and listened in silence to all that had happened. But it was singular that none of them were surprised at the wonderful phenomenon, or at the sound of the feeble voice, and they resumed their song: " My beloved is white and ruddy ; the chiefest among ten thousand. His head is as the most fine gold, his locks are bushy and black as a raven; his lips like lilies, dropping sweet-smelling myrrh."

Soon after this event, Abishag was promised in marriage to a young man by her parents. On this a youth appeared to her with hollow cheeks, and threatened to accuse her before the Besdin, as she had already married him on the evening, when he put down his hand and pronounced the words of the marriage ceremony.

Abishag was very much shocked, and went and told the Head Rabbi of Jerusalem what had befallen her. The Head Rabbi with his Besdin recognized the validity of the marriage with the hand, but postponed the ceremony for a whole year.

The maiden's parents refused to submit to this decision, and erected a marriage canopy, and led their daughter Abishag, accompanied with the sound of cymbals and of drums, to the expectant bridegroom. But the small, white hand again descended, and a feeble voice said: " If I may not have thee to wife, at least favour me with a kiss."

The bystanders said, " You may have twelve if you like."

They heard the sound of the kiss, which the invisible one bestowed on the young bride. It was the kiss of death—she sank on the floor and her lips were silent for ever.

### A FAMILY " MEGILAH."

The circumstance we are about to relate occurred in the year 5167, in the reign of King Saragasanus, who resided at Saragossa, where many Jews lived and worshipped Jehovah in twelve splendid synagogues. It was an ancient custom, when the King entered the Jewish quarter, for the oldest Rabbis of each of the twelve synagogues to advance to meet him with the sacred thora rolls of parchment, which were kept in ornamented boxes. They were joined by the whole community, and when the Rabbis, at the sight of the crowned head, pronounced the usual benediction, the whole community cried " Amen."

Such was the custom from the earliest times. But it so happened that some of the most pious Rabbis entertained doubts, whether it might not involve a violation of the precepts of the talmud to carry thirty-six thora rolls to salute the king, whenever he entered their quarter. It was, therefore, resolved that, on the occasion of the royal visits, they should only take three empty boxes, covered with rich hangings, from each of the synagogues, and thus advance to meet the king. This was done, and for many years they continued to meet the king with the empty boxes.

There was then living at the court of King Saragasanus, a wealthy Jew, of the name of Chajim Schamai, who was his chief favourite. But he apostatized from the faith of his fathers, and assumed the name of Marcus; in this way he acquired more influence at court, and, like all apostates, was a greater hater and calumniator of his own nation than those who were Christians by birth.

After Saragasanus had happened to pay a visit to the Jewish quarter, where the ancient marks of homage were exhibited towards him, he began to praise, as he sat on his throne in the presence of his whole court, the loyalty of his Jewish subjects, and expressed his appreciation of their pious custom of saluting their king with the object which was dearest to them on earth, even with the word of God. Then arose Marcus and said: "Think not, O my Lord, that the Jews are really so devoted to their king. These beautifully ornamented boxes, with which they advance to meet you, are empty, and do not contain their holy thora rolls." The king and the court were astonished on hearing this; Saragasanus was highly indignant, and ordered all his courtiers to hold themselves in readiness to accompany him the following day to the Jewish quarter, and swore that if Marcus's statement was true, he would kill all the men, sell the women and children as slaves, and confiscate all the money and property of the Jews for his own use.

While the king was uttering these angry words, the servant of one of the synagogues, the pious, virtuous, venerable Ephraim Baruch, was quietly sleeping on his couch. All at once he awoke, and saw a man of majestic appearance, with a long beard and a leather girdle round his loins, standing before him, and he immediately recognised Elijah, the prophet of God, who thus addressed him: "Art thou asleep? Haste, get thee up, go to the synagogue, place the thora rolls in each of the three empty boxes, then return and lie down again. But tell no one that I have appeared to thee, otherwise thou art a dead man." The pious servant rose from his bed in terror, and did as he was ordered; then he lay down again and slept.

The same thing happened to the servants of the other synagogues, who also did as they were told, and each of them believed that he alone had been favoured with this vision.

The fatal day arrived; it was the 17th of the 11th month Schebat, in the 13th year of the reign of King Saragasanus, and the 5180th year after the destruction of the second temple, when King Saragasanus suddenly appeared in the Jewish quarter, almost before the red dawn of morning had chased away the dark shadows of night. The traitor Marcus walked on his right hand; behind him followed all the nobles of the realm, and a company of 300 soldiers with drawn swords, ready, at a given signal from the king, to strike down all whom they met.

The Jews were very much surprised, and hastened from their beds to salute the king and to do homage to him; the Rabbis advanced to meet him with the thirty-six thora rolls. As they approached to the king, Saragasanus said to them, "I wish to look at the scrolls which contain the law of your prophet Moses, in whose name ye bless me."

Deadly fear fell upon the Jews, and the Rabbis said one to another, "Woe to us! What misfortune is this, that God has brought upon us." They little suspected with what fatherly care the Lord had watched over the safety of His pious followers. The servants of King Saragasanus rode up and opened the boxes which contained the scrolls on which the law was written. Judge of the astonishment of all at seeing them there, and when they were spread out, the first passage which was presented to view, was the 44th verse of the 26th chapter of the third book of Moses: " And yet for all that, when they be in the land of their enemies, I will not cast them away, neither will I abhor them to destroy them utterly and to break my covenant with them; for I am the Lord their God." The same thing happened when all the thirty-six boxes were opened.

When King Saragasanus had satisfied himself that Marcus was a foul slanderer, he became very gracious, thanked the Jews for their devoted loyalty, and, as a proof of his respect, relieved them from the payment of all taxes and public burdens for three years. But he had the slanderer Marcus hanged on the spot; his body was thrown to the dogs, and all that the dogs left was burned with fire.

The community held a festival to express their gratitude and their joy at their miraculous deliverance, and passed a law that for all time coming, the 17th day of the month Schebat should be devoted to the worship of God, to fasting and to prayer, and that the wants of the poor should be amply provided for; but that the evening, after reading an account of this occurrence, should be spent in rejoicing, in feasting and in singing.

Even at the present day, after the lapse of 436 years, there is living at Jerusalem a family originally connected with Saragossa, which possesses an ancient megila written on parchment. It is always read on the 17th of Schebat, and the day is concluded with a feast.

## THE LIFELESS LIVING.

The celebrated cabalist, Schalom Scherebi of Jemen, who was Head Rabbi of Jerusalem, in the year 5525 after the creation of the world, was sitting one morning in his *jeschibah*, dressed in a white robe, and a white *talith* with green stripes over it. He wore the *tephilim* folded round his left arm and his head. His servant entered, and informed him that the *mikweh*, the women's bath, on the Batrak, as it was called, in the Patriarchs' street, did not contain the quantity of water prescribed by law. The pious Rabbi started up from his seat, and, without waiting to remove the *talith* and the *tephilim*, hastened after his servant to examine the mikweh.

When they came to the Batrak, a young Mohammedan was standing there, who considered the green stripes on the Rabbi's talith an insult to his religion, as green is the sacred colour of the Mohammedans, and none are allowed to wear green turbans except the descendants of the prophet. He drew the dagger which he wore at his girdle, and aimed a blow at the Rabbi, but his hand all at once became rigid, and could not reach the Rabbi.

The Rabbi, being in haste, did not observe the young man's attempt on his life, but entered and examined the bath. On finding that it contained the quantity of water prescribed by law, he returned to his own house by another way.

But the young Mohammedan remained rigid and rooted to the spot, where he had made an attempt on the Rabbi's life; his hand was extended and held the glittering dagger in the same position as when he raised his arm to strike the fatal blow. He looked like a statue of stone painted in different colours.

The people who passed could not understand this singular phenomenon. When they addressed the young man, he stared with open eyes, and his lips remained motionless, and yet they could perceive that his body, though lifeless, was still alive. Intelligence of this soon spread over the whole city, which poured forth its population in crowds, till, at length, a violent tumult arose. His parents also hastened to the spot, and were horrified on seeing the condition of their son. In vain they called him by his name; he gave no sign or movement in reply.

Every one was expressing his surprise and questioning his neighbour, but no one could explain this strange sight, till one of the bystanders declared that he had seen the youth draw his dagger against the Head Rabbi of the Jews, who quietly continued his course, while the youth remained standing in a state of rigidity. The affair was clear to all; they knew exactly how the case stood, and what had to be done.

His parents hastened to the Head Rabbi, and fell down at his feet, and besought him to deliver their son from the state of rigidity in which he stood. The Rabbi now learned for the first time the danger to which he had been exposed, and from which the God of Sabaoth had delivered him. But he refused to set the young man at liberty. Then the Mohammedan inhabitants of the city, who had followed the unhappy parents to the Rabbi's house in a body, promised that, for the future, not even a hair of a Jew's head should be touched. The Rabbi made them swear a solemn oath, that they would no longer insult or injure the Jews, and they swore it with a loud voice.

The Rabbi then went to the place, where the petrified youth stood, and addressed him in the presence of the speechless, listening multitude.

" Lower the arm with the glittering dagger."

The arm of the youth was lowered.

" Look with the eyes."

And the eyes began to move, and to be faintly lighted up.

" Speak with thy mouth."

And the youth said :—" Blessed be Allah, Mohammed is his prophet, and all men are his children."

" Go."

And the youth went.

The crowd raised a shout of joy, and two men seized the Rabbi, raised him on their shoulders, and carried him to his abode, followed by all the inhabitants of the city.

But the Jews, as long as this pious man lived, were treated with the greatest consideration, and no one dared to injure them either by word or by deed.

### RABBI KOLONIMOS.

In the year 5480 after the creation of the world,

Rabbi Kolonimos held the office of Head Rabbi of the Aschkenasisch community at Jerusalem. One Sabbath, before daybreak, the Rabbi rose from his couch, and went, as he was wont to do every morning, to the western wall of the temple, to raise his thoughts to God in solitary ardent prayer. He had scarcely laid aside his shoes and leaned his forehead against one of the stones of the wall in a meditative posture, when the servant of the synagogue ran up to him pale as death, and tremblingly informed him that the community was exposed to the greatest danger, as the armed Moham- medans had surrounded the Jewish quarter, broken open the door of the synagogue, and were now threatening to massacre the whole community, if the Head Rabbi was not delivered up to them.

" But what do they want with me ?" asked the Rabbi.

" Master, I dare not repeat the horrible charge."

But the Rabbi continued : " The body of a murdered boy has been found before the synagogue, and the mad- men assert that I am the murderer."

The servant, wondering where the Rabbi had ob- tained his information, answered : " Master, thou hast said."

The Rabbi continued with calm dignity : " Heaven forbid that I should shed human blood. They speak lies, mere lies, and the truth will be brought to light."

As he was saying this, a fierce mob came raging up, threatening the Rabbi with their drawn swords and clenched fists. They seized him and dragged him to the court of justice before the cadi, and cried, "We bring thee the murderer."

The blood-stained body of the murdered boy was extended on the floor of the court of justice; the eyes were open, and the blood flowed from the breast.

The cadi sternly asked: "Why hast thou murdered this boy?"

A breathless silence pervaded the court, while all listened for his answer.

The Rabbi answered: "I have done no murder."

The crowd again broke out into a tumult; loud cries and imprecations were uttered against the Rabbi, and several rushed upon him to kill him. The cadi ordered silence, and asked the accused: "How wilt thou clear thyself from the suspicion of murder?"

The Rabbi answered: "Give me pen, ink, and paper, and thou shalt hear the name of the murderer from the lips of his victim."

After being supplied with pen, ink, and paper, he wrote mysterious characters on the paper, and laid it on the lips of the murdered boy. And then, to the horror of all, the body started up and sat staring at the crowd with open eyes, till, with a sudden spring, it seized a Mohammedan, and cried with a loud and fearful cry, which pierced every heart: "This is the murderer." After these words the blood-stained boy fell down again on the floor a corpse.

The murderer, terror-struck at this appearance, confessed his bloody deed, and was hanged on the spot, the servant of the cadi acting as executioner.

The parents of the boy now threw themselves at the Rabbi's feet, and besought him to exercise his mysterious power and restore their son to life.

The Rabbi answered: " *That* I dare not do. I have only been permitted to save the community of God."

The pious Rabbi spent the rest of his life in penance and fasting, as he had desecrated the Sabbath by writing. He lived for many years, and was highly respected by all. On his death-bed, he gave orders that, for a hundred years, every one who passed his grave should cast a stone on it, as, in ancient days, every one who profaned the Sabbath was stoned to death.

And this was done for a whole century after his death, till, forty years ago, the last stone was hurled at his tomb. On the south-eastern side of the Mount of Olives may still be seen the heap of stones beneath which Rabbi Kolonimos, the thaumaturgist, lies buried.

### SUPERSTITION.

If a Rabbi should happen to die at Jerusalem at a time when the rain, which fills the cisterns, has been long in coming, and much anxiety has arisen in consequence, a piece of the dead man's shroud is cut off, dipped in water, and then placed in his hand, in order that he may not forget to pray for rain, when he reaches the other side.

When two deaths occur in one house in the course of the same year, a cock is killed, if the deceased are men, and a hen, if they are women. The head and the feet are buried; the flesh is distributed among the poor.

A miser, on his death-bed, contrived to swallow his pearls and diamonds. His servant observed this, and dug up his body, in order to rob it. But the body said to him: " I was a Rabbi, the spirits have carried off the miser, whom you are looking for, to my grave a long way from this. But they conveyed me to his grave, and thus rewarded my life of piety by giving me a grave in the holy land of our fathers."

The spirits have feet like hens; are sometimes large and sometimes small, but always black.

Asmodai, whom King Solomon kept confined in his signet ring, is no more; his son Daniel now reigns in his stead.

In the days of Asmodai, a man put down a bucket full of water, as he thought, with very great care, but all at once he felt a pain in his foot. A chacham looked into the water in the bucket, and said: " What hast thou done to the man there?" Asmodai, the spirit, answered from the water: " Don't you see that he has put the bucket on my foot?" Then the chacham said, in reply: " Thou, being a spirit, canst see the man, but the man cannot see thee."

The water-carrier immediately lifted up the bucket, and politely begged Asmodai's pardon, on which the pain at once left his foot. But the place where the bucket had stood was marked as if with the print of a hen's foot.

There are houses in Jerusalem in which men and

women cannot dwell together: the Schedim, the evil
spirits, will not allow it, and thus they are occupied by
women alone.

" Ajin rah," the evil eye, is also very much dreaded,
at Jerusalem. When they whitewash a house, they
paint a hand with outstretched fingers—" *chamsa* " five,
—on the wall. They bind a little gold or silver hand
to the heads of their children. When a person is
unwell, and believes that the " ajin rah" is the cause, he
sends for the male and female exorcists, who pass a
comb, or a knife without a handle, over the head of
the patient, and pronounce, at the same time, the
names of the patriarchs, Abraham, Isaac, and Jacob, and
the name of Moses, the teacher. An old Sepharedisch
woman, and a young Sepharedi, at Jerusalem, derive a
very considerable income from acting as exorcists.

One night the spirits stole a child, when no one was
watching by the poor woman, who had just been confined. A pious believer went straight to the synagogue, where he saw the spirits carrying the child, and
took it from them.

Women in an interesting condition measure the
western wall of the site of the temple with a silk thread
and wind it round their bodies, so as to prevent acci-
dents, or they wear it round their necks in a string
fastened with a small lock, the key of which is thrown
away. Barren women pluck the grass from the clefts
among the stones on the western wall, boil it, and drink
the juice.

Indulgence is a superstitious mode of healing by sympathy, as it is termed, and is employed in the case of any violent shock, or mental excitement. On such occasions, it is an evil spirit that has gained the mastery over the sufferer. The spirit must, therefore, be coaxed (*indulgere*—hence indulgence) till he leaves the patient.

There are two kinds of indulgences; the one lasts nine, and the other forty days.

During the small indulgence, the patient must drink a draught of pulverised mummy, dissolved in sugar and water, half an ounce to be taken at each dose. Before this the patient must be washed, covered with white linen, and placed on a white bed. On certain occasions, women must not remain in the house, as their presence would be hurtful to the patient and to themselves. The patient remains alone, all kinds of animals, and especially poultry, being excluded from the house. The smell of garlic, or of onions, must carefully be avoided. During the nine days, the patient must taste nothing but milk, butter, and bread.

When children are panic-struck, sugar is strewn from their bed to a neighbouring cistern. The spirit, having a taste for *bonbons*, follows the track, and tumbles into the water.

The Jews in Africa slaughter a black cock at the end of the period of indulgence, and believe that they have killed the spirit.

My task was now happily accomplished. I prepared, therefore, to take my departure, enriched, indeed, with experience of a peculiar kind, but overpowered with a deep feeling of sorrow. It was not from this place, that the songs, which I have devoted to the Holy Land and its prophets, drew their inspiration; they owed their birth chiefly to my own imagination.

Accompanied by Count Pizzamano, I went to take leave of Effendi Abdala Wafi Nakib, *i.e.*, judge, when any quarrel arises among the green-turbaned descendants of the prophet, of the wealthy Suleiman Ibn Dschari and the Pasha of Jerusalem.

My residence had as lively an appearance as an annual fair. Articles of all kinds, which I wished to carry home as pilgrim's gifts, lay scattered about in strange confusion. Earth from the valley of Jehoshaphat, wine from Hebron, oil from the Mount of Olives, clay pipes and soap from Jerusalem, garlands of roses and crosses from Bethlehem, photographs of holy places and monuments, bottles of Jordan water, roses from Jericho, stones from the Dead Sea, flowers from Zion and the tombs of the kings, the foundation-stone for the new temple at Vienna, Schofar and Ezchajim, amulets, fragments of the wall of the temple, scrolls of parchment and books, skulls from the field of blood, Bedouin cloaks, &c., &c.

Rabbi Motche Schnitzer, the stone-cutter and manufacturer of charms, reduced this chaos to order in a miraculous manner. While engaged in packing he kept humming at songs set to music of a strikingly original character, and it is my firm conviction that these songs were supernatural incantations, as everything reached Vienna in safety.

On the 6th of July, which happened to be a Sunday,

the Arab Christian Matthia, who had been recommended to me as guide and interpreter by Count Pizzamano, was waiting before my door with two horses, a mule to carry my luggage, and a donkey for the use of the servant who was to accompany us. I distributed some money among the Jewish beggars who had assembled around the house, and walked slowly with Doctors Fränkel and Neumann in the direction of the Jaffa gate. There the keeper of the gate demanded a backschiesch, and, on receiving a small sum, thanked me in the most courteous manner. I parted from my two friends with sincere feelings of regret. I felt that I could never repay them for the able aid and support which they had afforded me. They came in for a share of the insults which were heaped upon me, but I was treated by them with the warmest hospitality and the kindest sympathy.

I sternly shook the dust of Jerusalem from my feet, sprang into the saddle, and cantered up the side of the hill. On reaching the summit I turned round, took a last, lingering look at the city, at Moriah, Zion, and the Mount of Olives. I then gave the reins to my horse and Jerusalem had disappeared.

As it would be a fortnight before the ship, which was to convey me to Egypt, could reach Jaffa, I employed this interval in travelling through the different towns of Palestine and the land of the ancient Phœnicians.

On the 6th of July, as I have already mentioned, I left the Holy City. I was not followed by a stately caravan, as when I crossed Mount Lebanon. I was now only accompanied by an interpreter and a servant, with two mules to carry my luggage. In order to avoid the expense, I took neither a tent nor a *batterie de cuisine* along with me, and I was thus entirely dependent on such casual hospitality as might be offered or refused to me. But I had the fullest confidence in the dragoman Matthia, whom Count Pizzamano had recommended to me, and who knew the road thoroughly.

We already know the route from Jaffa to Jerusalem; the appearance of the country is exactly the same, only at the small villages which we pass the corn is cut down, and is lying on small, open places, arranged like walls and hillocks. In the middle of each of these round places two or three oxen were driven round in a circle by a man or a woman, to tread out the ears of corn. As we passed these threshing-floors, children ran up to us with earthen pitchers and offered us tepid water to drink. When we passed these places, the landscape became solitary, the rocks and the surface of the country destitute of vegetation, and the hot rays of the sun were reflected from the mountains of Judah with dazzling intensity.

After a nine hours' ride, we reached Ramleh, and stopped at the Austrian Consular agency, the red and white flag unfurled on the roof of which could be seen at a considerable distance—at the house of Mr. Antonio Ajub, a Syrian Christian, to whom I was recommended.

I had now spent some months in the East, and had met numerous caravans of camels, without having as yet enjoyed a ride on this picturesque animal. I therefore commissioned Matthia to hire one for our journey of three leagues to Jaffa, so as to have a little practice on the plain, before travelling through the desert. The camel humbly bent down his knees, I clambered into the wooden saddle covered with a piece of carpet, and while holding on by it, I felt as if I had been tossed into the air when the animal stood up. It gives one a peculiar sensation to find himself suddenly elevated so much above surrounding objects, and left entirely to the will of this animal, notwithstanding its high character for patience. There are no reins to guide the movements of the ugly monster, which, at every large step, gives a rocking motion from side to side. This rocking motion produces much the same effect on the highly-sensitive nerves of the stomach as sea-sickness. I soon felt myself quite at my ease, after I had got accustomed to having my body bent forward at every step, and even indulged in a chibouque. As the rider has nothing to do with the management of the animal, I endeavoured to read, as a means of keeping off *ennui*. Matthia and the mules, which went at a slow trot, had some difficulty in keeping up with my phlegmatic, slow-stepping camel.

We reached Jaffa about ten o'clock in the morning. As we were passing through the luxuriant gardens near the town, we observed an immense crowd. We could perceive that they were animated by a strong feeling of joy, and could hear their huzzas and the sound of fifes and tambourines. We at length halted near the gate, to see what could be the cause of this commotion. We observed in the middle of the crowd a woman with a white veil, walking at a slow pace between two boys, the one fifteen and the other twelve years of age. Both of them wore white turbans, and carried long muskets over their shoulders. It is a mother with her two sons, and all this music, jubilee, and shouting are in honour of her.

There is a singular event connected with this procession. The reader of these pages will remember the wild scene which occurred during the night which we spent in the monastery at Ramleh. A Turkish husbandman was shot by three Bedouins, who had come to carry off his crop, which had just been housed, on their camels. Two of them escaped with the loaded camels, while the murderer was seized by the inhabitants of Ramleh, and handed over to justice. After having spent forty days in prison, he was escorted by four armed men to Jaffa.

This excited the suspicion of the family of the murdered man, as the prisoner ought properly to have been conducted to Jerusalem, and tried before the Pasha. In Jaffa he might contrive to escape by bribery or by flight. The widow went with her two sons to Jaffa to prevent justice from falling asleep. The murderer rode quietly in the midst of the armed men, little suspecting that death was dogging his heels.

Two shots were fired at the same moment, as if at a given signal, from among the gardens of Jaffa, which are enclosed with high hedges of cactus. The murderer fell from his horse, shot through the head and the heart, and the armed men rode off. The boys of fifteen and twelve years of age have avenged the death of their father. They come forth from behind the hedge, and glory, before the assembled multitude, in their deed, which is appreciated and praised by all.

" The happy mother!" shouts the crowd. "Behold the mother of two heroes!" "Look at the lioness with her two whelps!" Then followed shouts of joy, mingled with the sound of cymbals and drums.

I left all my luggage at Jaffa, and started for Khaifa by sea. Mussa Mustafa was the name of the proprietor of the small boat which was waiting to receive us, with its white sail floating in the breeze. He was a handsome, grave-looking man, and was aided by two rowers. We sailed joyfully along the coast. I was quite delighted with this new mode of travelling, and cheered by Mussa Mustafa's assurance, that we should reach Khaifa before the moon rose. The sea was blue, and smooth as a polished mirror, and the downy heights of the coast swept rapidly past. The freshest of breezes was blowing in our favour, and we lay quite comfortably beneath the sail, protected from the scorching rays of the sun. We sped along in this way for two hours, when all at once the breeze died away, and the sail hung flapping against the mast. The rowers did their best, but our progress was scarcely perceptible. Mussa Mustafa grew anxious, and expressed his fears that we might be detained at sea for twenty-four hours, or even longer. This announcement was all the more unpleasant, as I had calculated beforehand how each day was to be employed during my journey, so as to enable me to be at Jaffa in time to catch the ship. At length I felt a dizziness in my head, the precursor of a violent attack of illness. Matthia and I were scarcely quit of it the whole time; we were perfectly miserable. Mustafa prepared coffee, and half filled the cup with rum. He then added a considerable quantity of pepper, and, on drinking this mixture, I felt a burning in my stomach, and a drowsiness, which soon delivered me from the worst part of my sufferings.

All at once I awoke; the clearest of moons and the brightest of trembling stars were suspended over me. The sea was rippling softly against the sides of the boat, which rocked gently in the water. I could see the shadows of the rock-bound coast, against which the waves were breaking with a sullen roar, while all around me was calm as a lake. Mustafa was enveloped in his cloak; the two rowers sat on the benches asleep; the oars had slipped from their hands. Matthia was motionless. The scene and the grouping of the figures were so striking, that I could not withdraw my attention from them. I looked at my watch; it was past midnight, and the thought lay heavy on my heart, that every hour thus lost might interfere with the execution of my intended journey. I felt myself very weak and drowsy.

I was awakened by a rustling sound, and opened my eyes again; it was broad daylight, the sail was fluttering, and the boatman wished me joy, as "the invisible

angel of the wind" was with us. The promontory of
Carmel gradually appeared in sight. The rowers aided
the slight breeze which played with the sail, and
Matthia began to prepare coffee.

At nine o'clock in the morning, after a voyage of
nine-and-twenty hours, which might easily have been
completed in seven, we reached the small neglected
harbour of Khaifa, and had reason to bless the wind
that it had only made us lose half a day. The boatman assured me that it sometimes takes three days to
go from Jaffa to Khaifa by sea. We entered rather an
imposing-looking coffee-house, furnished with white marble tables and cushioned divans, near the harbour. The
room had no ceiling, and we could see the wooden roof
above. Several hundred bottles filled with spirits were
arranged along the walls. The landlord, a Greek, must
have observed that I had been suffering from sea-sickness, as, in place of the usual cup of coffee, he placed
before me a bottle of Cyprian wine.

Matthia went to leave my letter with Mr. Skopo-
vich, the Austrian Consular agent, and my card with
Mr. Rogers, the English Vice-consul. During his
absence I entered into conversation with a Spanish Jew,
who had entered the coffee-house to offer me his services as dragoman. I examined him concerning the
number and condition of our co-religionists, and received the following meagre information. "We form a
very small community, almost the smallest in the Holy
Land. It does not contain more than a hundred souls.
We support ourselves with difficulty as small traders,

and nobody thinks about us, while our co-religionists at Jerusalem, Hebron, Safed and Tiberias, receive large contributions from every part of the world. And how do they employ all this money? In eating and drinking of the best, and spending their lives in idleness, except when they are employed in begging. God will give man nothing, however much he may pray; he must work, and then God will help him. Our synagogue is a small, miserable building; there are no schools for our children, and they are quite uneducated. They are debarred from learning any trade, as we could not venture to bind them apprentices to Turkish masters. Better poverty than crime."

Matthia now returned and informed me that both gentlemen were out, and that the horses which were to carry us to the monastery on Carmel were ready. We rode through the gate of Khaifa, before which are several threshing-floors. The mode of obtaining the corn was somewhat different from that which we had seen practised on the plain of Sharon. A wooden machine, constructed of planks, and about six feet square, was placed on the ears, which were arranged in a large circle. It was drawn by a pair of oxen under the guidance of a man, who stood upon it. The ears were thus separated from the corn by the treading of the oxen, and by the heavy wooden machine which they dragged behind.

We soon began to ascend through olive trees, some of which were very old ; on our right were fields, which separated us from the rocky coast, with the ancient brook Kishon flowing through them to the sea. On the left of the steep path, which we ascended, were perpendicular rocks, in which might be seen the dark openings of caverns. Olive trees and luxuriant laurels make the mountain look verdant, and we reached the summit in half an hour.

We halted before the gate of the large handsome monastery, while Matthia went to announce us. He soon returned with a young Carmelite, who gave me a friendly welcome, and led me up a broad light staircase into a large room, furnished with divans and overlooking the sea, which dashes against the rocks 600 feet below. Soon after, the sub-prior, a Maltese, made his appearance, and asked me from what country I came. When he heard that I was from Austria, he expressed his deep regret that the Archduke Ferdinand Maximilian had not visited the mountain monastery when he came to Khaifa. The French Consul would not allow the French flag, which extends its protection over the monastery, to be lowered, and the Austrian flag to be hoisted in its place.

" Thus we have been deprived of the visit of one who is said to be a very talented prince, and he has lost a pleasing reminiscence."

The prior asked me what were my plans, and when I told him that I was still suffering from sea-sickness, he advised me to lie down for a little in one of the neighbouring rooms, and to let him know when I awoke, as he wished to conduct me himself to the holy places.

I entered a bed-room, remarkable for its cleanliness,

and all those adjoining to it were exactly the same. A bible in the Syrian language, and a history of the monastery in Italian, were lying on a table. I had previously met the founder of the monastery at Rome in 1838, and at Vienna in 1841. Giovanni Batista was the only monk who escaped, when the monastery was destroyed by the French and afterwards by the Turks. He fled to Rome, from which he was sent back to Carmel in 1819, without attendants or money, to restore the monastery. When Abdalah Pasha heard of the monk's intention, he ordered the ruins of the monastery to be blown up, being afraid that the monks, during the Greek revolution, which had just broken out, would give signals from the mountains to the enemies of the Turks, as they sailed through these seas. In the year 1826, the Carmelite obtained by his own personal efforts at Constantinople a firman for rebuilding the monastery. He hastened back to Carmel, and, while seated among the ruins, first conceived in his own mind, and then executed in black lead, the plan of a noble building. He had only a hundred francs at his disposal, and he calculated that the execution of his plan would cost 400,000.

Giovanni Batista is an example of what can be effected by enthusiastic faith and unbending energy, when aided by good sense. During his journeys between Carmel and Nazareth, he had noticed two ruinous mills on the Kishon; his first thought was to restore them, and to commence the building with the proceeds. The mills belonged to a family of Druses,

who would have considered it sinful to sell any landed
property to Christians, but they were prevailed on to
grant a lease. A Mohammedan who was kindly disposed to the monk lent him a small sum without
interest, and thus three men, all belonging to different
religions, undertook the restoration of the mills, on
which depended the founding of a Christian monastery.
Giovanni Batista travelled through the different
countries of Asia, collecting money, and ever returning
again to Carmel to resume building. Though more
than sixty years of age, he never lost courage, or
yielded to fatigue. Afterwards he visited Europe, and
collected alms with his hat for the ancient holy Mount
of Carmel. At length he was successful in the execution
of his sacred undertaking.

After some hours, the prior made his appearance
again, and had the kindness to conduct me through the
light rooms of the monastery, and down some steps to
the church, which is built in the grotto in which the
prophet Elijah is said to have lived. The church is a
pretty large rotunda, and is lighted from the cupola.
The walls are painted in imitation of marble, the floor
paved with black and white marble. We descended by
some steps from the rotunda into a low apartment,
cut out in the rock, where there is an altar, lighted by
lamps.

The prior knelt down and prayed.

As I remained quietly standing, I considered it my
duty to inform him that I was not a Christian.

" You are a pilgrim to Jerusalem," he answered,

" and that is enough to make you a welcome guest among the monks of Mount Carmel. Without the aid of one, who was not a Christian, this building would, perhaps, have never been erected in honour of God."

We entered the library, where the books, chiefly of a religious character, in the Latin, Italian, and Spanish languages, are arranged in four large cases. The room had that dank, disagreeable smell which is usually found in places that are seldom opened. I presented the library with my " Hebrew Elegies," which the poet Letteris has admirably translated into Hebrew. The gift was politely accepted by the prior : " It is the only book which we now have, or which the monastery has had, perhaps, for thousands of years, written in the sacred language, spoken by the prophet whom we honour here."

The really tolerant views of the worthy prior, as well as of all the monks whose acquaintance we made on Carmel, were very pleasing, and formed a striking contrast to the bigotry of the Franciscan friars at Ramleh, who refused their hospitality to a fellow-traveller because he was a Jew.

I spent the afternoon and the evening in walking on the mountain. A white-bearded Spanish monk, and a Belgian, who spoke a little German, acted as my guides. The whole mountain range of Carmel, but especially the side, which slopes down toward the sea, is celebrated for the richness of its flora. In early ages its aromatic herbs were sent to the kings of France ; they were considered highly valuable in the healing art. The vegetable kingdom here has a threefold character: one peculiar to the mountain, another to the valleys, and another to the coast, and presents a rich variety. The mountain rises more than a thousand feet above the monastery, and is covered with a small species of oak, *quercus crinita*, the acorns of which are edible. Numerous insects of different colours were flying and jumping around us, and the birds poured forth a delightful chorus.

On reaching the summit of the mountain, we had a magnificent view. Before us was the blue sea, rolling in the distance, and covered with sails, while the roar of its breakers was softened by distance. We saw the extensive bay, at the extremity of which lay the picturesque outline of the ancient Ptolemais, with its walls, its towers, its battlements, and its cupolas. On turning round, we saw the snow-covered ridges of Lebanon, glittering in the rays of the sun.

As I stood on this height, I could easily understand, from the effect produced on my own imagination, how, since the most ancient times, inspired poets and prophets used Carmel, which, in the Hebrew language, signifies a " fruitful field," as the symbol of splendour and prosperity. When Isaiah, in his sublime language, describes the desert as rejoicing and blossoming as the rose, he exclaims: " It shall blossom abundantly, and rejoice even with joy and singing; the glory of Lebanon shall be given unto it, the excellency of Carmel and Sharon." In the song of songs, the inspired bard says to the bride, as the highest compliment: " Thine head upon thee is like Carmel." Jeremiah promises to the people, if they will remain faithful to Jehovah, that He " will bring Israel again to his habitation, and he shall feed on Carmel and Bashan." Amos, in denouncing the judgments of the Lord and a period of adversity, says: " The Lord will roar from Zion, and utter his voice from Jerusalem, and the habitations of the shepherds shall mourn, and the top of Carmel shall wither." It was here that all the people fell on their faces when Elijah caused the fire to descend from heaven on the bullock offered in sacrifice, which " consumed the burnt sacrifice, and the wood, and the stones, and the dust, and licked up the water that was in the trench."

It is a striking fact, in the early periods of the civilisation of nations, that they delighted in offering up prayer on mountains, where they stood with outstretched arms, like statues on their pedestals. On Moriah the patriarch erected an altar; on Horeb God appeared to Moses in the burning bush; and on Sinai he received the tables of the law, in the midst of thundering and lightning. The meaning of Mount Tabor is pointed out in the book of Judges, and it was on the heights of Mizpeh that Samuel judged the people. It was on Mount Ararat that the ark rested, and Lebanon was considered sacred. In the early history of almost every nation, the mountains are the first columns of the temple erected by the hand of nature, and David sings, that God delights to dwell on the mountains.

The original mountain worship of the Canaanites seems not to have been without its influence on the

worship of the Jews.   Carmel has been sacred to
"gods many."   It was a sanctuary of Zeus.   Tacitus
calls the mountain itself a god supporting his own
altar.   The Phœnicians worshipped not a god, but that
godhead which is majestically revealed in the page of
nature, on the heights of Carmel.   Pythagoras is said
to have spent many years in solitary meditation on the
sacred Carmel, before he gave his system of philosophy
to the world.

All these nations have passed away, their bones are
dust, and can no longer be distinguished from the dust.
I descended from the sacred mountain, proud with the
thought that I am the son of a nation which has sur-
vived all others.

As we approached the monastery, we found the
monks walking solitary or in pairs in the garden, which
is partly a continuation of the terrace, and partly slopes
down the side of the rocks.   In the middle of the
garden, which is adorned with walks overgrown with
vines, with mulberry, pomegranate and cypress trees, is
a stone pyramid, to mark the spot where the ashes of
the Frenchmen, who fell in battle here, are reposing.

There are twelve monks in the monastery, all of whom
belong to different countries; my native land was
represented by a lay brother, John Zwittlinger, from
Hohenfurt in Bohemia.   He is a joiner.   His feelings
of piety led him to Rome, where, after a residence of
seven years, he was sent here, and has continued to
practise his honest craft in the monastery ever since.
He was confined to his bed with fever.   I visited him

with one of the monks, who acts as physician and apothecary.   The monk listened very attentively, as we conversed in the language of our distant home, which he had never heard before.

In the evening, I discussed my plan of travelling with Matthia.   I had a keen desire to visit Nablous, which, a few months before, was in a state of revolt, in consequence of a missionary having unfortunately shot a Mohammedan beggar.   The Austrian Consular agent at Beyroot would not allow me to travel by Nablous to Jerusalem, when I wished to do so.   I inquired about the condition of the town at every place I visited, and the monks informed me that matters were quiet again, although none of the representatives of the European Powers had returned.

Matthia was of opinion that we might visit it with perfect safety, the more so as I was dressed quite like a Frank.   I did not exactly understand his reasoning, but he explained to me that wearing the Arab costume in the East sometimes exposes one to danger, and is never of the least use.   The natives suspect that it is worn to avoid recognition; while they are accustomed to see Franks, who come to examine the country and its ruins.   Besides they know at once that they have to deal with a man who is travelling under the protection of a European power.   I made up my mind to visit the ancient Samaritans.   Matthia marked how much of the journey was to be accomplished each day, and told me that a Bashi Bozouk, on his return from the recent campaign, had arrived at Khaifa with three horses. He advised me to hire the horses, and thus to secure at the same time the protection of an armed man.    I warmly approved of the proposal and dismissed the lay brother, who came to ask if I wanted anything, with a friendly good night.

At 5 o'clock in the morning our horses were saddled. An excellent breakfast was on the table.    The prior came to wish me a happy journey, and gave me a *bouquet* of dried carnations, the small petals of which were of such a bright blue purple that they reminded me of the celebrated purple shells of the neighbouring Sidon.    Their fame on Mount Carmel is well known.

We left the monastery of Carmel at 6 o'clock in the morning, and then rode down the side of the mountain, through Khaifa, and along the coast, so close to the sea that the white foam of the rolling waves often gushed between our horses' feet.    The sea was rather rough, and the large green waves came rushing on and then broke against the shore with that thundering music, which never fails to excite a sort of ecstasy of delight in certain minds.    On our right were bleak and barren hills of sand, with here and there the graceful form of a palm, which thrives in such a soil.    The scorching rays of the sun were softened by the coolness of the sea breeze.    The sea here represents a large semi-circle, with the majestic Carmel and its monastery at one end, and the ancient Ptolemais, glittering with its battlements and walls, its cupolas and minarets, at the other. And above this splendid view the heaven was extended like a blue flag of victory, embroidered in silver with

the sun and his dazzling rays. What different thoughts
are suggested by the contemplation of such a scene,
some of them soaring aloft with eagle wing, and others
skimming gently along the surface like doves, while the
imagination luxuriates in an ecstacy of enjoyment.

After a ride of nearly three hours, we reached the
walls of this town, which has played such an important
part in ancient and modern history. The traces of the
events of the last war are still clearly visible. Gaps in
the walls, overturned columns, and ruinous houses did
not present a very cheerful view. The bazaar was not
very extensive, and it was in vain that I looked for a
riding-whip. Many shops were closed. A Khan, with
a court of an oblong, quadrangular shape, two sides of
which were adorned with ten Corinthian columns of
marble, was the finest building that I saw. The streets,
like those of almost every Oriental city, are narrow and
dirty, and few of them exhibited anything like a lively
appearance.

We halted in the middle of the town before a coffee-
house; the water which was offered to us was tepid, and
all Matthia's efforts to obtain a citron to make lemonade
were in vain; a sweetish insipid decoction of cubebs was
offered to me as a substitute.

My stay was too brief to allow me to obtain much
information about the Jews at St. Jean d'Acre; I only
learned that 120 are settled here, and support themselves as fishermen, tradesmen, and shopkeepers. They
have a synagogue.

After an hour we again left the town, in order to

take our usual noonday rest in the garden of one of the inhabitants outside the town. Though it was very pleasant there, I should have preferred remaining in the town. But I was assured by Matthia that the beggars of St. Jean d'Acre would not even have left me time to eat my dinner.

After a two hour's ride through the fruitful plain of Sahel Aka, we reached the pretty village of Berue, and a mountain ridge. Ascending a rocky path, we had on our right a fruitful valley planted with trees, and, when we turned round on our saddles, we could see the sea. We then entered the charming little valley of Schahur, which is planted with olives. The trees are planted on the slopes of the hills which enclose the valley; between it and the path we are ascending, are fields covered with fig and pomegranate trees. The plantations of maize and tobacco grow more luxuriant as we advance, and at length we see on a hill, glittering in the sun, what appears to be a handsome town. We soon find, as we approach, that it is only distance that lends enchantment to the view : it is the village Masd el Krum.

All is lively in the village; the people are busy in their fields and gardens. Matthia wished to rest here for the night, but as the sun was still high, I resolved to push on to the next village, so as to be able to reach Safed before noon the following day. We refreshed ourselves at the cool village fountain, and resumed our journey.

We still rode along the same valley for about an hour, when the olives gradually disappeared, and we came to undulating hills, which compelled us to ride more slowly. On the left we see a small village. After another hour we see glittering in the red rays of the evening sun, and shaped like a fortress, the village of Ramé, which is situated on a hill and partly surrounded with indented walls.

For a considerable way before we reached the village the road was very stony, and then we rode through rich plantations. Here we came to a well, where women were drawing water, and carrying their pitchers on their heads up the steep hill. About the middle of the hill was a drinking-place for cattle, enclosed with immense stones, which were polished smooth by time, and may have been lying there for countless ages. A negro was giving water to a snow-white dromedary, the first I saw in Palestine. We dismounted, removed our horses' bridles, and allowed them to enjoy a refreshing draught.

We reached the summit at sunset, and turned into the house of the Christian Daut Jaub, or David Jacob. We halted in a lofty flat-roofed entrance-hall, which looked like a wide and pretty long gateway. It contained two camels, some asses and goats, with poultry running and fluttering among them. The mistress of the house was busy milking the camels, and brought me some of the milk in an earthen vessel. It was the first time I had tasted it, and I did not find it very palatable, but I soon got accustomed to it.

Early in the morning I woke Matthia and Achmed. The horses, which, throughout the whole journey, were never stabled, but fastened to a ring in the open air, were saddled, while the landlord prepared coffee and narghilés. At five o'clock we mounted our horses, and rode down the heights of Ramé. Several women were already busily employed before their houses in the cool morning air; I was struck with the ornaments which they wore on their heads. Two of them wore a projecting silver horn, similar to those we had already seen on Mount Lebanon, while the usual frontlets of strings of silver coins, which the others wore, descended from the temples and were fastened at the chin; they looked like the sides of a helmet.

After riding through a thick grove of olives, we ascended a hill for about an hour, and found a beautiful waterfall, at which we enjoyed a cool draught. A boy, mounted on a loaded ass, came up at the same moment. There could be no mistake about his features, or the ample locks which covered his temples; I recognized him at once as a Jewish countryman. His name was Herrschel, and, being in a state of complete destitution, he had entered the service of a Jewish shopkeeper at Ramé. This was the only case which came under my notice of a Jewish settler in Palestine living apart from his countrymen.

The green hills were covered with vegetation: in a ravine we observed the village Betanan, and above it, on the top of the hill, another village, called Farada. At length the beautiful cone of Mount Tabor, and part of the Sea of Galilee, appeared in the distance. Having crossed the hill, we observed on our left the village of Samoi, sloping into a deep green valley, and beyond it, on the side of a hill, the far-stretching outlines of Safed. On reaching the bottom of the valley, we observed, far up among the hills, the village of Marun, which is crowned with a series of white, glittering sepulchres. One of them contains the remains of the author of Sohar. The Jews of Palestine and Syria, and also of the other more distant countries of Asia and Africa, used to undertake pilgrimages to his tomb, and to spend three days and nights in tents, in the midst of singing and music and the liveliest enjoyment; I heard numerous legends, chiefly of an amusing character, in connection with this burying-ground.

The path which we now ascended became so rocky and steep, that we were obliged to dismount and to lead our horses behind us for an hour, till we came to a plain of mowed corn. Descending this plain, and ascending a barren hill, we found ourselves before Safed. We were suffering from exposure to the sun even more than from our five hours' ride, and were glad to reach the town, which we had seen an hour and a-half before, and believed to be much nearer. Before Safed, on our right, we saw a small hamlet, called Ein Masatum.

## CHAPTER VII.

A Jewish Inn—" I don't Eat with Jews "—Jewish Beggars—The
Rabbis of Safed—Misery of the Jewish Community—Their
Past History—Earthquakes—" Our Misery Speaks for Itself "
—*mai de pays*—The Jewish Population—A Colony of Jewish
Husbandmen — The Synagogues — " Our Light is Extin-
guished " — A Peaceful Scene—The Sea of Galilee—" The
Stones of the Christians "—Magdala—Tiberias—A Wander-
ing Jew—Appearance of the Town—The Tomb of Rabbi
ben Sakai — The Tomb of Rambam — Romantic Story of
Rabbi Akiba—The Jordan—Herod II. and Josephus—The
Warm Baths—First Night at Tiberias—Visit from the Rabbis
—Misery of the Jewish Community—Their Mode of Subsist-
ence—A Fearful Scene—A Leaf from the Chronicles of
Tiberias.

I ENTERED the house of Mr. Schmul Barner, a Jew
from Zombor in Galizia, who had made his way to
Safed thirty-seven years ago, along with his father, and
now keeps a tavern for the entertainment of strangers.
I passed through a neat court into a small room, and
then entered another, which was comfortably furnished
and perfectly clean.

A strengthening meal was soon spread on the table,

and I invited Matthia to join me. He refused, and on being pressed, said curtly and doggedly : "I don't eat with Jews." It now struck me for the first time, that during our journey, he had never tasted the meat which we had brought with us from Jaffa. On the other hand, my friend, the Baschi Bozouk, enjoyed the mutton all the more, from having seen it killed before his eyes by a Jew, while he certainly would not have touched it, if it had been sold by a Christian butcher. What better subject could there be for a chapter on the weaknesses and inconsistencies of our common nature ! Here were three men, with three palates all exactly the same, and yet food touched by the one would have been an abomination to the other two. We have all heard of sacred places, but here were sacred palates.

My arrival in Safed was soon known, and my land-lord had considerable difficulty in keeping the beggars, who had assembled before the house, at a distance. Even Lot could not have found it more difficult to keep back the Sodomites, who tried to storm his house, and to bring out the men who were his guests. I gave notice to the crowd, that, on leaving, I would hand over a certain sum to the president of the community for distribution, but that at present I would not give any alms.

I had now to receive five Rabbis of Safed, three of whom belonged to the Sepharedisch and two to the Aschkenasisch community. They at once began to describe the poverty which prevailed at Safed. One of them spoke :—

"We have suffered severely from war, from robbery during the prevalence of peace, from earthquakes and pestilence. Death is to us a matter of indifference, but we cannot live. We might work, erect *fabriques,* cultivate the soil, open schools; but who will assist us to do this?"

"And yet you receive money from every part of the world for your support."

"Yes; we receive money, much money; may the blessing of God rest on the humane contributors! but we require it all to keep the people from dying of hunger. The sympathy of all is expended on Jerusalem, and only on Jerusalem."

"It is the city which we all esteem to be most sacred. Safed is not mentioned in the Holy Scriptures, and it is doubtful whether Josephus alludes to it in his chronicles under the name of Zeph."

"The misery of the present, and not the splendour of the past, should decide whether our brethren will help us. There are fewer difficulties in the way of doing good at Safed and Tiberias, as in these holy cities we Aschkenasim and Sepharedim are united, and not split up into different communities, all hostile to one another. Should not our brethren in the West take Safed also into account when they found schools? Do you not know what the Christians do for their priests, and yet the Jew has a better heart!"

"The priests are only single men, they do not add to their number."

"Not individually, but there are always new ones arriving."

" A single man does not require so much as a family."

" We are temperate ; and a Jewish family with many children does not eat and drink so much as a priest."

My visitors were now joined by Mr. Diamant, a surgeon from Lemberg, who had served in the Turkish army, and now practises his profession here. He had some knowledge of the previous history of Safed, and gave me the following information :—

" There can be no doubt but Safed was inhabited by Jews at a very early period; there are tombstones here 1,200 years old, and probably these are not the oldest, as many of the inscriptions are not legible, and many of the tombstones, as was often the case in ancient times, may never have had any. The Jewish pilgrim from Tudela found no Jews in Safed. Since the close of the fifteenth century, there have always been Jews settled here. A century later they had already seventeen synagogues and a printing press."

Mr. Rabbi Schwarz, of Jerusalem told me that the the Court library at Vienna contains a defence of the work " More Nebuchim," by Maimonides, which was printed at Safed.

" It is very fortunate," continued Mr. Diamant, " that this honour was conferred on the inhabitants of Safed in ancient times; the Chassidim of the present day might have burned the work as well as the author."

Mr. Mordachai Segal from Poland, whose acquaintance I had made at Beyroot, now began to give me an account of the earthquakes with which the inhabitants of Safed had been visited. One occurred a hundred years ago, during which 200 Jews lost their lives, all their houses were damaged, and twelve synagogues reduced to ruins. Half a century later, the plague broke out and the inhabitants fled. Far more destructive than the pestilence was the insurrection of the Arabs against Mehmed Ali's son Ibrahim in 1834. They were joined by the Bedouins, and a fearful plundering ensued. All that resisted were slain, and scenes occurred which make humanity shudder. An Arab slew his mother, because she reproached him for his cruelty toward a former good neighbour. Every kind of horror was perpetrated, till the Emir Beschir of Lebanon received orders from Ibrahim Pasha to advance with his Druses and to put a stop to these ravages. The Jewish population was now poor and helpless, when a fresh source of destruction delivered them from their actual misery. In the year 1837 an earthquake buried 1500 Jews in a few seconds beneath their houses, and next year the Druses, who had revolted against Ibrahim Pasha, plundered the city which they had formerly marched to protect. Has any city on earth experienced such a fearful fate? Does not our misery cry aloud to heaven? The inhabitants do not require to weep and to implore; our misery speaks for itself."

The tears rolled down the worthy man's cheeks, and the other Rabbis seized the hem of their robes and kissed them.

There is an innate feeling in the human heart, which ever attracts a man to the land of his fathers, and leads him to long to return to his native home. The earth may quake, the flames may burst forth from the mountains, all may be reduced to ruins, and nothing but life may be spared, and yet men return to that place, and erect their hovels on their native soil, though they all know how comfortless it is. Is it its hidden treasures, is it the force of habit, is it the undying remembrance of the early scenes of their youth, that always leads men back to the place of their birth, where they are exposed to destruction and misery? Who can tell?

We were specially struck with this singular phenomenon at Safed. There are 2,100 Jews again settled there, of whom 800 are Sepharedim, and 1,300 Aschkenasim; 400 of the latter are from Galizia and Hungary, 900 from Russia. Among the whole there are only 41 tradesmen, viz., 4 masons, 2 joiners, 5 tinsmiths, 7 tailors, 4 shoemakers, 15 shopkeepers, and 4 scribes.

I was informed that there is also a Sepharedish community in the village of Perkyin in the vicinity of Safed, which contains only 50 souls, and has a small church; they support themselves exclusively by agriculture and the rearing of cattle. When I asked why the Jewish inhabitants of Safed did not imitate this good example, I received an unsatisfactory and evasive answer.

It was now almost evening, the time for prayer. The heat of the day had disappeared, and I requested my guests to conduct me to their synagogues. We first entered "Raw Ari," the most ancient of all, on the ruins of which Jizchag Queda, the wealthy merchant of Trieste, caused a handsome stone building to be erected in the year 1855. Descending a stone staircase, we entered a large quadrangular court, from which we passed into a hall with painted wooden galleries for the women extending along the walls. Three steps led to the ark, which contains the law. It was enclosed within a lofty gate, beautifully carved in wood, which had been brought from Damascus a few days before, and was very much admired. Mr. Queda paid 6,000 piastres for it, and 2,000 more had still to be expended on it. The whole building, the execution of which cost 70,000 piastres, produces a fine effect, and is well adapted, if it is not destroyed by an earthquake, to remain a visible memorial of the pious founder for centuries to come. The floor is paved with beautiful Dutch tiles, brought from Trieste. On both sides of the staircase at the entrance, are two cisterns, at which the worshippers wash their hands on entering, and where, on feast days, when the service lasts for several hours, and the heat of the day is oppressive, they can enjoy a cool draught of water.

The synagogue "Stambuli," is a small building supported by four arches. The *almemer* is of wood; the curtain of the ark is without any inscription; there are a few lamps attached to a coarse tin lustre. All the Jews from Constantinople worship in this synagogue; hence its name.

The synagogue "Jischak Abiat," the roof of which

is supported by four arches, and the windows partly open and partly provided with wooden lattices, presented the same miserable appearance. When I remarked that the eternal light was not burning in the lamp before the ark containing the law, a Rabbi said :—

"You see, sir, that our light is extinguished."

A beautiful tree was blooming in the court before the entrance; forty children, instead of enjoying its cool shade, were squatting close together in a dark hall and reading, or rather singing aloud from a book, while they bent their bodies backward and forward. There are five school-rooms of the same kind in Safed, where the children are taught to read prayers which they do not understand.

The synagogue Zadik Rabbi Joseph differs little from those which we have just described, save that the court, in which a fig-tree and some maize have been planted, contains the white-plastered tomb of the founder.

In the Bet Hamidrasch, "Maranembet Josef," which was also founded by Mr. Queda, in the year 1850, and the "Bet din," are small collections of books, but no specimens of ancient printing or manuscripts. All these have been lost during the different calamities with which Safed has been visited.

All these synagogues belong to the Sepharedim; the following are the property of the Aschkenasim :—the synagogue of Rabbi Eisik is in a most neglected condition; the fragrance of the roses of red silk embroi-

s 2

dered on the curtain of the ark is not sufficient to
drown the odours of a very different description, and
the two embroidered lions, supporting a crown with
their claws, only served to remind us that, as the light
of Israel is extinguished, so also the crown has fallen
from her head.   When I directed the attention of my
Russian-Polish co-religionists to the indescribable filth,
they could not understand me ; the muddy streams of
Polish and Oriental uncleanliness have here met and
coalesced.

The synagogue " Chewra " is larger and less dirty:
as also a third, which is said to have been founded by
Ari.   There is also a Bet-Hamidrasch connected with
the last.

As we left the last of these buildings, the sun had
already sunk behind the mountains, and there was such
an air of gentle peacefulness spread over the beautiful
valley, richly planted with all kinds of trees, that one
could scarcely believe that the earth could ever have
been otherwise than fruitful and fraught with blessings
to man, or that the destroying angel could have gazed
on such a scene without a thrill of pity in his heart.

We started earlier than usual, at 3 o'clock in the
morning, and enjoyed the delightful coolness and the
gradual break of day, which seemed to have less difficulty in breaking through the dark clouds than in the
West.   We rode down the stony hill on which Safed is
situated, with a deep green valley on our right, and
then began to ascend another hill.   From the summit
might be seen in the distance the shaded outlines of a

round hill; it was Tabor, a grey streak like a sheet of lead, stretching in the distance far down below, was the Sea of Galilee; the floods of light which poured down from the neighbouring mountains proceeded from the rising sun.

We now descended through olive trees and fields of mowed corn, till we reached the fountain Ainkale, situated in a green ravine. Having been two hours on horseback, we halted for breakfast beside the fountain. At a short distance was a solitary stone-house, the inmates of which were already astir. Behind it rose a series of steep barren rocks of a reddish colour, which seemed to extend for more than a league.

After a delightful rest, we rode up the ravine, and then ascended a hill. Before us, glittering in the full light of the sun, lay the Sea of Galilee, stretching far away in the distance. We had seen it twice before through clefts in the hills, or from their summits, and had twice lost sight of it again. On our right lay a series of masses of rock, full of gaps and fissures, like quarries, from which men had obtained stones for thousands of years to erect their palaces, temples, and pyramids, without having exhausted the supply. Passing them, we descended declivities covered with dwarfed oaks, till we reached the shore of the sea, and rode along it till we came to Tiberias.

Matthia said to me : " Do you see these rocks ? It was there that Christ fed the hungry with five loaves and two fishes. Christian pilgrims show their respect for this sacred legend by kneeling down and praying at some blocks of stone, which are shaped like loaves, and named by the Arabs Hadscher el Noazra, " the stones of the Christians."

He pointed out to me, on the opposite side, Capernaum, and the shore, where the wildest Bedouins, almost inaccessible, assert their ancient nomadic liberty. Barren hills, lofty and steep, extend for miles along the sea. There is no ship, boat, or traces of life on its waters. Our road lay sometimes quite close to the sea, and at other times was separated from it by meadows and fields. The green vegetation and the red blossoms of the oleanders give it a lively appearance. These plots, which must be flooded by the waves of the sea during a storm, have a pleasant look. During our ride of several hours, through the ancient possessions of the tribe of Naphtali, we had not met a single living thing, and the sight of the flocks of sheep and goats feeding on the downs was a pleasant change. A shepherd was playing on a reed, and we were delighted even with his barbarous music.

We passed some camels grazing, and observed on the road thousands of round, porous, black and brown stones, varying in size from a melon to a pigeon's egg, which reminded us that we were riding over the closed craters of ancient volcanoes, which, remembering their violent overthrow, still sometimes quake before the power which subdued them.

We met a singular group; a boy leading a camel by a halter; a large basket is suspended on each side, with a woman seated in it. Both of them veil themselves as we approach.

The rocky path now begins to ascend; we are more than twenty fathoms above the level of the sea. Achmed, probably inspired by the musical shepherd, has, for a long time, been indulging in a horrible shrieking song, which, while it is almost martyrdom to me, seems to afford him the most intense delight. We do not wish to mar his pleasure, but, to save our ears, we give the spur to our horse. But the heat of the sun is sharper than the spur, the poor brute is tired and thirsty, and, after a faint attempt at a trot, relaxes into its former pace.

The road grows broader, and opens up into a plain; we see the village of Magdala on our left. It consists of some clay huts with terraces. On the latter are erected light arbours, supported by four poles, and thatched with reeds, like the tents of the Jews during the feast of tabernacles. The inhabitants leave their mud hovels, and take refuge in these, when the season during which fever is prevalent approaches.

The heat of the sun now became almost intolerable; the water which was offered to us in Magdala was tepid, and our desire to reach Tiberias increased with every turn of the road; but another rocky height always appeared in view. The sea, which we could see almost from end to end, looked like a molten sun, and the glare, which poured down from above, was intensified by the refraction of the sun's rays from its surface.

Ruinous walls, the cracked cupola of a mosque, a palm tree, a broken gate, with several threshing-floors before us; all these are passed in succession, and we reach Tiberias.

We lodged with Mr. Chajim Weismann, from Brody, who occupies a house with two large airy rooms and open verandahs. He has converted it into a hotel for travellers, and professes, as physician and apothecary, to cure all the ills which men and beasts are heir to.

He has led a strange and chequered life. In order to avoid learning lessons, he ran away from his parents, when eight years of age, and after wandering about the country for a long time, came to a large town, which, he was told, was called Jassy, but, disliking it, he extended his travels, and arrived at Bucharest. A physician, who found him destitute and starving before his door, received him into his house, and employed him for many years as his servant. The boy had a taste for the healing art, and as he always attended his master with the medicine chest, he had an opportunity of observing the symptoms of different diseases, and the remedies which his master employed. After some years, believing that he had learned all that his master could teach him, he left him, and still anxious to increase his knowledge, he engaged himself to several physicians in succession. When fifteen years of age, he was again seized with a desire to see something more of the world, and travelled through almost every country, healing such patients as would entrust themselves to such a youthful practitioner, or when practice failed him, supporting himself by begging, or by the exhibition of certain tricks which he had learned. His experience must have been rather extensive and varied during his two years' wanderings, before he came to Tunis. He was now a handsome youth, and having confidently asserted that he could heal some desperate diseases, where all hope had been given up, accident proved favourable to his boldness. He soon attracted attention. Pilgrimages were undertaken to the house which he occupied by those who believed that the touch of his hand, or the glance of his eye, or the medicine which he dispensed, could restore them to health. He was admitted into the palace of the Dey of Tunis as his body physician, and lived there three years in the highest esteem. His lively restless spirit would not allow him to remain longer; one day he escaped with 10,000 golden ducats, which he had saved from his earnings. He had been seized with an irresistible desire to see the Holy Land, of which he had heard his father continually speaking in his early home. His next appearance was at Tiberias, where he arrived in his twentieth year, accompanied by his wife, an African Jewess, whom he had suddenly married, and her younger sister. He built houses, the finest in Tiberias, and lived like a man of independent fortune, who only practised his profession from feelings of humanity without charging any fee, while the sick, for miles around, attracted by his fame, flocked to consult him. During the earthquake of 1837, he and his wife and family were buried beneath the ruins of their house. After eighteen hours he was dug out alive, but his wife and children were dead, and all his houses destroyed. At this time Prince Pückler-Muskau arrived at Tiberias. Weismann acted as his interpreter and guide through all the neighbouring country of Galilee. He advised him to open an inn, which has proved of great service to others as well as myself.

I had so arranged my journey as to be able to spend the Sabbath here, and as it was Friday, I had to make myself acquainted with the environs and the baths of Tiberias on the day of my arrival.

After a short rest I ordered two horses to be saddled, and rode with Reb Mosche from Berditschew, the servant of the synagogue, whom Mr. Weismann had recommended to me as very intelligent, and well acquainted with the localities, to visit the numerous sepulchres of the most illustrious men of the Bible and of Jewish history. The little town, through which we had to ride, resembled a heap of ruins. Fallen walls, broken terraces, here and there a doorway still standing, while the house itself had disappeared, a ruined mosque, with a palm tree in the court stretching aloft its green arms to heaven—such was the scene that met our view. The very houses, all of which seemed to be inhabited, are built of nothing but ruins, selected at the caprice of the builder. None of them are plastered, and all of them are the abodes of poverty and gnawing hunger. Who could venture to build strong houses on such a soil?

"We live," said my guide, when I alluded to the miserable appearance of the town, "from day to day, and are always prepared to die. We offer up thanks every morning, more than any other men in the world, that we have lived to see the light of another day, and that the earth has not opened during the night and swallowed up our wives, our children, and our brethren. In Tiberias we learn to be pious and to think only of a future life."

After ten minutes, we left the town by a ruinous gate. The heat of the day—it was two o'clock P.M.— was fearful, and was rather increased than diminished by the strong breeze which was blowing; we felt as if we were inhaling flames of fire, and with every breath the sensation was much the same as that which is felt on approaching a charcoal kiln or a furnace in the height of summer. I found the heat more oppressive here than I afterwards did in the desert. The thermometer stood at 40° R.

We rode up a height, to the right, before the gate, and stood before the grave of Rabbi Jochannan ben Sakai, the same to whom we have previously alluded in this work, and in whose synagogue we worshipped at Jerusalem. A rough stone without any inscription is placed on a strong foundation of square stones, which represent two steps. This stone covers the mortal remains of this immortal, learned, and brave man. Four of his scholars are buried on his right, and one on his left. Behind these tombs are two short columns half projecting from the ground; they mark the tombs of Raw Ami and Raw Aschi.

These tombs are situated on a place paved with

small stones, which is twenty yards long and fifteen broad, and enclosed on three sides with a wall only two feet high. Twenty yards farther on, there are four steps leading to an inclosure of rough stones; it contains a sarcophagus of white plaster, slightly arched above, which posterity reverences as containing the ashes of Rambam. Here lay countless numbers of small stones, which visitors had placed there, and which my guide increased by the addition of one more. On the evening before every new moon, prayers are offered up at this tomb by the community. It is frequented for the same purpose by some worshippers every day and at every hour.

We now rode down a pretty steep hill, which contains the remains of Rabbi Akiba and his 24,000 scholars. " I will relate the most beautiful of stories;" such are the words with which the Koran introduces the history of Joseph in Egypt. They might serve also as an introduction to the history of the learned, pious, and illustrious teacher, before whose tomb we are now standing.

Rabbi Akiba ben Joseph was a shepherd in the employment of the wealthy Kalba Zebua of Jerusalem, whose sepulchre is still identified by the Jews with the " Tombs of the Kings," as they are called. He loved Rachel, his master's daughter, and the heart of the maiden responded to the poor shepherd's passion. She bestowed on him her affections on condition that he should go away and make himself a learned man. Akiba, who was no longer in the first bloom of youth,

travelled to distant lands, and enrolled himself as the
pupil of the most celebrated masters. Kalba Zebua
disowned his daughter, because she had become Alkiba's
wife. She waited till her beloved husband returned after
years, surrounded with the splendour of a great name,
when she proudly hailed him as her own. Her father
remained inexorable. The thirst for learning was so
powerfully excited in Akiba, that, encouraged by his
noble wife, he again left his home, to pursue his studies
in other lands under the most celebrated teachers of the
law. She waited for years, without for a moment
doubting the affection of her husband, though she was
reduced to such poverty that she had to cut off locks of
her dark hair to make rings, which she sold. The
whole world was filled with her husband's fame; his
original and able explanations of the law had themselves
all the authority of law. His reputation rose so high,
that a Rabbi, who had formerly opposed him, affirmed
that he who gave up Rabbi Akiba gave up everlasting
life, and that his spirit of divination had restored all
that tradition had forgotten. His scholars asserted
that he knew the meaning of many passages of the
law of which even the prophet Moses himself had
remained ignorant. A wonderful, hyperbolical, but—so
far as regards Akiba's reputation for learning—characteristic legend relates that the prophet asked the Lord
what was the meaning of certain marks over some of
the letters in the law. The Lord answered that after
many generations there would arise a man of the name
of Akiba, who would explain the secret meaning of

these marks. The prophet begged the Lord to shew him the figure of the man; on which the Lord ordered him to sit down, eight rows of spirits behind Akiba. The prophet heard Akiba speaking and expounding, but he could not understand him. After many years, Akiba returned home, followed by his 24,000 scholars. All the people went forth with joy to meet him. Then his wife forced her way through the crowd, fell down before him, who was happier in her love than in all his fame, and, bursting into tears, began to embrace his knees. The scholars were about to remove the woman, whom they did not know; but the master said to them: "Leave her alone; all that I am, and all that you have become through me, is the work of this noble woman." He raised her from the ground and kissed her. The stern father was now reconciled, and bestowed on his children abundant wealth.

A projecting rock, more than half-way up the hill, commands a view of Rabbi Akiba's simple monument, of the hill itself, of the fields that extend round its base, of the town, of the sea, and of the rock-bound shores of Hauran on the opposite side. In the sea may be seen the dark outline of a stream, which proudly refuses to mingle its water with the waves, though it flows from the one end to the other. It is the Jordan. This phenomenon has been regarded as symbolical of the Jewish people, which marches through the flood of other nations without coalescing with them, or losing that liberty and keenness of intellect, which they owe to the mountains of their native land.

The tomb is visited by the community of Tiberias, and by pilgrims from all the sacred cities of Palestine, on the thirty-third day of the Sefira. All offer up prayers with burning lights, and erect tents, beneath which they spend a day and a night at the tombs of the 24,000 scholars. Behind the tomb is a deep hole, for holding cool water for the use of the worshippers.

About 30 feet below the tomb of Rabbi Akiba, is the sepulchre of Rabbi Chia; on the right and left those of his two sons. The place is open and unenclosed on three sides, and there is a cavity behind it. Another sepulchre contains the ashes of Raf Hamnuna the Elder, where the Jews go to offer up prayer after a long drought. Those who are labouring under any bodily ailment undertake pilgrimages to the sepulchres of Meier ben Nesz and of Zacharia Akana.

We had now to dismount from our horses and to lead them down the steep declivity of the hill, so as to reach a narrow neck of land between the hill and the sea. It contains the Turkish burying-ground, with its columns of grey granite, standing erect or prostrate on the ground. I counted nineteen which were entirely destroyed; only one was perpendicular, and two oblique, and elsewhere I saw many stones which bore traces of the chisel. The Jews believe that Herod II. built his palace here on the ancient sepulchres, and curse his memory, as also that of a man of the name of Josephus, who became a proselyte to Christianity, and employed the stones of a temple, which had been commenced during the reign of the Emperor Adrian, in the erection of a church. Many kinds of enchantments were employed to arrest the progress of the work, but he proved himself a still more powerful magician. Along this undulating neck of land are walls of rock, separated from the hill which we descended, by a ravine, which contains numerous sepulchres with enclosed entrances.

My guide, rich in legendary lore, informed me that on the summit of these rocks once stood a castle which belonged to King Solomon's mother, while he pointed out a ruinous building at the foot of the hill as the farm-yard of Abraham's mother.

A handsome building, about half a league from Tiberias, marks the locality of the warm baths, so celebrated in the days of antiquity. They are a few feet above the level of the sea and about twenty yards from it. We passed through two open halls into a rotunda with a cupola supported on columns. Around it are marble passages leading to the different bath-rooms. It was Ibraham Pasha who erected this building, as well as the beautiful baths of white marble in the halls adjacent to the rotunda. I had a bath, but I was obliged to have two-thirds of the water brought from the sea, and even then I found it very warm.

There are four springs, and on immersing my thermometer in one of them it rose to 49° R. The water has a sharp, saline, bitter taste, and smells of sulphur. It is singular that the water of each of these four springs, when flowing to the sea, leaves a deposit different in colour from the rest; one is red, while the rest are yellow, white, and green. The water has never been subjected to a careful analysis, or the result has never been published. Pocock's experiment, which was not strictly analytical, showed that it contained a considerable quantity of thick, strong vitriol, some alum, and a mineral salt. Dr. Turner is of opinion that the deposit, which consists principally of carbonate of lime and a little common salt, is exactly the same as that of the Dead Sea.

It was now close on sunset, and the sun again poured over mountain, sea and sky, that wonderful light, which is only seen in the east. We now rode close along the shore of the sea, where we saw a beautiful column of granite washed by its waves, and several fragments of chiselled stones. My guide pointed out a pretty large rough block of stone in the sea, about 10 yards from the shore, as the very stone which Moses struck with his rod, and thus procured a supply of water in the wilderness.

After half an hour we passed through the broken gateway, and found ourselves again among the modern ruins of this remarkable town. Mr. Weismann was waiting to conduct me to evening prayer in one of the seven synagogues of Tiberias. The Polish costumes, the wonderful snuffling intended for singing, the whole arrangements of the synagogue caused me for a moment to forget that I was standing on holy ground, consecrated by legends and history, by folly and wisdom.

At night we ascended a stone staircase and found ourselves on a terrace which covered the whole house, and on which carpets with linen sheets were spread out

for our use. Mr. Weismann wound a piece of thin
white woollen cloth round my head as a turban, remark-
ing sententiously, " The head must be kept warm"—an
opinion directly opposed to that which prevails in
Europe! Then he filled some unvarnished earthen
pitchers with sea-water, in order to cool the air by
evaporation, and requested me to lie down, so as to
allow him to place some heavy stones on both sides of
the sheets, to prevent them from being blown away by
the strong breeze, and me from being exposed to the
night air when asleep.

I could not yet tear myself from the magnificent
view which was seen from the terrace. The large
bright stars were flickering in the dark firmament.
Over against me rose the hill with the 24,000 sepulchres; and, though I could not see the sea, I could
hear its roar at the distance of twenty yards. The
town of Tiberias was illuminated with thousands of joyful lights. Lamps were burning in every room occupied by Jews, and, gently borne on the breeze came the
sound of those familiar but wonderful melodies, sung in
honour of the angel of the Sabbath, while here and
there might be seen the white fluttering night-robes of
men walking on the terraces.

I found that the demons of the night could climb as
well as creep, and awoke before sunrise with my whole
skin in a state of violent inflammation. When I mentioned this to Mr. Weismann, he was indignant.

" When you are lodging with a doctor, why don't
you consult him? The warm bath with its salt has

done you harm. Come as quick as you can, and let us have a dip in the sea."

" Could we venture to bathe at Tiberias on the Sabbath ?"

" We should all soon succumb before the fearful heat, if we did not bathe several times every day. At Tiberias we have permission from the Rabbi to bathe."

We went both together to the sea, wearing nothing but our white turbans, a linen sheet, and wooden slippers. It was glittering like a sheet of polished steel, and its waves were calm after the storm of the previous night. We met several bathers even at this early hour, and remained in the cool reviving water till the sun rose and illuminated everything around us with his dazzling light. I could not attend the synagogue, and was obliged to spend the whole day on the divan, enveloped in wet sheets. It was only in this way that I could obtain relief from the burning pain, and I could not avoid a hearty laugh, when Mr. Weismann told me that there is a proverb well known through the whole of Galilee: " The king of the fleas holds court at Tiberias."

After breakfast, which was served at six o'clock in the morning, and after divine service, I received a visit from Mr. Schmul Chajim Cohen Conarti, the worthy Head Rabbi of Tiberias, with seven Chachams. All of them wore wide white cloaks, with broad blue inwoven stripes, and fringed at the end. Such was the primitive shape of the *talit*, with which the Jews in country synagogues still cover the whole body, including the head. T 2

Mr. Conarti, in the course of his travels in Europe, had twice visited Vienna; in the year 1838, after the fearful earthquake with which the town was visited, and in 1848. His object on both occasions was to obtain relief for his unfortunate community. I was met here with the same complaint as at Safed; they could not understand why all the sympathy of the West should be bestowed on Jerusalem, while the Jews in Africa and Asia think also of Safed and Tiberias.

"Are we not also on the sacred soil of God? Have we not also suffered, when Jerusalem was already in ruins? Have not the sacred martyrs of our holy faith made Tiberias honourable, and was it not here that learning was saved from destruction, and revived, and sent forth its life-giving rays throughout the whole world? When Messiah comes, no doubt He will make His first appearance in Jerusalem. But what are we to do in the mean time? We are poor and miserable, and, O God! we have almost ceased to hope. Far be it from me to say a word against our pious brethren at Jerusalem; but at Tiberias we lead holier lives, because we are united."

"How many Jews live at Tiberias?"

"Oh, sir, do not ask that. We were numbered when Sir Moses Montefiore distributed alms at so much a-head; and then came the pestilence, as in the days of King David, and swept off many of us."

Mr. Weismann said to me in German :—

"He means the cholera, but what do the common people know about the difference between pestilence and cholera! *I* cured them with opium, and *they* gave all the credit to their psalm-singing."

I had a constant succession of visitors, and by examining all of them, so as to test their veracity, I obtained the following statistical information. The Jewish population of Tiberias amounted, at the period of my visit, to 1514 souls—881 Aschkenasim, and 633 Sepharedim. They form only one community: the latter have two synagogues and a *mederesse*, the former five synagogues and five *mederessen*, or schools. The Sepharedim have twenty-three houses. Among the Aschkenasim are 200 natives of Austria, from Galicia and Hungary; the rest are chiefly from Russia. The education of youth, as throughout the whole of the East, is entirely neglected. Ignorance has established a strong hold in the town, where the learned synhedrim sat, and the wisest men lived and taught. When I asked whether the children learned Arabic, which is so necessary for the daily intercourse of life in Palestine, Mr. Weismann said:—

"Arabic! Ask rather why they do not learn to speak their own language properly?"

"But do the children not learn to write?"

"To write? For what purpose? Have they ever any occasion to write?"

All receive alms from their native land, but they do not receive so much as their co-religionists at Jerusalem and Hebron. Most of them devote themselves entirely to the study of the Talmud; they despise commerce, because it pollutes the soul and leads it away from God. Only a few of them are handcraftsmen—

one smith, two masons, one joiner, three tailors, one shoemaker, two watchmakers, one fisherman, six shop-keepers.

About ten o'clock in the morning, the heat became so oppressive that even the natives felt weary and languid. It was in vain that they tried to cool themselves by lying on the bare floors of the cellars of their houses. I slept for several hours, and spent the time the best way I could till the approach of evening. Before sunset we again went and bathed in the sea. I made the acquaintance of the whole of the Jewish inhabitants in the water. At a short distance from us was the ladies' bathing-place, enclosed with high latticed walls.

On returning to the house, we found dinner on the table: cold fish swimming in oil, dreadfully fat mutton, green onions—which, though only pulled yesterday, were already quite dry—cold eggs, and a cake dripping with oil. I could not venture to touch any of these dishes, though I had tasted nothing since morning; I confined myself to bread and wine. It was only after the close of the Sabbath that I could get anything fresh cooked.

Other visitors arrived. Each of them had some fearful scene connected with the earthquake to describe; there was not one of them who had not lost a mother, a brother, a child, a wife, or a sister. Many were present whose whole earthly possessions had been swallowed up. About 300 of the 2,000 inhabitants disappeared in a few minutes. One man told me that he was coming down a hill, about a league from Tiberias, along with his son, who was a few yards in advance.

All at once he saw the earth open, his son sink in the chasm, and the ground close again. He was lost in astonishment, and stood motionless with terror, while he felt the earth shaking beneath his feet. He ran as fast as he could to Tiberias, and found there only a heap of ruins.

In the evening Reb Mosche, who had acted as my guide to the sepulchres and baths, brought me a valuable silver cup, on which the figures of all the kings of Poland were skilfully executed. His grandfather had received this cup from Stanislaus Augustus Poniatowsky, the last king of Poland, as a reward for his faithful services, and his grandson wished to sell this valuable heirloom. He wished to buy a boat with the money, and to become a fisherman, as he was sure that he could thus support his numerous family. I preferred to pay a certain sum for a chronicle of Tiberias, written in Hebrew, containing passages of history, and wonderful stories, and prayers, and poems in the Hebrew and Spanish languages.

While its former possessor is perhaps at this moment fishing in his boat on the sea of Gennezareth, we shall treat the reader to an extract from his chronicle, which contains an account of an event which has never appeared in any historical work, which gives a sort of importance to the city, and is worthy of being known.

"In the year of the creation 5,500, or 118 years before the present date, during the reign of Sultan Mohammed, God incited the holy spirit of our teacher, Chajim Abulafia, that he should go to the holy city of

Tiberias, for the purpose of rebuilding the ruins, and fortifying the place. For seventy years Tiberias had remained uninhabited, desolate, and waste; it had no synagogue or place of learning, and since its destruction no *kadisch* or prayer for the dead had been heard in it. Rabbi Chajim Abulafia was fortunate in all his undertakings, and so he went confidently to Tiberias in the month Sivan of the same year. As soon as he entered the country, by the blessing of God, he gained the favour of the men of the city, and especially of the Scheik Dahir-al-Amar, whose fame was great in the whole of Palestine.

Under his government the roads, which formerly could only be passed by armed caravans, became safe. The whole land was at peace, and all the men of the city were subject to the scheik, and called him Schech al Maschech, the lord of lords. He had entirely destroyed several tribes of Bedouins, who had made the roads dangerous, so that every one could travel, without fear, with money in his hand. The scheik was equally renowned for his liberality; his house was open to all, and travellers of all nations and creeds were treated with the same hospitality.

Two years before the arrival of the Rabbi, he was living at Asmir. When the scheik learned that the Rabbi was about to visit the land, he sent him letter after letter with these words:—" Get thee up and take possession of Tiberias, the land of thy fathers."

Indeed, the grandfather of this Rabbi, Jacob Abulafia, was Rabbi in Tiberias before it was destroyed.

When the Rabbi came to Tiberias, the scheik showed him great honour, and caused him to be clothed with valuable, almost regal robes. He did whatever the Rabbi desired, and, in about two years, streets and houses were built for the Jews; a splendid synagogue, superior to any in Palestine, was restored ; noble baths, and a bazaar supported on arches, were erected, and the whole land was intersected with roads. Men tilled the ground, planted vineyards, daily the popularity of the Rabbi increased among the men of the city, and all the inhabitants were very happy and contented.

In the year 5502, after two-and-a-half years' peace, such as prevailed in the days of Solomon, there came suddenly on the 22nd Ab a letter from Damascus to the Rabbi; it was from two distinguished men, Mr. Chajim Parchi and Josef Luschati, who were bankers to Soleiman Pasha of Damascus.

The letter ran thus:—" It is well that you should know the sudden and stern order of the Sultan to the Pasha of Damascus ; he is commanded to advance against Tiberias, to take the town by storm and to put Scheik Dahir to death. The Pasha is now preparing an army with much ammunition, and engines which can hurl stones six bowshots, and kill twenty men at that distance. The lives of the people of Tiberias are in danger. Hasten, O Rabbi, with all the holy community from the city, and flee to Safed ; the Pasha will send people there to protect the Jews. But have all your goods and property conveyed to Akka."

Rabbi Abulafia was very much disquieted by this

letter, and hastened to the scheik to inform him of its contents. But the latter said that the thing could not be true, for three reasons. If the destruction of Tiberias had really been resolved on, the Jews of Constantinople would have obtained previous notice of it. As Tiberias belonged to the province of the Pasha of Sidon, the execution of the order would have been confided to him, and not to the Pasha of Damascus. Besides, he could not imagine any reason why such an order should have been given, as he was entirely devoted to the Sultan, and punctual in the payment of the annual tribute. The letter, he added, had been written at the instance of the Pasha of Damascus as a means of extorting money from the inhabitants of Tiberias.

When the Rabbi heard these words he was very glad, and wrote immediately an answer to Damascus that there was no truth in the report; but, after five days, came a second letter, in which the threatened destruction was still more confidently announced. Again, the scheik said the thing could not be true, as the Pasha of Sidon had assured him that he stood very well at court.

On the fifth of Ellul the scheik was informed that the Pasha had left Damascus with a large army to march against Tiberias. The scheik now began to prepare to receive him, and garrisoned the places that were least secure. When the Jews saw this, they did not know what course to adopt, and hastened to the Rabbi. He advised them to remain in Tiberias, as God would save them even here. Next morning he ordered the elders to visit the holy sepulchres, and to offer up prayer there.

Next day—it happened to be a Friday—might be seen from the heights a great army approaching with tents and engines of war. The scheik was sorry that he had not sent away the defenceless inhabitants; as he could now no longer protect them. It is true that he was encouraged by the Pasha of Sidon to march forth and anticipate the arrival of the Pasha; the scheik sent to his brother Saat, who dwelt in the fortress Tirchanah, requesting him to advance with his men to his assistance.

On Sabbath, before sunrise, Soleiman Pasha encamped before the town, and, having attacked the tower, the garrison discharged a stone, which killed 14 men, and the army retreated to a considerable distance. In the evening, the Pasha threw up entrenchments, with the intention of bombarding the town. But, wonderful to relate, not a man or a beast was injured; most of the bombs fell into the sea. The Jewish children thought they were balls, and rolled them before them in sport. Some of these bombs are still preserved in the house of the Rabbi, and shown to pilgrims.

As the firing had no effect, it soon ceased, and the scheik, thinking that the Pasha might be disposed to come to terms, sent to him a woman with presents, as is the custom of the Arabs. He took the presents, and sent back the female ambassador with the message, that he would not grant them peace till the scheik was given up. The people of Tiberias were very much troubled on receiving this message, but the scheik comforted himself with the expectation that his brother would come to his assistance. The Pasha commenced a heavier cannonade, but it was attended with no better result than before.

The Jews prayed without ceasing, morning and evening, in the synagogue, and in other respects lived joyfully in their houses, trusting in God, and never thinking of leaving the town, though they had permission to do so. When the people now began to murmur and to say, " The army from Tirchanah must have deceived thee," he reassured them with the words : " My brother will not act on the offensive, lest it should be said that he attacked the Pasha while engaged in a pilgrimage to Mecca."

The Pasha now tried to cut off all communication between Tiberias and Acka, so as to deprive the besieged of the means of existence, but this attempt was also unsuccessful. The scheik, acting on the advice of his friends, again tried to come to terms with the Pasha. But the latter insisted that the citadel should be destroyed, and that his army should be allowed to march through the city ; the scheik would not consent to this.

The Pasha now had recourse to another stratagem, in order to get possession of the city. He arranged his forces, as if he were about to attack the north side of the town, in the hope that the defenders of Tiberias would be attracted to that quarter, and thus allow him to seize the tower. But the tower was not left ungarrisoned, and when the Pasha applied his scaling-ladders, on the Sabbath Bereschit, they were all thrown down, and not one of the assailants escaped.

Then came an ambassador from Constantinople, who, in the name of the Sultan, ordered the Pasha to undertake immediately a pilgrimage to Mecca. But the Pasha still hoped to accomplish something by mining. He sent for the chief engineer, and asked him : " How long will it take you to finish the work?"

" Eighteen days, my lord. But God leads the mines the wrong way, and they are always receding farther from the walls; this is owing to the enchantments of the Jews. Give orders, my lord, that Jews also be employed in the work."

Jews were brought from Safed; but as the chief engineer could effect nothing with their aid, the Pasha ordered his head to be cut off. When the head, stuck upon a pole, was elevated above the walls of the town, the Jewish women who were in an interesting condition thought it was a moon-flower.

At length, the ambassador from Constantinople forced the Pasha to retire. The fifteenth day of the mining operations was the eighteenth day of the siege, or the Hebrew number " Af," *i.e.*, anger ceases, which signified that God had turned away his anger on this day. The Pasha withdrew with his army ; but he swore that he would return, after he had finished his pilgrimage to Mecca.

The Jews of Tiberias now learned that a pestilence had been raging in Safed, and had swept away most of the inhabitants. They then gratefully acknowledged that it was the will of God which had prevented them from fleeing to Safed. But the day on which the Pasha raised the siege, the fourth of Kislaf, was observed as a festival, and devoted to songs of triumph. This festival is still observed at Tiberias.

The Pasha, on his return from Mecca, was laughed at by his countrymen, on account of his unsuccessful siege. This, and his oath, induced him to resume the siege of Tiberias. On the 12th of Tamus came another letter from the Pasha's Jewish Seraph to the Rabbi of Tiberias, announcing that preparations were being made. Most of them wished to flee, but the Rabbi again advised them to remain, and did not take any steps to lay in a supply of provisions ; for he asserted that the Pasha would never reach the city. This time the preparations were more extensive, and all communication with Tiberias was at once cut off by the enemy.

The Pasha embarked, and reached Akka, and then Lubei, two leagues from Tiberias. On Friday, the third of Ellul, came the intelligence that the Pasha was marching from the neighbourhood of Lubei. All the people of Tiberias were very much troubled.

On the same evening, the son of the Rabbi read the Haforah : " I, even I, am He that comforteth you," and on the Sabbath the Rabbi preached from the text : " I will not fear what flesh can do."

Next day it was announced that the Pasha was ill and lying unconscious. On Tuesday he died, and on Wednesday the Vizier fell back on Akka, and conveyed his dead body to Damascus. On the seventh of Ellul, the day of the Pasha's death, the Rabbi offered up a prayer of thanksgiving, and it was agreed, with the approval of the community, that this day should be observed as a feast of rejoicing for all time to come.

# CHAPTER VIII.

I MADE up my mind to leave at 9 o'clock in the
morning, so as to reach Nazareth before the hottest
part of the day had set in. I had another dip in the
sea; the stillness of midnight rested on the soft mur-
muring waves and the mountains. The breeze was
cool and refreshing. The only thing that disturbed me
was Mr. Weismann's unceasing tattle. He wished me to

stay another day, and offered to row me to see the
places where the Jordan enters and leaves the sea, and
to conduct me to a ravine, where the "Anoschim" and
the "Imahot" are buried. He told me that this ravine
contained the ashes of Abigail, of Queen Esther, of the
patriarch's handmaids, Bilhah and Zilpah, and of Zip-
porah, the wife of the prophet. Then he wished to
take me to the neighbouring Chetien, to the sepulchres
of Jethro and of Jochebed, the mother of the prophet,
and to a cavern in which the Emperor Antoninus and
Rabbi Hakadosch used to have secret meetings, and to
converse on philosophy. This land of Galilee is rich in
legendary lore, which plays around the imaginations of
those who choose to listen, like the mysterious voices of
the winds and the waves.

Our horses were now saddled, we breakfasted on
coffee and Polish brandy, and laid in a stock of provisions for some days. When I asked Mr. Weismann
for the reckoning, he said :—

"What! do you think I would charge anything from
a brother practitioner?"

He said this with the air of a man who had made up
his mind, and I was glad when he allowed me to have
some ancient coins, stamped at Tiberias, which he had
shewn me the day before, at double their value.

We began to ascend a hill, and reached the summit
in half an hour. An extensive mountain-plateau opened
up before us; we turned round to have a last look at
the sea, but it had disappeared, and the day began to
dawn. We were joined by a man driving two loaded

asses. On the right and left were fields of mown corn, and the whole face of the country was covered with the white down of thistles, which at a distance looked like snow. The summit of Tabor was visible in the blue horizon. Above us rose the joyful song of the lark, and, as it is exactly the same as at home, it awoke many pleasant reminiscences, and almost made me forget where I was, till Hadschi Achmed, from the land of Mizraim, began a shrill Arab ditty, which he continued with stentorian voice and unflagging breath for six hours, till we reached Nazareth.

After two hours we met eight donkeys driven by two men, from the village of Lubieh, which is situated to the left, on a hill planted with fig and olive trees. There is another hill of a similar character opposite to this, and our road, which is enclosed with hedges of cactus, lies between. A herd of cattle was feeding before the village, but we did not see a single human being; it had a lifeless look.

Our ride grew ever more lonely and sad. Nothing was to be seen but naked hills with narrow valleys sometimes lying between, or large plains strewn with white stones of considerable size. The sky was covered with grey clouds, a phenomenon which I had not seen for months together, and which imparted a still more melancholy appearance to the landscape, after the sunny days to which I had been accustomed. A soft breeze was blowing, and this day we did not find the heat oppressive.

We halted on this stony plain, and partook of a

slight repast on a large stone, which served as a table. Three women, leading two loaded camels, passed us. We broke up and resumed our way through the dreary solitude, through rocky hills scorched with the sun, and destitute of vegetation, and valleys whose only crop was the white stones already mentioned. Could these valleys, these hills have ever been green and fruitful? Was this their original condition? We have mentioned all the people that we met to show, by their small number, how uninhabited these regions are. The soul becomes oppressed with a mysterious feeling of disquietude, and I felt the same desire to escape from the scene, as a bird may be supposed to have to escape from the vacuum of an air pump. Never before did I experience, to the same extent, the dread sublimity of utter solitude.

After some hours we came to a miserable village, Kefr Kenna, which is pointed out to pilgrims as the Cana, where Jesus changed water into wine at a marriage feast, an act of hospitality which is supposed to have been his first miracle. More recent researches prove that Kefr Kenna, as the name shows, is not the Cana of the marriage feast, but Kana el Jelil, which is situated on the north of the plain el Butt, about three leagues from Kefr Kenna. In fact, Kana el Jelil was always pointed out in ancient works as the Cana of the New Testament. It was only in the sixteenth century that the monks, overlooking all difficulties connected with the name, substituted Kefr Kenna, because it lay at a more convenient distance from the road pursued by the pilgrims. Here is shown the house, or at least the heap of stones that represents it, and the earthen vessels in which the miracle was performed.

We rode down through the village, behind which is a large watering-place, with some gardens, enclosed with hedges of cactus. Women and girls, in wide blue woollen dresses, with red veils descending over their shoulders to their ancles, and bands of silver coins on their foreheads, were carrying earthen pitchers on their heads, and holding them firm with their hands. Broad rings were sparkling on their handsome arms. They did not veil themselves as we approached, but when we courteously saluted them, there was a general titter. Matthia remarked: "Women in the East are not accustomed to such acts of courtesy."

We drank from the cool fountain, and continued our way up stony hills, in one of the clefts of which, on our right, we saw the small village of Renie, on the sloping side of a hill. The road, which passed over heaps of stones, over naked ground, and natural staircases of rock, reminded me of my dangerous ride over Mount Lebanon. We had now been six hours in the saddle; Nazareth could not be far off, and on reaching the top of every hill we expected to see it, but found only another hill in advance.

Hadschi Achmed from Egypt, whose shrill song had followed in the rear ever since we left Tiberias, now suddenly passed us, and rushed up the hill, so that he soon left us a good way behind. He had never behaved in this way before, during the whole journey, having always remained behind to protect us or to show his respect for us. Matthia, who had a growing dislike for him on account of his uncleanliness, said : " Has the devil entered the pig ? "

But it was no mean motive that led Hadschi Achmed from Mizraim thus to hurry up the rocky path. On reaching the top of the hill, he drew his crooked sabre, and, turning round in the saddle, he pointed with it in advance, and shouted to us, " En Nasirah ! "

When we reached the crest of the hill, we saw a deep valley below. On the slope of a hill lay Nazareth, a Syrian village, built of stone, and hidden among green trees, above which rose the cupola of a mosque, a solitary palm, and the castellated monastery.

Achmed the Mohammedan, who also acknowledges Jesus to be a prophet, dismounted from his horse, and stood holding him by the reins.

Matthia, the Arab Catholic, knelt down and engaged in prayer.

I remained in the saddle gazing on the scene, and was reminded of the words of Nathanael in the New Testament : " Can any good thing come out of Nazareth ? " And this was the man of whom Jesus said : " Behold an Israelite indeed, in whom there is no guile."

Achmed again mounted his horse, while Matthia led his by the bridle. In a quarter of an hour we reached the fountain of the Virgin. A negress, with wide red trousers, a short blue dress, and a turban round her head, was drawing water.

Opposite the monastery, at only twenty yards' distance, stands the new house for the reception of pilgrims, a fine-looking building, with a handsome public room, and numerous light cells in a state of perfect cleanliness. I met here with the kindest reception from Fra Angelino Costa, a native of Genoa, who gave me a most refreshing draught of raspberry vinegar, and then showed me the cell which I was to occupy. He announced to me, at the same time, that the guardian for whom I had a letter from the Father President at Jerusalem, would receive me at his house in the afternoon. Fra Angelino was delighted to hear that I knew the "haughty" city of his birth, which claims as her children the two greatest discoverers of modern times, who have enlarged our knowledge of geography and music. Every time we met, the old man alluded to "la superba Genova," which he never expected to see again.

Worn out with the ride and the heat of the day, I lay down for some hours; since my visit to the monastery on Mount Carmel, I had not enjoyed such an excellent couch, or such delightful cleanliness; and, although in the course of the night, the demons of darkness gave certain indications of their presence, the gauze curtains and a certain magical powder from Persia, strewn on the floor, served to keep them at a distance.

Having rested myself, I went to the monastery. After knocking several times, a large iron gate was opened. On both sides, in the interior, is the burying-ground for the monks and the congregation. Passing through an arched entrance, I reached a large quadrangular space, paved with broad tiles, which contains a fountain. I passed through an ante-chamber in a corner of this court, and ascended by a stone staircase to a broad, shady passage, full of doors, leading to the cells of the monks. The interior of the monastery is almost the same as that of similar estab-lishments in Europe.

The guardian, Angelo Veneziani di Caprarota, a fine-looking man, with a black beard of surprising length, received me in the most friendly manner. I gave him the letter, which he read with evident interest. I may mention that the religious persuasion to which I belong was expressly mentioned, which made me appreciate more highly the genuine hospitality and amiable toleration with which I was treated.

A peculiar task had been confided to me at Nazareth. When Duke Maximilian, of Bavaria, was travelling in Palestine, Dr. Bayer, his body physician, died at Nazareth of the plague. The amiable prince wished to erect a monument to his friend and physician. King Louis was of opinion that a monument was not a proper mark of respect for any one at Nazareth, and that it would most likely soon be destroyed. I learned all this from Dr. Röser, body physician to the King of Greece, who was anxious that I should obtain some information at the monastery of Nazareth regarding the prac-ticability of erecting a living memorial of a different kind, which might prove useful to others. He had conceived the idea that the money, which had been set apart for this purpose, could be turned to better account if it were invested in the funds, and the interest devoted to the support of a medical man, who should reside at Nazareth, and give the inhabitants of the town and of the neighbouring country, who are at present without medical advice, the benefit of his professional knowledge.

The guardian, like the Father President at Jerusalem, took a lively interest in this proposal, the advantages of which he at once recognised, and promised to support it in every way, provided that he obtained the approval of the Father President, of which, considering the character of his letter, he entertained no doubt. The medical man could board and lodge in the *Casa Nuova*, till he got a house of his own, and could live comfortably with a servant on 600, or, at most, 800 silver florins. I conveyed this information to Dr. Röser at Athens. The guardian conducted me to the burying-ground, which I had crossed when passing from the gate of the front court to the monastery, for the purpose of showing me the grave of Dr. Bayer, " the martyr," a name to which he was fairly entitled, as he fell a victim to his own zeal and over-exertions in succouring those who were attacked with the plague. We entered a quadrangular space enclosed with walls, in the centre of which is a small stone column surmounted by an iron cross. Not a single grave is distinguished by a stone, a cross of iron or of wood, a tree or a flower. If I had not known it before, I should never have imagined that I was in a burying-ground, as there was not a single mound to remind one of the presence of the dead, all the graves being on a level with the surface. All the graves were overgrown with vegetation. Dr. Bayer's grave, which is close to the wall on the left of the entrance, is slightly elevated, and has a thistle growing on it. Palestine has always been fruitful in thistles and thorns for weaving the martyr's crown. We passed from this place to another opposite to it, exactly similar in character, where a palm-tree—the only one in Nazareth—raises its graceful head, and sings its lullaby over the dead. An arbour of vine-branches, resting on a quadrangular enclosure of low pillars, forms the entrance to the grotto, and the flat surface above is planted with tobacco. " Pulvis et umbra sumus," said the guardian. Playfully alluding to the tobacco, I replied, " Fumus, reverendissime domine."

Fra Angelino invited me to dinner in the *Casa Nuova*, where a cover was laid for me alone. When I told him that I had brought a supply of provisions with me, he said : " If you cannot conscientiously partake of our food, we cannot refuse to make you the offer, and to fulfil the sacred duties of hospitality." And thus, on each of the three days which I spent in the monastery, I was provided with an abundant meal.

After I had drunk some black coffee, the guardian, accompanied by Padre Wenzelaus Kichel, from Stams in Tyrol, and Fra Joachimo, from Valencia in Spain, returned my visit, and invited me to see the holy places. I have visited them all, and received from my guides the most minute details connected with their sanctuaries. Countless descriptions of these places have been given, and it is not necessary for me to increase the number. I shall therefore confine my observations to a few works of art, which are scarcely mentioned in the numerous works on Nazareth. I was most struck with a beautiful painting of the Conception by Antonio Darallo, and a black Christ with the noblest Caucasian features.

" Unfortunately, it is only a copy," said the guardian, " the original was appropriated some years ago by the Consul Catafago, who has been so much praised by travellers."

The pieces of tapestry with which the walls of the church are covered produce a very fine effect. As they are not contrasted with Raphael's productions, as in the Vatican, they afford almost a higher amount of pleasure to the spectator than those at Rome, the effect of which is weakened by the thousands of other objects of art by which they are surrounded. These productions of art at Nazareth were really to me an oasis in the desert, as for a long time I had not seen any painting worthy of the name. On the tapestry may be seen the bold outlines of artistically arranged groups ; the marriage of Joseph and Mary, the annunciation, the birth of the child, and the adoration of the three kings, are embroidered in lively colours and executed with considerable skill.

After visiting Mount Tabor we returned to the

monastery. I rose at the earliest dawn and ascended one of the hills, to meditate in solitude on the scenes which surrounded me. Here, in the miserable hut of a carpenter, was born a child who grew up in silence without attracting public attention. He gazed on these declivities and rocks, on this fountain embedded in trees, on Tabor with its covering of green verdure, on the snow-capped Hermon, and the sparkling Mediterranean, stretching away in the distance, as I now gazed on them after the lapse of twenty centuries. These sublime scenes, on which solitude is now slumbering, were imprinted on his soul and awoke within him thoughts and feelings which were afterwards to change the outward appearance of the world, and to give an impetus to the human mind, the influence of which was to be felt through future ages.

The Jewish Rabbi Jischo (Jesus) little dreamed of the revolution he was destined to effect, but his word at an after period was the only sound in a cold world, that could roll the avalanches from the mountains. They buried, though this was not intended, the eternal principles of Judaism, the religion, which before the advent of Christianity had announced the doctrine of love on its tables of stone at first only to one people. He did not come to destroy the law of Moses, but to fulfil it, and to impart the knowledge of it to the many nations still sunk in heathenism.

The imagination is ever attracted towards this man, and longs to reach the source of the mighty stream, to see and examine him closely in his early childhood. I was now standing at the source of the stream, whose mighty waters overflowed the whole world.

On Sinai and Golgotha, on the heights and in the depths, wherever one of the world's religions has taken its rise, the soul of the pilgrim is agitated with mingled feelings of sublimity, of terror, and of veneration, and is incited to pious thoughts. Every spot on God's earth is sacred on which a light has shone forth and become one of the beacon lights of the world.

Are we to believe that the eternal will is immutable and absolute? What shall be the destination of humanity in future ages? The imagination cannot scan the secrets of the future, but it can wing its flight across the stream of future ages, and declare itself a citizen of future worlds yet undreamed of.

Boys and girls passed me on their way to church, as the signal had been given for morning prayer. I looked at them with something of veneration and awe, not only because each had a future, but because the thought was half suggested to my mind, that one of these children might be called to solve the problem of the world's destiny. But the soil which has given birth to one great man does not produce a second, the far-spreading tree imbibes all the strength of the soil in which it grows, and leaves no vital force to strengthen the growth of another planted on the same spot.

All these imaginings owed their birth to the appearance which Christianity presented to my mind during my stay at Nazareth, and the impressions which I had received in early youth from association and education were soon revived, and I could explain on pure psychological principles the prudential motives which induced the Rabbis to proclaim it unlawful for Jewish children to attend Christian schools, and the French bishops to pronounce the reading of the Greek classics in the schools dangerous. It is on the same principle that governments have prohibited certain songs and airs which, having been learned in early youth, tend to rouse the people to revolt, when the familiar sound is heard.

Religions also have their Alpine ranges and lunar rainbows.

I descended from the hill to the fountain of the Virgin. It is probable that the mother and her child were in the habit of visiting this spring, as it is the only one in Nazareth.

A motley group of women were drawing water. Some of them approached with their two-handled earthen pitchers placed horizontally on their heads, others carried them perpendicularly, and held them fast with one or both arms. These women had olive complexions; most of them had blue rings beneath their eyes, and their lips also painted blue. All wore wide blue robes, fastened at the waist with a piece of blue cloth. A white or red veil descended from the head over the rest of the body. Only two or three of them were veiled—a proof that they were Mohammedans.

Here, still less than elsewhere, could I understand those ecclesiastical painters, who look upon the pious

Jean Bellino, the chaste Francia, the naturally ideal Raphael, as much too sensual in their representations of the leading figures of Christianity. Giotto and Cimabue, who appear to them the highest masters of severe Christian art, would certainly have given richer representations of life, if their knowledge of art had been sufficiently developed. I have always been struck in their productions with a certain longing sense of dissatisfaction, a sorrowful aspiration after that perfection, which the immortal masters of painting who succeeded them were alone destined to attain. But the modern adherents of the ascetic school of painting regard their incomplete efforts in art as intentional, and think that they have attained to the highest perfection when they paint an emaciated Byzantine angel, or a spider-legged saint, while inspired by the music of the organs kept in their *ateliers* for the purpose of exciting their imaginations. No doubt the typical figures of the Byzantines approximate more closely to the original forms. But we cannot understand why the sacred painters of the present day should imitate original paintings, produced at a period when art was imperfect, and become the servile adherents of those who felt their weakness, and aspired to something higher than they could produce. A journey to Palestine and Egypt, where the type of humanity has remained unchanged even in the very matter of dress, would be far more serviceable to them than a visit to Rome, where Christian art has been so much influenced by that of Greece, that many of its productions are altogether heathenish. I have never seen more beautiful models for the representation of the leading characters of the Old and New Testament than in the land of the Bible.

The finding of Moses in the Nile, painted by a French painter, and seen by us some years ago at Vienna, is the most lively illustration of the remarks we have just made. Horace Vernet owes his noblest triumphs to his travels in the East, although there is too much of French frivolity in his delineations of Biblical characters.

I discovered a very close resemblance between the women of Nazareth and of Egypt, which did not appear in the women of other parts of Palestine, and still less in those of Syria. Mary, by the descent into Egypt, belongs as it were to both countries, and forms a connecting link between them. Antoninus Martyr in the sixteenth century describes the beauty of the women of Nazareth, with which more recent travellers have also been struck, though they do not ascribe it, as he did, to the influence of Mary.

Nazareth was inhabited exclusively by Jews till the reign of the Emperor Constantine; at the present moment there is not a single Jew among the three thousand inhabitants, one thousand of whom are Mohammedans, though no fanatical hindrance has been opposed to their residence, at least on the part of the Turks. The principal cause of this may be found in the fact that this place, which is not mentioned in the Bible, has no historical or religious attractions for them.

Leaving the fountain of the Virgin, I walked through the little town and explored every part of it. The artizans and tradesmen were everywhere busy at work. I remained for a long time standing in an open place, and indulging in all kinds of thoughts, as I watched a carpenter giving shape to a tree, and drinking from a leather bottle which his wife, who carried a child in her arms, had brought to his place of labour.

On my return to the *Casa Nuova*, Matthia told me that Fra Joachimo had been twice to see me, and requested him to let him know as soon as I returned.

Fra Joachimo is a native of Molina, in Spain. When eighteen years of age, he entered the " Convento de Sta. Maria de las puertas extra muros del Orca in Murcia," where he remained seven years. Sent by his superiors to Jerusalem, he lived there fifteen years, and has now spent other fifteen at Nazareth. He is now fifty-five years of age, but slender and erect as in his early youth; his profile is nobly designed and full of expression, his eyes a lively blue, his hair black, his beard grey.

Having a strong natural inclination for medical studies, he had read the whole of the limited supply of medical works contained in the library of the monastery, so as to be able to prescribe for his brethren when sick, and to enhance his usefulness, he was in the habit of tending them, and of performing those more menial offices which are more within the province of the apothecary.

The experience which he had acquired in this way,

aided by a certain amount of natural talent, had encouraged him to attempt the cure of the simpler forms of disease, and his reputation had gradually increased to such an extent that he was entrusted with the management of the apothecary's shop at Nazareth, and consulted as the only physician for miles around.

At the instance of Dr. Röser, he was chosen a member of the Royal Greek Society of Physicians at Athens, and this gentleman had also given me a letter to Fra Joachimo. He now called upon me to invite me to accompany him in his visits to the sick of Nazareth. "I begin," said he, "my visits in the morning and the evening, in order that I may drink from the fountain of the Virgin. I regard hydropathy as an extremely successful, because it is a natural mode of cure. Is it known in Germany? Unfortunately there is so little water in Nazareth, that when this fountain is dried up in the height of summer, the women are obliged to go half a league farther to obtain water from another source."

Wherever we went, the men remained standing, and saluted the venerable man; many of them kissed his hands. "Those who do this," said Fra Joachimo, "are Christians; not merely Catholics, but also Maronites and Greeks. The Greeks form the most numerous portion of the population of Nazareth, as there are more than two hundred and twenty families; the Mohammedans rank next in point of numbers; there are a hundred and twenty families of them. There are only sixty-seven Roman Catholic, and sixty-two Greek

Catholic families. The least numerous section of the population consists of forty Maronite families. The inhabitants all live together on the most peaceful terms, and there is almost more friendly intercourse between the Christians and the Mohammedans, than between the members of the different Christian sects. God loves all men alike."

Sometimes during our visits, men and women remained standing, and stretched out their hands to allow the physician to feel their pulses, without saying a word about the nature of their ailments. Fra Joachimo occasionally gave some advice with respect to regimen, or sent the patient to his house and promised to visit him. We entered about fifteen houses, and this gave me a welcome insight into the family life and economy of the inhabitants of Nazareth. In almost every case the windows had no panes of glass, and were only closed with shutters, or, in Turkish houses, with wooden lattices. I did not see a single bed-frame; in every case the patient lay on a carpet and some cushions, spread on the damp clay floor, or on the flat slabs. The Mohammedan women veiled themselves when we entered, but they drew aside their veils when questions were put to them. The children were playing about in the rooms, for the most part in a state of perfect nudity. Most of those whom we visited were suffering from ague. "This people," Fra Joachimo observed, "cannot restrain themselves in the heat of summer, and are always eating at melons, which gives rise to fevers, especially in the case of the Mohammedans, because they abstain from wine. It is in vain that I advise them, since they *will* eat so many melons, to sprinkle some finely-ground tobacco over them."

Fra Joachimo has repeatedly visited patients attacked by the plague; he considers it non-contagious, and treats it as he would do any other fever. "At the commencement of the pestilence, almost all who were attacked died, then the number of convalescents gradually increased, though the symptoms were the same as at its first outbreak. I tried hydropathy as a cure for the plague; but only in a very few cases, when two of my patients died and one recovered. I would not venture to draw any conclusion from this."

We concluded our round with another drink at the fountain of the Virgin, and then lay down beneath a fig-tree. It was eight o'clock in the morning, and my thermometer had already risen to 30° R. in the shade.

The books of Hippocrates were the only classical works with which Fra Joachimo was acquainted; he inquired with the liveliest interest about the remedies employed for the cure of different diseases in the West, and noted them down carefully in his diary. "How happy I should be," he continued, "if this noble and humane idea were carried out, and a properly educated physician established at Nazareth. How much I could learn from him, and what useful information I could communicate to him in return!" We now returned to the monastery, where a considerable crowd was already waiting before the apothecary's shop. Many had come from leagues around to obtain medicine and advice for themselves or for their sick friends in the different villages.

I now retired to my cell to rest myself.

Fra Joachimo had scarcely finished his duties, when he despatched a servant with a cooling draught, extracted from different fruits, for my refreshment, and soon after he joined me himself, and presented me with his chibouque, which had a beautiful head made of green glass. "It is filled with tobacco," he said, "which grew on my own grave. I shall never see my beautiful fatherland again. How beautiful it is—my fatherland !"

He had much to tell me about his cloister-life, and his conversation was composed of a strange mixture of Spanish and Italian expressions and idioms. I obtained a deeper insight into his noble and pious character, his amiable and humane disposition. It may be long before he meets with another who will listen to him with the same warm sympathy. He took his leave, as duty summoned him away, but I was delighted, when he requested, almost as a favour, to be permitted to return when the heat of the day had passed away. "You will so soon leave us," were his parting words.

After the dinner—served as a matter of ceremony—had been removed, and Matthia had supplied me with part of the provisions which we had brought from Tiberias, I had another visit from Fra Joachimo, who came to drink coffee with me. He brought me another present, a small box carved from the wood of a fig-tree, which he had brought with him from the home of his fathers. I really felt myself very much embarrassed by his kindness, and the only return I could make was to present him with a small microscope, which I had used during my travels. I could only persuade him to accept it by showing him how useful it might be to him in the examination of the morbid matter of certain diseases.

We had another walk through Nazareth, and examined the Greek Catholic Church, which is situated above the fountain of the Virgin, and then rested ourselves in a court, where an arbour twelve feet square, formed by a vine loaded with clusters, afforded a pleasant shade. We were joined by an Arab physician, who lives on terms of professional intimacy with Fra Joachimo, as the latter attends the sick gratuitously, and scarcely interferes with the professional gains of the Arabian charlatan. He remembered having seen Napoleon, after the victory which he gained in the plain of Esdraelon. He came to Nazareth, halted, and partook of a meal there. When I happened to allude to my travels in Italy, he asked me if I had been at Loretto. I answered in the affirmative, and then nothing would satisfy him but that I should describe the hut of the parents of Christ, which the angels carried from Nazareth to Loretto in one night, to prevent it from being desecrated by the Mohammedans. A Mohammedan boy ran to obtain from the Christian sexton the key of the " synagogue," in which Jesus is said to have taught when a boy. After we had seen the miserable, filthy, modern building, we ascended half way up the side of the hill, on which Nazareth is situated, to the hamlet, which contains the ruins of the ancient nunnery of Sta. Maria del Tremore. It is said to have been erected on the spot where Mary learned that they were about to cast her son down from the mountain. We found a hole in the wall, by which alone the monastery—which is surrounded with lofty walls—could be approached. At no great distance from these ruins is a cavity four fathoms in length and three in breadth, the walls of which are constructed of square stones. In these square stones may be seen artificial incisions and holes. From the bottom of the cavity, which is several fathoms in depth, rises a fig-tree, more than a hundred years old. We could not discover the object of this building, and even tradition, in this instance, is at fault. Fra Joachimo directed my attention to a hill, at a distance of about three-quarters of a league, with a white chapel on the top; this is said to have been the abode of John and James, the sons of Zebedee.

The sun sank behind the mountains of Nazareth, the peaks of which glowed with his parting rays, while the valley was already enveloped in the deepest shade. We gazed on this peaceful scene for a long time in silence. As we drank in its calm and holy beauty, we were almost tempted to believe that the whole world was at peace, and that the souls of men were purified from hatred, the lust of persecution, and every other evil passion.

Fra Joachimo, who, it struck me, had surveyed the parting twilight with a certain expression of sorrow, seized my hand, and said:—

"You leave this valley to-morrow; shall we ever meet again?"

"I suspect that I shall never visit this country again."

"We shall meet again; if not here, in paradise."

"Do you believe that Christians and Jews will both be admitted to heaven?"

"It would pain me to think"—and there was a tear in his eye—"that we shall never meet again. But God is gracious."

It was now dark. Both of us were labouring under strong emotion as we arose and returned to Nazareth.

We had dismissed Hadschi Achmed from the land of Mizraim, because we had reason to be dissatisfied with his horses. Matthia hired fresh horses at Nazareth, the owner of which accompanied us with a donkey, which carried our luggage. At the monastery, I was advised to take a Bedouin as an escort, as the inhabitants of Samaria are much addicted to thieving, and were still in a state of excitement in consequence of the recent accident at Nablous.

Fra Angelino brought me my breakfast, and expressed his regret at my departure. At the monastery "de terra santa," no one ever asks how long a guest will remain, he meets with every attention, and, when he leaves, he may give something to the monastery, or nothing at all, just as he chooses. I gazed on the scene for the last time, and lingered as long as I could before mounting my horse; I felt as if I could not leave

Nazareth without saying good bye to Fra Joachimo.
He was nowhere to be seen. At length we started, and
rode down the gradual slope of the valley for half an
hour, when we came to a fountain. Fra Joachimo
hailed me from a distance, and, when I came up, he presented me with a cup of fresh water and a small
bottle of spirits which he himself had distilled from
the vine. Here also we found the Bedouin, who
was to act as our guard, with his small, thin horse
drinking at the fountain. Fra Joachimo was too much
agitated to speak, he could only listen, and, when
Matthia gave the order to start, he gave me a silent
embrace and turned back. I felt as much emotion as
if I had been parting from a friend of many years'
standing.

We continued to ascend for another hour, till we
came to a steep, perpendicular rock on the left side of
the road. This is supposed to be the rock to which the
Jews dragged Jesus and threatened to cast him down.
It is not probable, however, that the riotous mob of
Nazareth, with such abundance of precipices close at
hand, should have dragged their victim for a mile in
order to put him to death. No monkish author before
the time of the crusades alludes to this rock, which,
however, is calculated, through its wild beauty, to make
a deep impression on the imagination, which can easily
conceive it to have been the scene of some fearful
event.

At length we reached the largest and most beautiful
plain of Palestine, known in the Bible as Jezreel, but

afterwards named Esdraelon by the Greeks. Extending as it does from Tabor to Carmel, and from Dschenin
to Nazareth, it seems fairly entitled to the designation
of " μέγα πεδίον," " the great plain," which Josephus has
bestowed upon it, while, at the same time, it is the most
fruitful part of the holy land, and, if properly cultivated,
would fill the granaries of a population thrice as large
as that which occupies Palestine at the present day.

Its fruitfulness was celebrated by Ethan the Esma-
lite :—

" Jezreel is a field of corn, no human hand has sowed
its seed, no mower has gathered its ripe ears."

This fruitfulness results from the peculiar nature of the
soil, and the large number of springs and rivulets by
which the plain is watered. As it was the month of
July when I crossed it, I did not see it in its full splendour; it rather resembled an immense pasturage,
scorched by the sun. Even the brook Kishon, in
which the bodies of the slain were swept away after
Deborah's victory, was quite dried up, and even during
the rainy season, it only attains the size of a pretty
large rivulet. The plain derived its name from the
town of Jezreel in the tribe of Issachar, which was the
residence of the kings of Israel. It was situated on the
projecting heights of Mount Gilboa, and is now a miserable village of some twenty houses, known by the name of
Zerin. There is nothing to remind us of the former
greatness of the town—three thousand years ago, when
it was inhabited by Ish-bosheth, the son of Saul, by
Ahab and Jezebel—except some remains of walls,

and eleven sarcophagi of basalt enclosed among the ruins, which seem to be of early Jewish origin. From the midst of the ruins rises a square watch-tower: it is in a very dilapidated condition, but it is still possible to climb to its summit. It is probably the one which is mentioned in the Book of Kings: "And there stood a watchman on the tower in Jezreel, and he spied the company of Jehu, and he came and said, I see a company. And Joram said, Take a horseman and send to meet them, and let him say, Is it peace?" It was not peace, but war and murder.

Below Zerin is a large fountain, which is supposed to be the Ain Jezreel, or fountain of Jezreel, mentioned in Scripture. The Beni Saker, an Arab tribe, call it Ain Dschal, and the fountain of Goliath. It was here where Saul and Jonathan encamped before they fell on Gilboa. The Christian army of Crusaders under King Fulco once encamped here. Even at the present day, the small pond connected with the fountain contains many small fish similar to that on which the Crusaders feasted.

The plain of Jezreel is known to the Arabs as Mevdj beni Amer, the meadow of the sons of Amer. For thousands of years up to the present day, this valley has been a highway for armies and plundering Bedouins, and the peaceable inhabitants have been exposed to war or oppression. They gradually retired from the valley up the side of the mountain, till at length they took up their abode among its almost inaccessible ravines and heights. It is in this way that this valley—

which is eight leagues in length, and five in breadth — has become quite uninhabited. It is not quite flat, but rather gently undulating, and the sameness of landscape is enhanced by the entire absence of trees.

At ten o'clock, we crossed a pretty long stone aqueduct and reached the village of Zerin, which is surrounded by gardens. I met here with my countrymen from the Dardanelles, whose acquintance I had made some weeks before. Overpowered with fatigue, I soon fell asleep in the garden, and, when I awoke, all was still ; the caravan had left, and the only proof of their presence was a present of fruit and a bottle of Hebron wine, which they had left for my refreshment.

At half-past two o'clock, we again mounted. I exchanged my horse for Mahmud's white mare Dschilfe, which seemed to have special objections to carrying a strange rider. Mahmud spoke tender words to her, smoothed her mane, stroked her face with his finger obliquely from the forehead to the eyes, which had a magnetic effect on the animal ; she became quite gentle, and carried me peaceably through the hills and dales of Samaria, the boundaries of which we had now crossed. We reached a small mountain plateau, on the opposite side of which was a village, which Mahmud called Abatie ; on one of the heights by which it is crowned, is a castellated building with two extensive wings. As we passed through the village, the inhabitants eyed us askance with dark and gloomy faces.

Matthia, who was not at all a timid character, ordered Mahmud, who usually rode in advance, to keep alongside of us. The village itself had a warlike appearance; every house was built of massive stones, so arranged as to form a small fortress. As we left the village, we met a Samaritan woman, returning from a fountain with a pitcher full of water on her head. At my request she gave me some water, and I must do her the justice to say that she was the only party I ever met in the East, who refused a backschiesch.

We rode through a series of beautiful, richly-wooded valleys till we passed a round hill, on the top of which is the village of Sanur, which, in the distance, looks like a fortress. In another half hour, we reached the village of Dscheba, where we intended to halt for the night. Here, for the first time in all my travels in the East, we were treated with inhospitality. None of the inhabitants would receive us. Matthia observed: " These inhabitants of Samaria are always insolent and rebellious, and in this village of Dscheba, as I have just learned, they expelled the scheik three days ago, otherwise none of them would dare to refuse us hospitality. But we are not far from Sebaste and Nablous, and the minds of all are still agitated with the recent insurrection against the Christians."

We were not provided with a tent, and it was dangerous to remain in the open air. We took refuge in a deserted house, with a broken terrace, near the mosque, and kept our horses beside us, as Mahmud said that it was not safe to leave them out of sight.

Matthia sent our Mahommedan servant to buy eggs and milk, but he returned without having accomplished his errand, with the words : " The people are gloomy and evil disposed."

# CHAPTER IX.

I was awoke by the chattering of the Arabs, which is often continued for hours on the most trifling subjects, as among the women of Europe. I felt a dreadful numbness in my head and an oppression of the chest. When I mentioned this to Matthia, he said: "The covering of your head and breast must have fallen off during the night, and the cold has affected you. That will disappear when you have become warm with riding."

Matthia pressed us to start without breakfast, as he was anxious to get away from the village as soon as possible. The sky was covered with grey clouds, and the landscape was concealed from view by a cold mist. We rode through a fruitful valley, planted with olive and fig-trees, and it appeared to us, throughout the whole journey, that Samaria is better cultivated than Galilee and Judea. We met two armed shepherds, with small flocks of goats, and two wild, savage-looking men, who, on our approach, removed their long muskets from their shoulders. We came to a deep, extensive valley, from the centre of which rose a steep hill, shaped like a cone, with the village of Silte on its summit. As we continued to advance, we saw several other villages on the sides of the hills. We soon left the mist and the mountains behind, but the sun could not pierce his way through the cloudy sky.

As the mountains retreated, the valley continued to expand, till we came to a narrow cleft among the mountains, where we saw eight columns, standing two and two, close to one another, with a solitary column standing erect behind them. A shepherd was feeding his sheep among the ruins of Usbaste, as the remains of the Hebrew city of Schomrom are called at the present day. Schomrom is the same city as the Samaria of Josephus.

We rode past these columns through gardens enclosed with low stone walls, and then began to ascend the steep hill. We came to the ruins of a building, which can still be recognised as a gate or triumphal arch, and, turning to the left, we rode through a double row of still erect but half-shattered columns, which are 16 feet high, and not quite 2 feet in diameter. There is one column 8 feet, and a row of columns 50 feet distant from the rest. Broken capitals of the Ionic order are scattered on the ground. I rode slowly for a quarter of an hour among these columns, and, on counting them, found that there were 90 altogether. These columns, now lying on the platform of the hill, which is planted with corn and trees, are supposed to be the remains of the magnificent temple which Herod erected on the top of the hill. We now came to the village, which consists of miserably-built houses, in the walls of which may be seen fragments of columns, capitals, and large cut stones. This is, or rather no longer is, the ancient city of Schomrom, which was built by King Omri, and formed the residence of the kings of Israel. I had never seen the force of the words of the prophet Micah so clearly as here: " Therefore, I will make Samaria as a heap of the field, and as plantings of a vineyard; and I will pour down the stones thereof into the valley, and I will discover the foundations thereof. And all the graven images thereof shall be beaten to pieces."

At the end of the village are the ruins of the church of John the Baptist, in which, according to the modern monkish legend, he was buried, but this is opposed to the account given by Eusebius, the church historian, who places the martyrdom and the tomb of John in the neighbourhood of the Dead Sea.

The gate of the town overlooks the western side of the mountain and the church the eastern. I waited for the guardian to shew me the ruins of this church, which has been converted into a mosque. When Matthia returned, he informed me that the guardian refused to admit me, and though I could have forced him to do so by appealing to the Scheik, he advised me not to do so, as the populace was still agitated by hostile feelings, in consequence of what had occurred at Nablous.

I had therefore to content myself with mounting the ruinous walls, so as to have a look at the beautifully paved court of the building. I observed a monument in a niche, and saw the small cupola of the mosque. Two stunted palms showed that this tree does not attain its full height on mountains. The whole of the interesting building is a mixture of Roman and Moorish architecture. Pointed and round arches stand side by side; the windows are lofty and narrow.

Within this church, in a subterraneous chamber, the Arabs worship the tomb of Nebi Vehva, the prophet John the Baptist.

The view from this highly-cultivated mountain comprehends an extensive landscape, abounding with hills, and explains why Herod covered it with a city and a temple, and made it one of his strongly fortified residences.

We descended the side of the mountain, which slopes down from the church, and is covered with olives and pieces of architecture that have rolled down, and found ourselves in a beautifully wooded valley. We halted for breakfast at a fountain shaded by fig-trees. Men and women were busy with hoes and shovels, deepening the stone water-courses, which convey the water of the fountain to their gardens, as the fountain in summer is partly dried up, or at least not so abundantly supplied with water. A young man came to our place of encampment, and offered for sale a copper coin, stamped with "Sebaste Syria" in almost illegible letters. He was delighted when I gave him a piastre for it.

We started early, so as to reach Nablous before the overpowering heat of the meridian sun had set in. Matthia, without explaining the reason, rode on in advance, and was soon lost behind the hills. I was left with Mahmud and the donkey-driver. Mahmud was one of the handsomest men I saw in the East. His head was formed after the noblest Greek model, and his complexion was a rich brown from exposure to the sun. As we could not converse together, he tried to amuse me by exhibiting his skill as a horseman. Sometimes he seemed to be rushing on a foe with his lance, then he passed through all the attitudes of a horseman bending to escape the spear which has been hurled against him, or to protect himself from his enemy's sabre. In order to give more life to this representation of a combat, he discharged his pistols, and while rushing through the valley, he contrived to load them again with wonderful dexterity, and then fired them off a second time. All that I have ever seen in a circus fell far short of the bold dexterity and noble attitudes exhibited by this handsome Bedouin. In order to express my admiration of his skill, I took out a piece of silver, and threw it up in the air. His falcon eye had seen it glittering, and, though rushing past at full gallop, he reined in his horse, which stood as quiet as if he had been rooted to the spot, and caught the piece of silver in his right hand.

We came to a spring surrounded by large blocks of stone, where several horsemen were watering their cattle, and camels were lying about, chewing the cud. Matthia came up carrying a cup of black coffee, into which he had poured part of the spirits given to me by Fra Joachimo at Nazareth, and ordered me to drink it. He had observed, he said, that I looked very pale, though, in consequence of our smart ride, this was no longer the case. For another half hour we continued our ride through a well-cultivated valley, with Mounts Gerizim and Ebal full in view, and after being six hours on the road, we at length reached Nablous.

Matthia had reason to be anxious about me, for as soon as we had entered the house of a Greek of his acquaintance, I was attacked with the violent headache which I had felt in the morning. I was seized with a sudden trembling and difficulty in breathing; my pulse rose to a hundred, and I was devoured with a burning thirst.

My strength failed me, and I sank down on a divan in the large room which had been prepared for me, and began to fear that this was the commencement of a serious illness.

This was the most painful moment in all my travels. On finding myself in a strange city, from which all the Europeans had fled, on account of the recent insurrection, without a medical attendant, and almost without money, for from prudential motives I had brought with me only what was barely sufficient to pay my way, I was seized with a deep feeling of depression, which added to the fever from which I was already suffering.

The woman of the house treated me with that kindness and sympathy which none but a woman can show. Often and again, when I felt thirsty, she descended the steps and brought me water from the fountain; she seemed to have a pleasure in doing so, and spoke to me every time in such soft and gentle accents, that I thought I could understand her words of sympathy and consolation. Sometimes she sent her little girl, who was only six years of age, or her little boy, who was not much older, to keep the flies away from me. They always brought me an orange-blossom or a pink, some lavender or rosemary, and seemed quite delighted when I made signs to them that I was pleased with their fragrant gift of love.

Matthia came to me repeatedly, and said that the mistress of the house was continually pressing him to send for a doctor, as there were several distinguished practitioners in the town.

I drank some hot lemonade and made them wrap me up in woollen coverings, and after waiting for some time almost in a state of unconsciousness, I was visited by that best of all physicians—sleep.

When I awoke, I found the room lighted by a lamp in a large lantern suspended from the roof. I was alone and felt myself weak as death; but I had got quit of the head-ache, and though I had all the symptoms of a severe cold, my pulse was less rapid. I considered it a good sign that I began to be attacked with ennui, and, as it was now eight o'clock in the evening, I ordered Matthia, as soon as he entered, to go for two of the most celebrated physicians of Nablous. I wished, come what might, to make the acquaintance of my brother practitioners, the Arab descendants of Avicenna.

After an hour, there entered two men of imposing appearance. One of them was an old man with a long snow-white beard, the other, a solemn-looking man with a black beard. When they afterwards began to talk over my illness, and engaged in a lively discussion—looking at their black and white beards—I seemed to behold Ahriman and Ormuzd—Light and Darkness— contending for a human soul.

Matthia supplied them with coffee and chibouques, and both of them seated themselves cross-legged on a carpet, near the divan on which I lay.

" I have sent for you, my honoured lords, to cure me of my illness."

" In that thou hast done well," said Ormuzd. " Thou art wise," said Ahriman.

I explained to them the cause of my illness, and described the symptoms. Ahriman felt my pulse with his right hand. An Arab physician never feels the pulse with his left hand, and the Arabs when eating never use it; it is unclean. Then, Ormuzd felt my pulse.

" Dost thou believe," said Ahriman, " that I can help thee ?"

"I should not have sent for thee, if I had not expected to be benefited by thy well-known skill."

"It is not I, but the medicine, that can help thee. Dost thou believe in the power of medicine, or in the mysterious powers?"

A pupil of the modern sceptical school of Vienna, I replied that I doubted the power of medicine and believed in the mysterious powers.

"Thine intellect, my lord, is clear, and thy heart is pious," said Ormuzd.

I had to strip myself naked and to lie down on my face. Light and Darkness began to stroke me gently across the shoulders and down the back. Then the hands of the mysterious powers ceased to act, and an extraordinary sing-song sort of conversation, which sounded like question and answer, began behind my back. I again felt as if a dry flame had been passed across my body, and heaven alone knows what colours an eye possessed of insight into the world of mysteries might have discovered on my body.

This was continued for about a quarter of an hour, and then Ormuzd anointed my forehead with a delicate fragrant oil, which Ahriman supplied from a piece of cotton, and wound a piece of cloth tightly round my head like a turban.

Both now began to converse, and after a violent discussion in Arabic, relapsed into silence. The old man sent his servant, who was waiting on the terrace before the house, home for some medicine.

"Didst thou not say that the mysterious powers would be sufficient to cure me?"

"The Iblis, the devil, the disease, must be fed, and will not go away if it is starved."

"Give him drink, my honoured lord."

Dreading the medicine, which I might have been obliged to swallow, I pretended to fall asleep, and whether it was from the effect of this magnetic treatment, or from fatigue, I cannot tell, but I *did* fall asleep, and awoke next morning when the hot rays of the sun were beating on the terrace, which I could see from my couch through the open door.

Near me stood a glass, which, judging by the odour and taste, I found to contain tincture of opium with a large proportion of water. Matthia had given each of the practitioners twenty piastres, in order, as he said, to spread the fame of my generosity through the town.

My pulse was now regular, but I was still suffering from headache and general debility, though not so much as at first. As I never intended to visit Nablous a second time, I resolved to conquer my weakness, and to have an interview with the Samaritans. Though they lived at no great distance, I ordered the horses to be saddled.

Matthia told me that Mahmud had turned back with the horses, as he would not accompany us all the way to Jaffa, and that he had hired other horses, which now carried us through the town to the abode of the Samaritans.

The streets, as in every city of the East, are narrow and dirty, but the houses are higher and more strongly built; they almost look like mediæval fortresses, and seem thoroughly adapted for enabling the inhabitants, when properly supplied with provisions, to hold out for a long time against an attack. The bazaar was more lively and more abundantly supplied with goods than I had expected. This, however, was doubtless owing to the fact, that this town is the entrepôt of commerce and of the caravans between Damascus and the cities on the coast.

The quarter of the Samaritans is situated at the foot of Gerizim, and consists of a succession of large and strongly-built houses. We entered the house which contains the synagogue. We passed through a court paved with marble, and planted with four orange trees, and entered a quadrangular vaulted hall opening into the court. In the wall, opposite to the entrance, was a marble tablet with a Samaritan inscription.

We waited in this hall for the arrival of the high priest of the Samaritans. There entered a tall, strongly-built old man, entirely covered with white robes with blue striped borders. A white turban was wound round his head. His face had a remarkable expression ; it looked as if it had been cut out of a weather-beaten rock ; all its features were strongly marked and full of energy, while the long, overhanging eyebrows, which met one another, gave his countenance an expression of sternness, which was increased by his stentorian voice. He ordered us to take off our shoes, and opened the door of the synagogue. We found ourselves in a rather large and lofty room, which was only lighted by a single window. On the right and left, opposite to the door, is a sort of alcove, of the same height as the synagogue, to which you ascend by a step. Five white circular tin lustres with lamps of white glass attached to them were suspended from the roof. The floor was covered with straw mats. This synagogue is 500 years old.

The high priest, Salameh Cahen, the same who corresponded with Sylvester de Lacy at the commencement of the present century, after he had seated himself on the threshold of one of the alcoves, which was concealed by a curtain, proceeded to inform me that he sprang from the tribe of Levi, while the rest of the Samaritans were descendants of Ephraim and Manasseh.

"I also am a Levite."

"Are you a Jew?" he asked in evident surprise, "and do you come to us, the Samaritans, who are despised by the Jews?"

"God despises no one—why, then, should a mortal man despise his brother?"

"You are not the same as the rest! We would willingly live in friendship with the Jews, but they avoid all intercourse with us."

"How large is the community of the Samaritans?"

"Our number is small, it only amounts to 150 souls. Formerly, about a hundred years ago, there were some Samaritans in Damascus, in Jaffa, in Askalon, and Gaza. During the last three centuries, there have been no Samaritans in the land of Mizraim. Is it true that there are some Samaritans in Genoa?"

I was surprised at this question, and answered in the negative, but I could not discover from what source he had derived this information. When I reminded him that Wilson* had saluted him in the name of the Samaritans of Bombay, he seemed only to have a faint recollection of this traveller; but when I mentioned the name of Sylvester de Lacy, he told me he knew that he was dead.

"We are," he began in a querulous tone, "alone in the world, and poor. If the English had not sent us £100 this year, we and our children should have died of hunger."

"Do the Samaritans, then, not earn their bread by labour?"

"We have a few tailors, shoemakers, and shop-keepers. We are a very poor people. We have suffered for centuries; but we suffer joyfully, because we maintain the pure law of Moses in the world."

"Will you have the goodness to shew me your celebrated sacred book?"

"I will procure you this blessing."

As we were talking, we were joined by the son of the high priest, who will inherit his office, and by two boys, his grandsons. His son was dressed in white and yellow striped woollen cloth, and wore a turban of bright red silk. They seated themselves beside us on the straw mat.

The high priest arose and drew back the yellow and

* Rev. Dr. Wilson, late missionary at Bombay, and author of "The Lands of the Bible."

white striped curtain, which extended from the roof to the floor, and concealed the alcove, before which he had been sitting. Behind this curtain we saw the ark of the covenant standing on a wooden desk covered with a piece of coloured cloth. It was turned in the direction of Gerizim, and was open and without doors.

The old man took out a long narrow copper case, which was skilfully inlaid with silver and adorned with the name of the workman who had made it 500 years ago. He opened the case, and we beheld in a cover of red silk that celebrated Pentateuch written on parchment, which is said to have been written by Abishua, the son of Phenehas, the son of Eleazar, 3,460 years ago. This Pentateuch is written on very yellow parchment, which is already very musty, cracked, and crumpled. It could not have held together so long, and would already have fallen to pieces, if it had not been placed with the greatest care on new parchment, which is sometimes pasted, or, when the rents are larger, stitched on.

I placed my finger on this thora-roll, which at all events is a very ancient one, and then kissed it in accordance with the custom which has been handed down in our synagogues.

" You do well. You have kissed the only genuine and authentic law of Moses in the world. We do not shew it to everyone."

Immediately after this remark, he began to laud the generosity of certain travellers, on whom he had conferred the same honour. I requested him to read a passage.

" My grandchildren shall do so, to show you that our children can read as well as write Hebrew."

He sent one of his boys for his copy-book; the other began to read in an extraordinary recitative, perfectly different from that of the Jews, so that if I had not known that he was reading from the Pentateuch, I should never have suspected that it was Hebrew.

I asked the High Priest if he could also read the El Assuri; he answered in the affirmative, but when I handed him my memorial " Kol mebasser," he had great difficulty in spelling the word Israel.

" What country do you come from?"

" From the great empire of the Sultan *njemsza.*"

He shook his head as a sign that he did not know it, and he did the same when I mentioned Austria.

" Is Hebrew not written in your country in the same way as in the Holy Land?"

The boy, whom his grandfather had sent for his copy-book, now showed me his Hebrew and Arabic writing, both of which were rather pretty. All the Samaritans speak Arabic.

I asked the High Priest if he read the talmud.

" None of the Samaritans do, because we do not believe in its contents. The law of Moses is clear and simple. If it had been the will of God that we should observe more commandments, He would not have left them to be explained by the Rabbis."

" Do you ever read any work in Arabic?"

" Certainly."

" Why not, then, the talmud also, not from a desire

to believe in its contents, but from a feeling of curiosity? The Karaites, also, do not believe in the laws of the talmud; they hold with you that the word of Moses alone is sacred, but still many of them read the talmud."

" What can it contain for us?"

" Will you give me one of your written prayer-books to use during my travels?"

" We never sell our books. If a traveller offered us its weight in silver for a prayer-book, we should refuse it. The English Consul aided one of our members in effecting his escape to England. He was an apostate, and stole fifty of our prayer-books."

" You tell me that you are very poor. Why, then, will you not sell some of your written prayer-books? Surely what is written by men cannot be holy."

The old man rose up, replaced the Pentateuch in the ark, drew the curtain, and bowed down to the earth. He then left the synagogue. There were two women in the court scouring copper vessels, who quickly veiled themselves. They wore silver bracelets three inches broad of a strange and singular shape. I asked them if they would sell them, and they at once agreed to do so. Thus I became the possessor of the ornaments of these poor Samaritan women, which now adorn the arms of the lady to whom I presented them.

I may here remark, because their conduct was quite exceptional to my experience of Eastern life, that we never received any kind of hospitality in the house of a Samaritan. The reason of this may have been that they wished to induce me to imitate the much-lauded generosity of the travellers who had preceded me. I left a sum of money for them and took my leave.

There is also a small Sepharedisch community at Nablous, all the members of which live in one house. It contains only 40 souls, and has no Chacham. I visited the house, which forms a small blind alley, on both sides of which are narrow, indescribably dirty rooms, which only obtain light through the doors. The women and their children, all miserably dressed, surrounded me and began to beg. There was only one elderly man present, who conducted me to the synagogue, which is situated in the same court. It was a sort of cellar, capable of holding about twenty persons, and had a miserable appearance. I asked the man if he had any intercourse with the Samaritans. The women retreated with a cry of horror, and one of them said: " Have you been among the worshippers of the pigeon ? "

I said that I had. The women again fell back with the same expression of repugnance, and one of them said : " Do you know that they offer sacrifices on Mount Gerizim ? Take a purifying bath."

I requested them to provide me with some dressed fowls for use on the journey, which they promised to bring to the house. The old man, who was at once the clerk, the circumciser, the butcher, and the amulet writer of this the smallest community I met with in the East, brought them to me, and also a cake steeped in oil, which I took good care not to eat. I rested till the heat of the day was over, as I still felt very weak, and wished to reserve my strength for the ascent of Gerizim in the evening. At 5 o'clock Matthia brought us a Samaritan, who was to act as our guide. We mounted our horses, and rode through a well-watered and richly-wooded ravine at the foot of Mount Gerizim, which, like Ebal on the opposite side, has a bleak, rocky appearance. Between the two, lies the narrow green valley of Nablous, among the splendid trees and fragrant gardens of which may be seen the massive stone houses, the sparkling cupolas, and the white minarets of the ancient Shechem. The houses, like those of Jerusalem, have all cupolas, and the valley between the Mountains of Cursing and Blessing looks like a lovely green stream. Damascus is the only place in the East which presents the same charming appearance, owing to the fruitfulness of the soil and the abundance of water.

We are indebted to Robinson for the important discovery that Nablous is situated on the water-course of the valley, in which the springs in the East flow toward the Jordan, and those in the West toward the Mediterranean sea. The valley is only 1,600 feet broad, and the two mountains are about 800 feet above it. The legend that the Mount of Blessing is fruitful, and the Mount of Cursing barren, can only be believed by those travellers, with Benjamin of Tudela at their head, who trust to the imagination instead of using their eyes. Both appeared to me equally barren and inhospitable. The legend that there are numerous sepulchres on Ebal, while Gerizim has none, is equally destitute of truth. After about a quarter of an hour we reached the summit of the mount, which forms an extensive table land. There is a *Wely* on a small elevation near the edge of the hill, where the Samaritans offer up prayer on the new year, the day of atonement, the feast of tabernacles, and the passover. On the last of these feasts they offer up lambs in sacrifice. The spot where this is done is marked by two rows of stones and a cavity roughly lined with stones. Behind this elevation are the extensive ruins of a fortress, probably erected by the Romans. These ruins, which were long supposed to be the remains of a temple, are known to the Samaritans as the castle. Below the castle are some flat stones of immense size. "Here," said our Samaritan guide, "are buried the twelve stones which the Israelites brought with them from Egypt." Benjamin of Tudela says that he saw the altar which the Samaritans had erected with these twelve stones.

As we continued our way, our guide told us to take off our shoes. I obeyed the order, though it was not at all pleasant walking over the stones. Matthia remained behind, while we advanced to a pretty large platform of rock, on which the tabernacle with the ark of the covenant is said to have stood. Around it, though now scarcely discernible, are the remains of a wall, probably the wall of the temple. Our guide said: "Up here we can turn and pray in every direction; but below we must always turn our faces toward Mount Gerizim. Here will appear the *el Muhdy*, the leader, who shall deliver us from slavery. The measure of the world's duration will soon be complete, and our deliverance is at hand."

Near this large platform of rock, I was shown the spot where Abraham was about to sacrifice his son Isaac. When I told him that this event took place on Mount Moriah at Jerusalem, where the temple of Jehovah stood, he replied : "It would be a sin for me to disturb your faith; but this is the place."

The Arabs call Gerizim El Tur; but the Samaritans still retain the ancient name, "The Mount of Blessing —Grisim." Contrary to the Holy Scriptures, as we have already seen, they affirm that the altar which Joshua built "on Mount Ebal" was on Gerizim, and that the introduction of Mount Ebal in this passage is a falsification of the text. The victorious warrior built the altar of undressed stones, which had never been touched with iron. He offered burnt-offerings and thank-offerings, and wrote the law of Moses on stones. "And all Israel, and their elders, and officers, and judges stood on this side the ark, and on that side before the priests, the Levites, which bare the ark of the covenant of the Lord, as well the stranger as he that was born among them; half of them over against Mount Gerizim, and half of them over against Mount Ebal, as Moses the servant of the Lord had commanded before, that they should bless the people of Israel." A more sublime act has never been witnessed in the history of any nation, than the swearing in of this religious-political constitution.

Where the city now stands, stood the ark of the

covenant, the sacred Palladium of the nation. Around it stood the Levites with their faces toward the East; thus they had Gerizim on their right hand, which, since the earliest ages, is the place of honour in the East, and Ebal on their left. This, perhaps, may explain why the voices on Gerizim pronounced the blessing, and the voices on Ebal the curse, though the altar was erected on the latter.

Sinai and Gerizim are the two beacon lights of the world, illuminated with the noble thoughts of the great lawgiver; the eyes of a nation that shall never die out have ever been directed toward them, and there is a beautiful Rabbinical legend, to the effect that when the law was given forth in a voice of thunder, all the yet unborn souls of the Jewish nation were assembled to hear it. "Has not my soul also stood on Mount Sinai?" may often be heard from the lips of a Jew, repelling some attempted wrong on the part of a wealthy co-religionist.

As we were riding down Mount Gerizim, some considerable time before sunset, our guide surprised me by asking if I would like to ascend Mount Ebal.

"I thought it was dangerous. Few travellers have attempted it."

"I will take you there and back again in safety."

"But the people of Nablous are more rebellious than ever, and there have been so many victims to their cruelty lately."

"The insurrection was occasioned by the French Consul having used his influence with the Pasha to get a boy of fourteen years of age appointed agent. The French flag on this occasion was torn in pieces and trampled under foot, and we hear that the Pasha will be deposed."

" I thought it was owing to a Mohammedan beggar having been shot by an English missionary."

"That was merely an accident, and used as a pretext for an outburst of angry passion which had long been restrained. You are not a Frenchman or an Englishman, and no one will injure you."

"But how can the people know that? If I am killed, it will be little consolation to me to have it shewn afterwards that I do not belong to either of the great nations."

"The Scheik has made enquiries about you at your house, and the two doctors whom you rewarded so generously have been talking about you."

I felt too weak, however, to attempt the ascent. We passed the beautiful fountain of Asal, and, after drinking some of its delightful water, we came to the burying-place of the Samaritans. I asked my guide whether the Samaritans had any peculiar funeral rites.

" We do not bury our dead ourselves, as the touch of a dead body is pollution. We employ Mohammedans to carry them to the burying-ground, and to place them in their graves. We go out a few hours after, and lament the dead over the closed grave."

I sent our horses on before and paid another visit to the beautiful fountain, where a number of Mohammedans from Nablous were enjoying the sunset and the cool air. They asked me how I liked the town, and I told them that it was superior to Damascus in beauty, and still more so on account of the bravery of its inhabitants.

"That is a man of noble thoughts," they sagaciously remarked to one another.

I directed the conversation to the two mountains before which we stood, and remarked that Ebal looked even bleaker and more desolate than Gerizim, when one of the men said :—

"That is quite natural. Ebal is more exposed to the sun than Gerizim."

I leave this explanation to the consideration of all legend-loving travellers. I then pointed to Mount Ebal, and asked them to tell me its name, as Ritter relates, that Robinson, after repeated enquiries, could not discover it. The men gave me the name Dschebel Emat e din, but I am not sure that I have written it down correctly.

I had the horses saddled at 5 o'clock next morning, so as to be able to visit Jacob's well, and to be back in sufficient time to resume my journey. The fresh morning breeze completed my recovery, and after half an hour's ride through the highly-cultivated valley before the city gate, we reached the well which the Mohammedans as well as the Samaritans believe to be that of the patriarch. The hole in the rock is partially covered with a stone. We could discover no traces of water by dropping stones into the well, which, however, may have been dried up, as this was the height of summer. The Christians, who call this well Bir es Samiriyeh, honour it not only on account of the patriarch, but also on account of the beautiful conversation with the Samaritan woman which took place beside it. Near it are the insignificant ruins of an ancient church—four shattered columns lying in a circle. The depth of the well has been differently estimated; when a traveller* accidentally dropped his bible into it, and an Arab was let down by a rope to pick it up, it was found to be 75 feet deep, but it may formerly have been deeper, as almost every traveller drops in a stone or two to sound its depth. There is a monkish legend which relates that the well overflows with fresh water once every year, on the day when Jesus conversed with the Samaritan woman.

About 300 yards to the north of Jacob's well, in a circular valley, formed by the surrounding mountains, may be seen a glittering white quadrangular building; this is Joseph's sepulchre. A more desirable resting-place could not be found; it is far preferable to that of Rachel between Jerusalem and Bethlehem. Before entering the sepulchre, I sat down on a stone, and opened my bible and began to read all the different passages connected with the scene spread out before me. Numerous and able as the descriptions of the Holy Land by uninspired pens unquestionably are, the simple, natural narrative of the bible surpasses them

* One of the deputation sent out by the Church of Scotland to inquire into the condition of the Jews in Palestine.

all. The manners, the customs, and even the dress of
the Orientals, are so little changed, that in reading the
bible we can almost believe that it treats of the present,
and not of the past. This, then, is Shechem, the
city of refuge on Mount Ephraim. This town was
visited by Abraham, and Jacob encamped before it,
before he went to Bethel. His sons went in the direction of Shechem to feed their father's flocks, and it was
here that they sold their brother to the Ishmaelites,
who were passing with a caravan to Egypt; just as at
this moment a similar caravan, consisting of camels and
mules, carrying white-turbaned armed men, is passing
along the road. The brothers encamped on this field,
before they went to the city to avenge their sister
Dinah's dishonour. I am sitting on the very field
which Jacob bought from the children of Hamor for a
hundred pieces of money. Joseph's bones were buried
here after the children of Israel had entered Canaan.
During the time of the Judges, Shechem was destroyed
by Abimelech, because it had revolted against him.
It was here that Rehoboam uttered the words, fraught
with such important results :—"My father hath chas-
tised you with whips, but I will chastise you with
scorpions." Then the tribes renounced his authority,
the first step which led to the destruction of the
Jewish nation. There are certain spots where the
great scenes of history have been enacted, which can
never be forgotten, and Shechem is one of them. It is
a singular circumstance, also, that in this very town,
where the history of the Jewish nation may be said to

have begun, are found the last remains of an extinct nationality, a people who claim to be the possessors of the Book of Books contained in a manuscript, more than three thousand years old, and who still ascend the mountain to offer sacrifice to Jehovah.

It deserves to be generally known that the learned German scholar, Olshausen, explained the meaning of the name of the town Mabortha in Josephus, which for a long time was unintelligible, in the simplest manner, by proving that this word in Aramaic means a pass. The town could not be more naturally described than by saying that it is situated in a pass between two mountains. The Roman name of the town, Flavia Neapolis, is still preserved on coins.

Let us now enter the sepulchre. We pass through a roughly-built entrance-court, and, turning to the left, enter another open space, which is surrounded by walls 15 feet high and 4 feet broad. On the right, opposite to the entrance, may be seen a white plastered sarcophagus, 8 spans long and 7 spans high, at both ends of which are white plastered columns of the same height as the sarcophagus. Both are hollow above, where the capitals should be, and exhibit traces of wood having been burned in these cavities. Opposite the entrance are two niches, one of which is adorned with two marble tablets; they contain, the upper *in basso*, the lower *in alto relievo*, all those passages of Scripture which refer to the death and burial of the patriarch. Opposite to these niches, on the left of the door, is a third, and a raised divan. To the left of the entrance in the corner of the quadrangular space, is a walled terrace, reaching half way up the wall. Three vines were growing on it, one of which I brought along with me as a *souvenir* of the patriarch.

Both Mohammedans and Christians believe that this is Joseph's sepulchre. The whole building differs little from a Mohammedan *Wely*, and it cannot be very old. It has been entrusted to the guardianship of the Jews, though neither the entrance nor the inner court has a door that will shut. It appears, also, that it is chiefly Jews who resort to the sepulchre, as I found a very large number of Hebrew names written in pencil or cut out in the walls; there were very few Arabian names. The Jew who acted as my guide told me that the building was erected by the Mohammedans, who respect Joseph as a prophet, and that they are in the habit of holding family feasts at this sepulchre.

Though we started from Nablous at nine o'clock in the morning, the heat already was almost insupportable. We had to bear the scorching rays of the sun, till we came to a well, shaded by a palm-tree, near the village of Refidia, where we halted for a little. Several maidens came from the village to draw water. They were dressed in white, their dusky features were lighted up by their sparkling black eyes, which shone through their white veils, while their arms were adorned with bracelets. As they withdrew with their pitchers on their heads, I could not but be struck with their proud and noble bearing. The habit of carrying everything on their heads, and supporting it with their arms by turns, makes the women of the East hold the upper part of the body erect; and all motion is confined to the lower part of the body. They have thus something of regal state, as they walk erect, with the chest expanded, and the head bent slightly back.

After an hour's ride we observed a village, to the right, on the side of a hill, which, our guide told us, was Sawata, and then the village of Ariet Dschid, which is surrounded with olives and plantations of maize and tobacco. We rode round the hill, and found a well-cultivated valley behind it, where we halted for breakfast. We then rode over the mountain ridge of Rasz el arnin, past the villages of Hedsche, Fundok, and Dschen Safur, till we came to the Wady Azun. The bed of the stream was quite dry; the sides of the narrow valley were covered to the summit with verdure, while the valley itself abounded with carob trees. We rode quickly through this *Wady*, which is not considered quite safe, but we did not see any one, and soon reached a mountain-ridge covered with ancient olive trees. We spent the hottest part of the day beneath their shade, and then rode down to the large plain of Hadschar en nus. We came to the village of Hable, where we had intended to spend the night, but as the sun had not set, we continued our journey to Dschel Dschule, a league farther on. I do not find this village marked in Robinson's map.

It consists of about forty mud-hovels, each of which is enclosed within a wall of mud, and contains a single room with open verandahs in an extensive court, where the inmates sleep and find shelter during the rainy season. Children were rolling about in the court, cultivating the acquaintance of the dogs and chickens. A horse and an ass were standing quietly in a corner. Three women were baking bread, of which every family requires a fresh supply daily. The oven was of clay, and about 4 feet high. The dough was moulded into round, flat cakes, about a foot in diameter. After remaining in the oven about half an hour, they were taken out, while soft. Here, as well as in Egypt, where the bread is thinner and harder, I was reminded of the unleavened bread which the Jews use at Easter.

I lay down on the floor, without undressing, and tried to sleep, while Matthia kept watch at the door. It was impossible to sleep; apart from other disturbing causes, the jackals commenced a lachrymose serenade, and all the cats in the neighbourhood lent their sweet voices to swell the chorus. We started at midnight, and soon left the village behind. All at once Matthia's horse stood still, apparently very much frightened. Matthia cried to me to cock my pistols, and to remain beside him. In a moment a leopard sprung across the road before us. We both fired, but it soon disappeared; this was the only wild beast I saw in Palestine.

We came to two mills, where several caravans had halted for the night. As I had ridden fourteen hours, and frequently fell asleep in the saddle, I was anxious to spend the remaining part of the night here, but Matthia thought it might be dangerous to associate with strangers. We, therefore, continued our journey and

soon heard the distant roar of the waves of the Mediterranean breaking against the shore.  We rode for two
hours across the sandy downs, and then, on reaching
the summit of a hill, we saw the broad ocean with its
silver sheen spread out before us, and the rising sun
shining on its bosom like an immense crimson rose.
And now we have reached Jaffa.

# CHAPTER X.

BEFORE leaving Palestine, I shall give a brief account of
my four days' journey from Jerusalem to Jericho, the

Jordan, the Dead Sea, St. Saba, Hebron, and Rachel's Tomb, which I previously omitted, so as not to interrupt the narrative. We left Jerusalem at 6 o'clock in the morning, and formed rather a formidable caravan. I was accompanied by three Germans, an English physician, and Mr. Endlicher, the architect. We had mules for our tents, and an abundant supply of provisions, while six Bedouins followed us as an escort. Mussa, the cavass, headed the procession.

Look at Mussa as he rides on before. He is a broad-shouldered, thick-set fellow, dressed as an Arab; he is armed to the teeth, with a scimitar on his left side, pistols and dagger sparkling at his girdle, and a musket laid across the bow of his saddle and ready for use at a moment's warning. His head is covered with a red and yellow turban, the loose ends of which flutter in the breeze as he rushes on before the caravan, or rides back to see that all is in order. Thus he rides over the road twice, while we find it quite enough to ride over it once. Mussa's face is a very striking one; it is burned brown and red, the eyes are lively, and the moustache grey. The expression is an odd mixture of good-nature and cunning, and few on looking at him would believe that he is capable of acts of the most daring courage or stern cruelty. When Ibrahim Pasha conquered Syria, Mussa acted as his executioner. He now holds the office of cavass to the Austrian Consul, and as such is known and dreaded throughout the whole of Palestine.

One day when the Consul General was engaged on a journey, his suspicions were excited by a distant group of Bedouins encamped by the side of the road. Mussa sprang from his side like a flash of lightning, rode his horse right into the middle of the Bedouins with the war-cry " Mussa Cavass ! " and ordered them to pile their arms in a circle. Struck with his reckless courage, they mechanically obeyed. Mussa remained with them till the caravan had disappeared, then saluted them and rode on.

On one occasion a thief was confined in the prison at the Consulate, and the Consul drew up     protocol of the affair, which was perfectly formal and perfectly fruitless. Mussa promised that if the matter were left in his hands he would soon settle it. As the Consul suspected nothing wrong, he agreed, and soon after a piercing yell was heard from the prisoner's cell. On entering, the Consul found the thief stripped naked and suspended from the roof by the feet with his head almost touching the floor. Mussa was critically examining a red-hot poker which he had just taken from the fire, and when the Consul, shocked at the sight, shouted to him to desist, Mussa answered with a quiet smile :—

" It is all right, your Excellency. I know where the stolen goods are ; the rascal made a clean breast of it, when he saw that I was going to spit him."

The Austrian Consul could not have a more careful, devoted, or amiable attendant than Mussa. It does one good to see him playing with a child or waiting on his master, while his face is beaming with good nature. His fearless bravery is not the result of momentary impulse, it is part of his nature, and his courage is only equalled by his coolness. Frequently, when his master had got involved in an altercation with a custom-house officer, Mussa has quietly asked him :—

" Shall I shoot the fellow ? " much in the same way as a servant in Europe on a similar occasion would say:—

" Shall I explain the matter ? "

At the smallest sign from his master he would have fired.

The road from Jerusalem to Jericho has been often described. The heat was excessive and my thermometer rose to 36° R. We were delighted to reach the fountain of Elisha, the Ain es Sultan. A draught of its cool water was the greatest of all possible luxuries. Our cattle smelt the approach of water and accelerated their pace, while the Arabs began to sing and the whole caravan got quite animated. When I asked Mussa what the Bedouins were singing, he said to me :—

" They are crazy and always repeat the same words : Snow in the sun ! Snow in the sun ! "

I was struck with the poetry of the expression they use to denote the vicinity of water.

We reached Jericho at 4 o'clock P.M. and found our tents already pitched beneath some large fig-trees. The men of Jericho soon assembled around them, and began to stare at us with indolent curiosity. I was struck with their dark complexions and the resemblance which their features bear to the negro type. It is possible that at some former period they may have intermarried with the Ethiopians, and this may account for the

sleepy indolence of character for which they are notorious. Their gross immorality reminded us that they
lived in the neighbourhood of Sodom and Gomorrah.

Both the Bedouins who accompanied us, and all
those whom I had previously seen, strengthened my
belief that they have sprung from the same root as the
Jews. They have the hooked nose, the projecting chin,
the want of flexibility in the lower jaw, the low, thin
figures, the expressive gesture with the hands in speaking, the brief, interrogative, cautious mode of speech,
the shrug of the shoulder, and almost all the other
marks which are characteristic of the Jewish race. The
peculiar smack of the tongue, expressive of admiration,
the nasal intonation in speaking, the preponderance of
gutturals in the Arabian language—everything, in
short, served to remind us that Ishmael was Isaac's
brother. But there was one striking difference ; the
Bedouin holds himself erect, with the air of one who has
never borne the yoke of servitude, while in the bearing
of the Jew may be seen the effects of long years of sub-
jection and persecution. But if the body of the Bedouin
be free, the intellect of the Jew is equally so, and the
latter is as superior to the former in intellectual
development as he is inferior in physical organization.

After we had rested till the setting sun had softened
his rays, we commenced our walk through Jericho. We
counted twelve miserable huts, built of mud and thatched
with straw, which contain a population of 200 souls.
Such is the city of palms, the paradise on earth, the
seat of the gods, as the ancient historian calls it. No

monuments of antiquity are to be seen except the ruins of an aqueduct and part of a street. In this almost tropical climate, where the productions of the tropics may still be seen, the palm tree yielded fruit, which it fails to do at Jerusalem, which is only six leagues distant from Jericho. By means of two large fountains, and water carefully brought from a distance, the town was once surrounded with such splendid gardens that it was known by the name of the "fragrant."

Passing through plantations of fig-trees, we came to the ruins of a tower, which is about 30 square feet in circumference and 40 feet high. The building is evidently the work of the Saracens, but it is known as the house of Zaccheus. We passed through a small court, ascended a staircase, and reached the terrace, where the Aga of the Turkish garrison politely received us beneath a verandah roofed with dry twigs, and supported by four poles. The Aga was surrounded by his soldiers, who wore Albanian dresses, while he himself was dressed as a Turkish officer, in a blue uniform with a red fez. He wished for information about the terms of the recent peace, and asked if "the hunger of the Russian wolf was yet appeased." After witnessing the magnificent sunset from the terrace, which is surrounded by a parapet with embrasures, we returned to our tents.

Here a lively scene was presented to our view. Some men had stolen an ox from a hostile Arab tribe, and were conducting it in triumph to Jericho. The people were loud in their acclamations, and assembled to receive part of the spoil. On a given signal, the men cut the sinews of the ox with their long knives: it fell to the ground, and then one of them cut its throat. It was skinned, eviscerated, and cut up in fifteen minutes, and then every male inhabitant of Jericho received his share.

While this was going on, the Scheik of Jericho was trying to persuade us that it was dangerous to visit the Jordan without an escort, and offering his services, which we declined. The gift of a Napoleon d'Or put him in good humour, and he willingly exchanged his brass signet ring with his name cut out on it, for one of bronze set with Bohemian stones, which I wore on my finger. I was struck by observing that he applied the ring to his nose and then handed it to the bystanders to smell. "Ah," said Mussa, "they know the pure metal by smelling it."

Our cook, a member of the community of the Sepharedim and a sort of Oriental *cordon bleu*, now announced that our meal was ready. We invited the scheik to join us, in the hope of obtaining some information about the balsam tree and the roses of Jericho. He knew nothing about the tree or the balsam, a shell full of which was brought to Alexander the Great every day, and which adorned Pompey's triumphal procession; like the city of palms, it has disappeared. But it is different with the roses of Jericho; they never bloomed there in the days of antiquity, nor are they to be found there at the present day. No botanist has ever found this wild flower, which is indigenous to the sandy plains of southern Palestine and Arabia and the lower part of Sinai, at Jericho. It appears that a passage in Jesus Sirach gave rise to this error. " I have grown up like a palm-tree by the water, and like the stem of the rose-tree, which is cultivated at Jericho." The rose of a hundred leaves is not to be found at Jericho, and the palm-tree has also disappeared.

Night set in while we were yet at table. Our cattle were lying before the tents, our arms and riding gear were hanging on the branches, and the Bedouins sat gossiping beside their long lances, which were stuck into the ground. The flickering stars looked larger and nearer than those we see in the west. All at once there rose from the neighbourhood of the huts a wild song, a sort of compromise between a quaver and a howl, accompanied with the clashing of cymbals. On inquiring the cause of this ear-splitting serenade, Mussa informed us that he had hired some warriors and female dancers to exhibit their skill for our amusement.

The barbarous music gradually approached, till at length we saw five women dressed in long, dark-blue robes with slit sleeves, which descended to the ankles. Their faces were as brown as a gipsy's, their eyes were painted, their lips, which did not conceal their dazzling white teeth, were tattooed blue, their breasts were uncovered, and a veil descended from their heads over their shoulders.

The men, ten in number, had a piece of cloth rolled round their heads, and wore nothing but galligaskins and short jackets. They almost appeared less formidable than the women. They brought a bundle of wood, which they laid down before our tent, and then set fire to it. The green wood smoked and pinched our eyes, as we reclined in a semi-circle on our carpets, scarcely expecting that the rest of the exhibition could be stranger or more picturesque than what we had already seen.

Four of the women took hold of one another's hands, and forming a circle round the fire began to move slowly. The fifth woman, who was not in the circle, but took her stand nearer to us, began a strange dance and kept time to the song which her four companions were singing. The *danseuse* held a long strip of cloth in her hands, which she swung backward and forward over her head like a hoop; then she dropped this scarf, and raising her arms aloft, she whirled them about so rapidly, that her long sleeves fluttered round her person like dark wings. She advanced and retreated, and twisted her body round and round, accompanying this gyration with a shrill quaver, produced by a rapid movement of the tongue, while her voice was raised to a violent shout. The four witches, who stood in a circle round the fire, accompanied her in this shrill quaver, and then resumed the monotonous air, with which she kept time. They used only two words, which were continually repeated, " Good arrival,"—" good health." Thus they danced, circled, sang, and shouted for half an hour in the midst of the smoke of the fire, which was always stirred by the men. While their movements could scarcely be termed graceful, they had nothing of that lascivious expression which I afterwards witnessed among the Almees in Egypt.

At length the women sank down on the ground, and were replaced by the men. They stood close together, without touching one another, holding their long, glittering knives in their hands, while one of them, armed in the same way, stood opposite to the rest. The former began to deride him, by continually shouting, "Eheb! Eheb! Eheb!" At first, he remained quiet, and brandished his knife without betraying any emotion. The men now pressed on one another, so that their shoulders met, and bending down, they advanced, still shouting "Eheb," so that their opponent was obliged to retreat. All at once, however, it appeared as if his composure and hesitation had been only assumed, he sprang forward, and struck his knife against those of his opponents, so that the sparks flew from them, and we could hear the clash, as he attacked one of his opponents, or struck aside the whole of their knives as if he had been using a sickle. The struggle grew fiercer and fiercer, while the women stood up and animated the combatants by their wild song. Their horrible quavers, the clashing of the knives and the continual shout, "Eheb! Eheb!" formed anything but a pleasant concert. We rewarded the wearied warriors with a bottle of arrack, and the female dancers with two dollars. We could hear their wild song long after they left, till at length it died away in the distance.

At five o'clock in the morning we struck our tents,

saddled our horses, and started for the Jordan. We passed threshing-floors of different sizes, where the oxen, which were treading out the corn, were muzzled with pieces of linen, in violation of the Mosaic law. After half an hour, we came to the ruins of some buildings and a number of dressed stones scattered about, which mark the site of the ancient Gilgal. In the eighth century, pilgrimages were undertaken to the church, which formerly stood here with the twelve stones which Joshua took from the Jordan leaning against the wall. We rode over desolate flats, past hills and rocks, which often rose from the sandy plain like square castles and towers. Sometimes one of our Bedouins rushed to the top of one of these hills to look out. As he stood there on horseback between us and the blue horizon, he looked like the statue of a horseman.

We were quite close to the stream before we saw its banks, which are covered with the most luxuriant vegetation. Tall reeds, tamarisks, poplars, and willows render it difficult to approach the stream. It is not quite so broad as the Tiber at Rome; at the place where we stood it might be almost called rapid, and its waves are of a yellowish colour.

I have always experienced a feeling of profound sorrow on comparing the naked rocks and valleys of the Holy Land, scorched as they now are with the burning rays of the sun, barren and unfruitful, with the luxuriant pictures of its fruitfulness presented to us in the Bible. True, the country is depopulated, and barbarism has ruled over it for many long centuries, but, even under the most favourable conditions, it could never have been literally such as the Bible and the prophets have described it. Whatever else may have changed, the climate is the same, and the mountains have undergone no change. One necessary condition of a fruitful soil, I mean springs and irrigation, no longer exists. But still this land, with its almost tropical temperature, could never have resembled a luxuriant garden. We can easily conceive, however, that a people, who had spent many years in the wilderness, on finding themselves suddenly transported from the desolate solitude of the desert to the green oasis of Jericho and the pleasant banks of the Jordan, would speak of the country in more enthusiastic terms than men habituated to similar scenes would employ. Even at the present day, the poets of the East employ the same language in speaking of a fountain and its green oasis, or of an umbrageous tree. Often my guides said to me, when they spoke of our halting-place at noon: "You will repose beneath the delightful shade of a garden." The garden was usually two or three miserable olives springing from the rocky soil.

Mussa told us to lose no time in bathing, as it is always dangerous to remain long in the stream; the Bedouins often choose their moment of attack when the pilgrims are in the water, and unable to offer any resistance. In former times, pilgrims, especially those from Egypt, used to throw balsam and spices into the stream, which was consecrated by a priest, before they entered it, and, even at the present day, the Greek pilgrims are always buried in the shirt which they wore when bathing. Such facts remind us of the worship which the ancient heathens paid to the Nile.

Mindful of Mussa's advice, we quickly bathed and dressed, and after partaking of an excellent breakfast, I filled some tin flasks with water, and cut twelve walking-sticks from the neighbouring willows, in memory of the twelve tribes of Israel. On my return to Jerusalem, I obtained handles for them from the Mount of Olives.

Before leaving the Jordan, a few words regarding the tribe of Bedouins who inhabit its banks may not be out of place. The Bedawin, as they call themselves, are Arabs, and greater fanatics than the Mussulmans, although they are almost entirely ignorant of the law, and only practise circumcision and fasting. The knowledge of the Koran is confined to certain holy men, known among them as fakirs. An assertion has no weight with them, unless it be confirmed by an oath. They hold themselves of royal descent, and acknowledge no ties of blood between themselves and the Mussulmans who live in the towns. While they prefer a life of wild independence among their native mountains, during the rainy season they are attracted by the warmer climate of the valley of the Jordan; nine tribes frequent the east and eight the west bank; the former are the sons of Edom, the latter the sons of Moab. A bloody feud has existed between them, since the time when some of the Bedouins on the eastern shore, who had fled with their wives to their brethren of the west in order to escape the pursuit of the Syrian government, were plundered by the latter. One tribe of the western Bedouins cultivate the soil, and have thus incurred the contempt of their nomadic brethren. If they ever become civilised, their liberty is at an end.

We mounted our horses again, and following the stream in its course through the flat, undulating, and gently sloping valley for an hour, we reached its debouchure by two different channels at the Dead Sea. For a considerable distance before it reaches the sea, the banks are quite barren.

The Dead Sea, or Birket Lut, " the sea of Lot," as the Arabs call it, now lay before us. It is 20 leagues in length, and is surrounded by reddish yellow, barren rocks, which sometimes rise to a height of 3,000 feet, and are covered in spring with a rich carpet of green, which produces a pleasant effect. The southern extremity of the sea is not visible with the telescope, being concealed from view by the peninsula of Mezraah. Its greatest breadth varies from 4 to 5 leagues.

Its shores are covered with blackened limestone, interspersed with flint. At the place which we visited, there was no lava, but we met with some bitumen, which had been washed ashore.

We bathed in the sea, but I had not the pleasure of enjoying a swim without being acquainted with that art. Two of my companions, both good swimmers, took me between them. I lay down in the water, while they held me. The moment they loosed their hold, I sank beneath the surface. Both of them assured me that the water supported a greater weight than the water of a pond or a river; but this phenomenon can easily be explained by the fact that its specific gravity is greater than that of the Mediterranean Sea, in consequence of which fish cannot live in it. The old legend, that birds in attempting to fly across drop dead into the water, is a pure invention. We saw several fly across in safety. The water has an oily feeling, irritates the skin, and has a bitter, acrid taste.

Among the countless, flat, kidney-shaped stones of different colours which were scattered along the shore, might be seen layers of salt, which looked like wreaths of snow. We were also struck with the appearance of some pretty large trunks of trees lying near the shore, the branches of which are encrusted with a coating of salt, which is almost petrified, and can scarcely be broken off. Though these trees may not be so old as those of the petrified forest which we saw in the Libyan desert, they must belong to the period when these barren mountains were covered with wood.

We may here be allowed to allude briefly to the apples of Sodom, which are beautiful to the eye, but full of ashes. They have hitherto been found at the southern extremity of the sea, on trees from 12 to 15 feet high. They are of a reddish yellow colour, like small oranges, and grow in clusters of two or three in a bunch. They are tender, the skin is easily broken, and the interior contains a sort of silky wool, which covers the capsules. They are soft and fleshless, and, as the traveller can derive neither nourishment nor refreshment from them, this circumstance may have given rise to the poetical fiction that they are full of ashes. The Arabs call this fruit Oescher, and extract from the bark of the tree a kind of sweet, milky juice, which is supposed to be a remedy for barrenness. It is not certain, however, that this fruit, which is described by Josephus and Tacitus as full of ashes, is really the apple of Sodom. More recent writers affect to have discovered it in a charred-looking fruit, which is produced by a species of acacia, known as *Logonychium Stephanarium*.

There is also a shrub, which grows in the neighbourhood of Jericho, and is known as Leimun Lut, or Lot's Lemon, which produces a yellow berry about an inch in diameter. The Arabs relate, that, in ancient times, they were as large as lemons, but when the people of Sodom and Gomorrah became sinful and corrupt, the Lord cursed the tree, and changed it into a shrub with small, bitter berries. This fruit has also been supposed to be the apple of Sodom, because it frequently happens that the cow-fly perforates the berry and devours the flesh, while the skin remains entire, so that, when crushed, it is found to contain nothing but dust.

After an hour, we again mounted, and, after ascending through sandy ravines, we came to a desolate wilderness, which the sun had changed into a sea of fire. We lost sight of the Dead Sea and came to a deep cistern,

which contained some green, brackish water. A
Bedouin stripped himself quite naked, and was let
down into the cistern by a rope, to fetch some water in
a leathern bottle. The water reached to his breast, but
that which the bottle contained was so hot and brackish
that, even after qualifying it with rum, we could not
drink it, and were obliged to remain content with the
few pomegranates which still remained. The heat was
so fearful, that we had scarcely strength to retain our
seats. A man, to enjoy travelling in the East, must
have a frame of iron. Often the most beautiful scenes
and the most interesting spots produce little impression
on the traveller, when his blood is boiling in his veins
with feverish heat, or his frame worn out by excessive
fatigue. It was almost with a feeling of indifference,
that I saw on our left the mountain of Nebi Musa,
where a white, glittering minaret near a mosque which
looks like a castle marks the spot where Moses is
buried, and which is frequented by Mohammedan pilgrims.

No place is pointed out more exactly in the Bible
than the place where Moses died, and Rachel's grave,
and yet Mohammedan tradition points to a different
spot, which has been regarded as sacred for more than
a thousand years. The beautiful legend of the Rabbis,
that Moses died of a kiss, is equalled by that of the
Arabs:—

"When the period fixed for Moses' death arrived,
it happened that he and Joshua, while walking in the
fields, came to a place where a man was digging a

grave. The prophet, whom the legend describes as having been of an inquisitive disposition, immediately asked : ' Whose grave are you digging?' ' Come down to me and I will tell you.' Moses descended, and the grave immediately closed over him. It was the angel of death, who, as he was not allowed to approach the prophet in a fearful form, enticed him into the grave, and carried off his soul without his knowing it. Joshua returned to the camp, and told the people what had happened. But they did not believe him, and ran to the grave with cries of sorrow, and opened it. It contained nothing but the prophet's heart, and the people, being convinced that his spirit remained in the midst of them, ceased to weep and to lament."

After some hours we reached the bed of the Kidron, which was quite dry, and saw before us the monastery of St. Saba, which looks like a mediæval fortress. Surrounded by mountains and by deep ravines, it stands there alone with its forty monks, separated from the whole world. When Mussa knocked at the heavy iron gate, an iron casement was opened above, and a basket let down; Mussa placed in it our letter of introduction from the Greek patriarch at Jerusalem, and, after we had waited for some time, the door was opened. It would be difficult to describe the interior, or to convey any intelligible idea of this picturesque building. The architect seems to have been guided by no fixed principles of art, and to have followed only the promptings of his own wild fancy. We met with the kindest reception, and our cook was provided with everything which we required to refresh us after our long ride, except meat. Before sitting down to table, we were shown through the monastery; it was quite a journey to walk upstairs and downstairs, through halls and passages, over terraces and battlements, through churches, cells, and apartments. We witnessed from the loftiest terrace the glorious sunset, and saw his dying rays shed their golden light over the battlements of a tower which is about 100 yards distant from the monastery. Its small iron gate can only be reached by means of a long ladder. Female pilgrims are lodged in this tower, which has been occupied by two well-known Austrian ladies, Ida Pfeifer, who visited this place sixteen years ago, and the Duchess of Brabant, who travelled through Palestine three years ago.

We left the hospitable monastery at four o'clock in the morning; in half an hour, we could see only two of its turrets peeping from the ravine, and part of the Dead Sea sparkling in the distance. These soon disappeared, and, leaving the desert behind, we came to cultivated fields, covered with scarecrows, built of stone. We passed two small encampments of Bedouins, each of which consisted of ten black, tattered tents, with some horses feeding before them. The men and women scarcely glanced at us, while the children ran up to us, offering tepid water and begging for backschiesch. On receiving a few small pieces of money, they rushed back to the tents with shouts of joy. These encampments were exactly the same as those of the gipsies in Hungary.

Here and there women were busy in the fields, gathering the ears of corn, while we occasionally met shepherds with small flocks of sheep and goats. Camels, carrying women, who veiled themselves as soon as they saw us, sometimes passed. Amid such scenes the imagination is ever active, and it requires no effort to recall the leading personages of the Bible; the patriarchs moving from place to place with their flocks, Eleazar conducting to his master his young bride, and Ruth gleaning in the fields.

After three hours, we reached the pretty little town of Bethlehem, and put up at the monastery, where we met with the kindest reception. I was struck with two portraits in the refectory, the only ones in the monastery, of Robert Daugian (Anjou?), and his consort. After breakfast we visited all the different places which the Christians esteem to be sacred, and of which descriptions may be found in every book of travels. I cannot, however, avoid alluding to the incredible hatred of the Christian sects, which rages quite as violently here as at the church of the Holy Sepulchre. I must, at the same time, do the monks the justice to say that they could not have treated me with greater kindness; they seemed almost to be more attentive to me than to my fellow-travellers. At all the sacred places we were attacked by crowds of the inhabitants, pressing us to buy crowns of mother-of-pearl and olive-wood, pictures, crucifixes, &c. The scene reminded me of the former Jewish fancy-fair at Prague, with this difference, that the latter was not held on sacred ground. We saw thin plates of mother-of-pearl before every house. Most of the inhabitants of Bethlehem support themselves by the manufacture of articles prized by the pilgrims. It were desirable that some real artist should be introduced into the school connected with the monastery. It is really surprising to see the progress which these self-taught artists have made, and they require only a little instruction to give a right direction to their natural talent. The inhabitants of Bethlehem, generally, are celebrated for the beauty of their features and their talented dispositions. Here, as at Nazareth, our artists might find many noble living models, far more worthy of their study than the productions of the Byzantine and Italian schools.

At nine o'clock, we reached a ruined, mediæval castle, known as Kasr el Burak, where we halted. A deep, fresh spring and a fountain, supposed to be the "sealed fountain," alluded to in the book of Canticles, supply Solomon's three large quadrangular ponds with water. They are cut out of the rock, and walled in with large cut stones. Even at the present day water is conducted from them to Jerusalem, and I have seen it gushing into a marble basin in the mosque before the residence of the cadi. Below, in a ravine, may be seen a beautiful green oasis, extending along the side of the water-course in the midst of barren rocks; it has been known from time immemorial as " Solomon's Gardens."

We rode through pretty valleys, between gently-sloping hills, covered with dwarf oaks and wild strawberries, till we came to a spring, with an ancient stone trough, at which some women were washing blue shirts, which they dipped into the water and then beat with flat stones. On a hill above this spring were the ruins of an ancient fortification, which the women called ed Dirweh. On a hill, opposite to these ruins, was a tower, the colossal foundation of which must be very old. Recent researches have established almost beyond a doubt that these scattered ruins are the remains of the ancient fortress of Bethsur. Two large flocks of black, white, and speckled goats, driven by four herds, passed the well, and were followed by an old man with two loaded camels. The women immediately drew water with leather bottles, and gave to the men to drink, and then filled the trough with water for the cattle. To make the biblical picture complete, I took two bracelets from my portmanteau, and gave them to the two women. They were overpowered with surprise and joy, and said to Mussa: " What blessed land has given birth to thy generous master?" At six o'clock we reached Hebron.

Nothing can be more delightful than the appearance of Hebron, when the traveller, leaving the desert behind, first comes in sight of its fruitful valley and its gently-sloping heights. The hills are covered with vineyards, in which may be seen the small towers of the watchmen, alluded to in the book of Canticles. The vineyards are enclosed by rows of fig and olive trees, the dark and silver-grey tints of which have a pleasing effect. We ride along the stony path between them till we reach a narrow valley, which gradually expands. Hebron extends from this valley up the side of the hill, and that cupola, which rises from the centre of the town, forms part of the mosque which contains the ashes of the patriarchs.

The city has no walls, but these scattered blocks of stone shew that we are riding through the ancient gate. We find our tents pitched on a gentle slope in an open space. There are several tombstones around us. To the left, on the eastern side of the valley, may be seen the arched roof of the haram, the mosque with its beautiful cupola. A little higher up are the ruins of a castle, which was known at the period of the crusades by the name of St. Abraham, and is supposed to have been the fortress of David when he reigned in Hebron. Perhaps future excavations may establish beyond a doubt what is now only matter of tradition. To the right is a massive building of one story, with a red flag, adorned with the crescent, floating on its roof. It is the Turkish lazaretto, which is under the management of Dr. Helbig, to whom we have forwarded a letter of introduction. He immediately called upon us, and invited us to accompany him in a walk. We ascended a rocky hill, covered with plantations of olive trees, behind the Turkish cemetery. We came to Abraham's well, which is very deep, and supplies Hebron with water all the year round. A still more rocky and difficult path conducted us to Jesse's—*i.e.*, to Isais' tomb. It is a small ruinous porch which covers a deep pit. During the whole of the month Elul, the Jews come here, morning and evening, to pray, and for a long time they believed that their prayers met with special acceptance, when a kind of fragrance issued from the pit. They are in the habit of throwing locks of hair, cut from the heads of the sick, and containing certain mysterious words, into this pit, and then offer up prayers for their recovery. The custom of slaughtering a fowl, or some other bird, on the evening before the day of atonement, is still prevalent among the Jews, and a few years ago, one of them threw a hen into this pit as a living sin-offering. Soon after, the guardians of the mosque, which is situated on the opposite hill, at the distance of half a league, heard the cackling of a hen beneath the vault of the haram. On searching, they found the hen, which the Jew had thrown into Isais' tomb. The odour of incense which had cheered the hearts of the Jewish worshippers was now explained; it proceeded from the mosque by the subterraneous passage. I have not found any allusion to this subterraneous passage, which connects the two buildings, in any book of travels, and it would be interesting to examine it.

Not far from this tomb is an ancient pistachio tree, which reminds us of the present which Jacob gave to his sons when they went down to Egypt, that they might find favour in the eyes of Joseph, the king's representative. The view from this hill, extending over the gently-sloping valley below, surpasses in beauty all that I have seen in Palestine. Ancient olives, here and there a walnut tree, the *juglans regia*, numerous fig, pomegranate, and apricot trees, exhibit every shade of colour on the green sloping sides of the valley. The hills, which are covered with vineyards, awoke still more pleasant associations, while deep in the background might be seen, with the aid of the telescope, Abraham's celebrated oak. Children brought us fragrant *bouquets* of flowers which they had gathered in the fields.

"Look at these olives," said Dr. Helbig; "they are all very old. None have been planted by the Turks for the last four centuries; and thus the rich vegetation of this fruitful valley is gradually passing away. It is the same with the fountains. I know a village two leagues from this, where there are a hundred springs, some of them of a mineral character, and where traces of a still greater number may be discovered. Everything here shews that there is no public spirit and no government. For example, it is with the greatest difficulty that I can obtain my monthly salary, which amounts to 900 piastres with a free house, from the Governor. The money is safe, but I have always to dun him for it. My salary just now is seven months in arrears. To obtain payment, I have only to keep back the official reports which I have to forward to the Government. The Governor, through whom the reports are transmitted to the Pasha, will then pay me in the most courteous manner every halfpenny of my salary. Society here is in a very primitive state, and I could tell you much that has been brought under my notice as a physician, which would appear incredible to a

European. For example, I have a joiner and a butcher as my colleagues in the healing art. The former is entrusted with the treatment of broken legs and arms, because he is very skilful in making splinters, and the latter, who, in virtue of his office, is supposed to have an extensive knowledge of anatomy, has to perform the different operations usually confided to a surgeon. Our vaccinator is a gardener; his mode of practice is very simple; he pricks the child's arm with a needle, and then rubs the vaccine matter over the wound with a fig. I am chiefly employed by the Jews, who are too intelligent to confide themselves to the care of the Arab physicians, who are skilful enough in the treatment of the particular diseases to which they devote their attention."

We visited the doctor in his comfortable abode, and ascended the terrace of the lazaretto, which contains lofty vaulted places for the reception of man and beast. There has been no outbreak of the plague, since the appointment of Dr. Helbig, who was formerly stationed at Bajezit. On returning to our tents, we found an abundant meal awaiting us. Some Jews had supplied our cook with flour, eggs, rice, live fowls, and wine. Wine is the staple article of produce at Hebron; the vine grows almost without cultivation, and the inhabitants are very careless in their mode of converting the grapes into wine. Most of the grapes are sent to Jerusalem for sale. More recently, the European mode of preparation has been attempted, and a wine produced equal to the vintage of our finest vineyards on the

Rhine. I brought with me to Vienna a hermetically-sealed bottle of wine, pressed from grapes which grew near the ancient sepulchre of the patriarchs at Machpelah. I visited Hebron on the 4th of June, and the clusters were already a foot in length, and the grapes were as large as the smallest pigeon's eggs. I doubt very much whether any of these clusters were ever so long and heavy as to require two men to carry them on a stick. Spies and travellers are always prone to exaggeration. I may also remark that there is no historical proof that Noah planted the first vine here. All the grapes are not converted into wine; many of them are dried, and more still boiled into a syrup, which is used by the inhabitants of Palestine as a substitute for sugar.

While we were at table, some men came and offered glass bracelets of every colour, rings, and blue coral for sale. None but Jews are employed in the preparation of wine, and the manufacture of glass is confined to the Mohammedans. It was introduced by Venetian Jews in the twelfth century. We bought a dozen of bracelets for a penny, and two dozen of rings for the same moderate amount.

I had employed a member of the Sepharedisch community to meet me at the earliest dawn, and to conduct me through the city to the different synagogues. When the sun began to rise over the grove of Mamre, he stood before my tent. We passed an ancient pond, resembling in form the pool of Siloam and Solomon's ponds, probably the one at which King David caused the assassins of Ishbosheth, his rival for the throne, to be hanged.

We first visited the mosque, which is reached by a broad lofty staircase. Before the entrance of the lofty gateway, which is faced with slabs of red and white marble, immediately in front of the mosque, is a corner, marked off with small stones. On the eve of every feast, the Jews assemble for prayer in this corner, which can scarcely hold ten people, closely crowded together. They are also allowed to ascend the third part of the steps which lead to the mosque, where there is also a hole, by which they can peep into the dark vault beneath the mosque. The Jews come and offer up prayer at this hole in behalf of those who are dangerously ill. On one occasion, when a cruel scheik ordered the Jews to pay a sum of money in coins, which were not to be found in Palestine, so as to make their destruction certain, they went to this place to implore the assistance of the patriarchs. Next day a traveller, who had crossed the desert, arrived with a bagful of the coins which the scheik had ordered.

Many years ago, Hebron was under the government of an avaricious Pasha. He threatened to burn the most distinguished Jews alive, and to sell the rest as slaves, if they did not pay him 50,000 piastres. As they were very poor, this order reduced them to despair. Then the Rabbis resolved to bring their strait under the notice of the patriarchs, and wrote an account of the whole affair on a sheet of paper. Tempted by a backschiesh, the guardian of the mosque promised to lower the paper into the sepulchre of the patriarchs by a thread—as even the Mohammedans do not venture to enter the holy place, and examine it through a narrow passage, which leads from the mosque to the vaults of the sepulchre below.

The same night, the Pasha was suddenly woke from his sleep; before him stood three venerable old men, who threatened him with instant death, if he did not give them 50,000 piastres. Such stern resolve was written on the features of the old men, and so murderous was the expression which gleamed in their eyes, that the Pasha started up in terror, hastened to his money-chest, and handed over to them a bag, containing the exact sum which they had demanded, in gold and silver coins.

Early next morning a loud knocking was heard at the gate of the large building, in which all the Jews dwelt, as they continue to do at the present day. It was the Pasha's armed followers come to demand the 50,000 piastres.

All had assembled for prayer in the synagogue, as they felt that their last hour was at hand. The presidents sent the servant to open the door; all at once his eye fell upon a bag of money lying in the window of the entrance-hall, where the Jews wash their hands before entering the synagogue. He brought it to the presidents, and then hastened to open the door.

The Head Rabbi and the presidents proceeded at once to pay the 50,000 piastres to the Pasha, for, on examining the contents of the bag, they found that it contained exactly this sum, not one para more or less. The Pasha had no difficulty in recognising the bag, which contained his own money, and addressed the Jews with feelings of deep respect :—

"Truly ye are a people beloved of God! It is He who protects and preserves you. This money was demanded from me by the patriarchs Abraham, Isaac, and Jacob, in order to save my soul from an evil deed. The Shepherd of Israel slumbereth not, nor sleeps. Since the patriarchs, who have been sleeping in their graves for thousands of years, rise up for your sakes, I also will show my respect for you. Accept of this money as a gift, and when I am threatened with adversity, I will send you notice, that ye may pray to the patriarchs in my behalf."

Even at the present day, the Sepharedisch Jews celebrate a *Purim taka*, so called from the Arabian word " taka," which means a window, because the money was found in a window.

The event we are about to relate occurred at Hebron, in the days of Eliezer Archi, in the year of the world 5360. The Jewish population was scarcely large enough to form a Minjan, and they could only celebrate divine service, when a Jewish traveller or pilgrim happened to visit Hebron. On one occasion, on the eve of the atonement, the sun had almost sunk behind the horizon, and yet no stranger had appeared to complete the number of ten, necessary for the Minjan. The Jews began to be very anxious, and sent out scouts in all directions, to look if they could see one of their brethren approaching.

Already the tops of the olives and of the vine-clad hills were tinged with the golden rays of the setting sun, when all at once a venerable old man was seen advancing in the distance near the Maahroth Hamachpelah, the tomb of the patriarchs. A white talar, which looked like a shroud, was floating around his lofty figure, a white turban covered his head, and a long, white beard descended over his breast. There was great joy when his mode of salutation proved him to be a Jew. All hastened to welcome him, and expressed their regret that, as night had set in, they could not offer him any refreshment. The noble-looking old man thanked them, and said that, with God's assistance, he would get over the fast-day without any inconvenience.

They then conducted him to the synagogue, and the service began. Throughout the whole night and the next day might be heard the sound of the penitential psalms. The community showed all possible respect to their beloved guest, who, during the whole 24 hours, proved himself a perfect model of devoted piety. They were struck with observing a sort of halo which played around his forehead, but they thought it might be the reflection of the rays of the sun, as it formed a singular contrast to his glazed and almost motionless eyes.

When the first star appeared in the firmament, and the first blast of the *schofar* was heard, every member of the community was anxious to have the stranger for his guest. They were obliged to decide the matter by lot, and he became the guest of the poor but pious clerk of the community. He joyfully led the venerable, noble-looking old man to his small house. He walked before his guest through the low door and a dark, narrow passage; but, on turning round, he found that the old man had disappeared. The poor Chazan thought that his guest might have entered some of the neighbouring houses by mistake, but no one had seen him.

After long and fruitless inquiries he returned home in deep dejection and threw himself on his couch, without partaking of any refreshment after his long fast. But his beloved guest appeared to him in a dream, and spoke words of comfort to him. "Worthy man! be not troubled about thy guest; I am Abraham, the father of nations. Your sorrow at not being able to have a *minjan* on the day of atonement reached my heart even in my grave at Machpelah, and I arose and appeared among you as the tenth person. But when the service was concluded, I returned to the place from which I came."

I have introduced these legends, because they show how deeply rooted in the Jewish mind is the remembrance of their past history, their sacred traditions, and their primitive faith, and prove their constant belief in the presence and protecting power of the God of their fathers. Even at the present day, the forms of those who lived thousands of years ago appear at times on the stage of time, to comfort and to succour their miserable descendants.

The mosque is surrounded by a wall 200 feet long and 150 feet broad, with a minaret at each of the four corners. The foundation-stones, like those of the western wall of the temple, are chiselled at the edges, and many of them are 38 feet long. I ascended the east side of this wall, and saw a chapel of an oblong shape standing in a court before the entrance of the mosque. It was originally a church, the period of the erection of which is unknown. In the sixth century the Jews were allowed to approach it, and to bring offerings of incense. Benjamin of Tudela relates that he entered the sepulchres. For several centuries no Jew or Christian has enjoyed this privilege.

Dr. Fränkel, my kind host at Jerusalem, told me that in the year 1843, soon after his arrival, he was called in to visit Abd el Rachman, the notorious Scheik of Hebron, who had been taken ill. He remained several days at Hebron, till the Scheik, who had formed a strong attachment to him, was recovered. He requested as a favour to be permitted to enter the sepulchres, and the Scheik, after using every precaution, allowed him to do so, and conducted him himself down the dark, narrow staircase. He saw three sarcophagi covered with curtains of green damask, and when these were drawn aside he observed the names of the patriarchs written in letters of gold in Hebrew and Arabic.

This description agrees partly with that of a Spanish renegade, who saw three other sarcophagi, which belonged to the patriarchs' wives. But it is probable that these monuments are only imitations of sarcophagi, and that the real ones are buried below, as in one of the first centuries of the Christian era there was obtained from this place a Greek votive tablet, which was placed over the tomb of the patriarchs. Some pretend, also, to have seen Joseph's sepulchre, though it is expressly related of him that he was buried at Shechem. My guide also told me that Adam's sepulchre was here, as the city was called Kirjath Arba, before it received the name of Hebron. Arba in Hebrew means four, and the talmudists explained it as referring to the father of the human race and the three patriarchs, in direct contradiction to that passage of Joshua, where it is said that "Arba was a great man among the Anakim." It is also related that Adam was formed from the red earth of a field near Hebron. Jerome, one of the fathers of the church, borrowed this legend, which was quite unknown to his predecessors, from his Jewish teacher. For centuries after this, Christians undertook at considerable risk pilgrimages to this field, threw themselves on their faces, and moistened it with pious tears, and also carried off some of the earth, which was supposed to possess certain healing qualities. As at the present day many places are pointed out as the scenes of remarkable events in direct opposition to the Holy Scriptures, so also in the middle ages a feeling of deep veneration was attached to a cave near Hebron, in which the patriarchs were said to have lived, and the place was pointed out where the first fratricide was committed. Those, whose interest it was to do so, counted on the credulity of the pilgrims, and all these stories met with the same ready acceptance as at the present day.

When my guide and I returned to the small space in

front of the mosque, I was importuned for "back-schiesch" by a Turk with a green turban, the proof of his descent from the prophet. I at once complied with his request, but, as he was dissatisfied with the amount, a lively altercation ensued between him and my guide, which was brought to a close by the Jew giving the Mohammedan a sound beating before the cave of Machpelah. I was at once surprised and shocked at this act of audacity, but it shows how much times are altered, when a Jew ventures to punish a Mohammedan before the mosque of Hebron, one of the wildest and most fanatical cities of the East. When I reproved my guide for his conduct, which might have been attended with unpleasant consequences to myself, he coolly replied: "They are arrant cowards, when they have got to deal with a strong, bold fellow like me."

We then visited the sepulchre of Abner, Saul's general, and passed through a narrow entrance into the small court of a Turkish house. A venerable-looking Mussulman was sitting on a straw mat beneath a tree, enjoying his pipe; he invited us to sit down beside him, and entertained us with coffee and chibouques. Then he led us down sixteen stone steps, on the narrow side of the court, where there is a chapel surmounted by a cupola. We found a small space beneath, which is divided into two parts by a curtain of coloured calico, to which two stripes of green silk are attached. When it was drawn aside, we saw a sarcophagus of white plaster, which was nine feet long. The Jews offer up prayer here every new moon.

I visited the two Sepharedisch synagogues, and the one which belongs to the Aschkenasim. Their miserable appearance was only equalled by that of the worshippers, who devote themselves to the study of the talmud throughout the whole night, relieving one another by turns. When one of them learned from my guide that I was a Jew, he went to the ark of the covenant and opened it in honour of me. I touched the thora rolls with the hem of my garment, and then kissed them. A Hebrew prayer for Sir Moses and Lady Judith Montefiore was hanging on the wall of the synagogue. The children had not yet assembled in the school; along the walls were ranged about 2,000 books, numerous copies of the Pentateuch and the talmud, prayer-books, and only one work in profane literature, a French-Arabic dictionary, which was exhibited with some pride as a gift from a French Rabbi. In our description of the Jews at Jerusalem, we have already alluded to the organisation of the two communities at Hebron. In point of intelligence there is no difference between them. There are about 300 Sepharedim and 100 Aschkenasim; very few of them are native subjects; most of them are under the protection of the European consuls.

Before leaving the sepulchre of the patriarchs, which has been honoured by the erection of a synagogue, of a church dedicated to St. Abraham, and then of a mosque, we shall introduce two beautiful legends, which the Arabs relate of Abraham, whom they call El Khalil: Nimrod attempted the life of the child

Abraham, because the soothsayers announced that he would prove formidable to the gods. His mother concealed him for fifteen years in a cave. When she thought that the danger was past, she led him forth from the cave for the first time.

It was a wild, stormy night. The angel of the wind was flapping his mighty wings; one solitary star peeped through a rift in the clouds. Abraham saw nothing but darkness, heard nothing but the sighs of the bride of the wind; then he thought that the pure light, which looked down so calmly amid the war of nature's elements, must be the Supreme Power, which had given unity and order to the universe. He fell down and worshipped it. But when the star faded away, Abraham saw his error, and cried: " I will never worship that which fadeth away."

The bright moon now arose, resplendent with light. Abraham cried: " This is my God," and fell down to worship her. But when the moon faded away, Abraham cried: " This is not my God; I will not worship that which fadeth away."

Then the sun arose in all his majesty and power, and the wonders of creation, illuminated by his rays, unfolded themselves to Abraham's astonished gaze. " This is my Lord and my God," he cried in a transport of delight, as he threw himself on the ground to worship. But the sun also finished his course, and sank beneath the western horizon. " This is not my Lord and my God," cried Abraham; "I will not worship that which fadeth away. I look up to Him, who has created the small and the greatest light, to the Lord of heaven and earth. He is my Lord and my God."

When Abraham was 199 years of age, he undertook a pilgrimage to Mecca; there he asked the Lord how the resurrection of the dead would take place.

" Kill four birds," said the Lord, " cut them into pieces, and mix their flesh together, put it into four pots, and place them on the four hills near Mecca. But keep the heads of the birds beside you." When Abraham had done this, the Lord said unto him, "Now call the birds by their names."

Abraham called them by their names, and the flesh in the pots began to be agitated, and came rushing down the sides of the hills, and all the different parts became separated, and were united in the same form as before. And when the birds stood on their feet, each bird resumed its own head.

And the Lord said, "Thus, also, shall men arise from their graves, and seize, each man, his own head, the essential mark of difference between them."

Mussa, the cavass, was impatiently waiting our return; he had sent on our mules before, and, with a forethought for which we could not feel too grateful, had spread out our breakfast beneath the oak in the grove of Mamre, where the patriarchs pitched their tents, and where the three strangers announced to Abraham the destruction of Sodom and Gomorrah. Flavius Josephus calls it a terebinth ; later authors have called it an oak, and the tree, which is now extending its shade over us, is unquestionably a specimen of the *quercus ilex*, which the Arabs call *sindian*. The gigantic oak stands in the centre of a gradually-sloping meadow. The trunk is twenty-two feet in circumference; some way up, it separates into three thick stems, one of which is divided into two a little higher up. The branches cover a space which is ninety feet in circumference; they are very dense, and covered with thick foliage. There is a well in the vicinity.

Botanists are justified in expressing their doubts regarding the great antiquity of this tree, our earliest knowledge of which does not extend beyond the fifth century. But the Jews believe another place, to the north of Hebron, to be the one where Abraham pitched his tent. The ruins of ancient walls are to be found upon it. They represent the two sides of a large quadrangular space, and consist of two immense layers of stones. This undulating space, which is covered with green verdure, contains a cistern: a huge owl, the only one I saw in the East, was perched on a stone.

In more recent times, it has been proved, by comparing passages in the Bible and the Talmud, that the Hebron of the Scriptures must have stood on this hill, which is about a league distant from the present city. Joshua mentions that the town was on the mountains of Judah. It is enjoined in the *Mischna Tamid* that the morning sacrifice shall be offered up at Jerusalem "as soon as the light begins to appear at Hebron." But it would be impossible to see the modern city of Hebron, which is almost concealed in a valley, from

Jerusalem. There can be no doubt but an accurate
examination of the heights where Abraham's tent
stands would lead to many important discoveries. At
a small distance, on an eminence, may be seen the ruins
of the mosque Nebi Yumas, of the prophet Jonah,
which we visited. The hill is encircled by the ruins of
a wall, which is almost on a level with the ground.
Mussa called the place Hulhul; it is probably the
Halhul mentioned by Joshua.

No tomb connected with the ancient world has been
more minutely designated than the one in which the
sorrowing patriarch buried his beloved Rachel, the
beautiful mother of his most beautiful son. " And
Jacob set a pillar upon her grave; that is the pillar of
Rachel's grave unto this day." The remembrance of
it has been transmitted from generation to generation.
While cities in the West have disappeared, and time
has blotted out all memorials of their past existence,
this small and almost insignificant monument has been
preserved by the devout feelings of successive ages.
If destroyed, it was at once restored. At one time
a rough pyramid of stones was erected over the
grave, at another twelve blocks of marble, representing
Jacob's twelve sons. A marble stone, erected in
memory of the patriarch, was carried off by the monks
of the neighbouring monastery of St. Elias to their
church; but, as often happens in legend, the stone
returned every night to its former place. In course of
time, these stones disappeared, and were replaced by a
cupola supported by columns, by an arched vestibule,

and then by a mosque. When these fell into decay they were always restored.

The adherents of the world's three great religions bent, and still piously bend, the knee before this tomb. Here they worshipped in peace, though scarcely had they sprung to their feet, and retired a short way from the tomb, when they began to destroy one another with fire and sword. How wonderful is the magic influence exercised by every spot, where a noble and truly pious heart has ceased to beat.

While the Jews and Christians worshipped here, the Mohammedans of Bethlehem, actuated by a deeper feeling of piety, selected this as their place of interment, and a scheik of the name of Mohammed, when the mosque had fallen into ruins, caused a building with a cupola to be erected over the tomb, 300 years ago, the outlines of which can be traced at the present day.

It is worthy of remark that the Mohammedans, who, from a feeling of fanatical jealousy, prevent all Giaours from entering their sanctuaries, have of late years committed the charge of this tomb, which was once adorned with a mosque, to the Jews, on condition that they pay an annual tribute of 5000 piastres.

When I visited this monument, after I had left Bethlehem, I found a Sepharedi waiting for me with the key. We passed through a broad, open, pointed arch into a small entrance court, surrounded by walls nine feet high. In a niche, opposite to the entrance, is a stone turban over a Mohammedan tomb. On the right, as you enter, is a small iron gate, through which

we passed into a hall, over-arched by a cupola. On a
stone step, beneath this cupola, is a sarcophagus of
white plaster, which looks like a coffer with a convex
lid. It is marked with the names of numerous
travellers. We walked round the sarcophagus; before
it, toward the entrance, is a square slab of marble, a
foot and a-half in size, which covers the mouth of the
vault. I lifted it up, and looked down into a dark
hole, where, after lighting a lamp, I could see nothing
but a few stones.

The Jewish guide is in the habit of bringing with
him lamps, which the pilgrims light in honour of the
wife of the patriarch. They then offer up the beautiful Hebrew prayer in memory of the dead.

What woman on earth has been treated with such
respect, for a period of four thousand years, without
having her name encircled by the halo of superstition,
or immortalized by any great historical event! Jews,
Christians and Mohammedans bend the head and the
knee with equal reverence before the form of a beautiful mother, cut off in the bloom of youth, who is known
to us only through the tender affection which she bore
to her husband and her children. It is a noble trait in
the human heart, that it delights to honour all that
appears to it beautiful and good. The intellect and the
imagination both aid in shedding a halo around it, and
man has always shown the deepest devotion to the gods
of his own creation.

The legend relates that Joseph was saved by the
spirit of his mother, when he was tempted to sin in the

land of Egypt; it was her spirit, also, that taught him the interpretation of dreams, the wisdom of the world, and the art of government. When he was stretched on his death-bed in the land of Egypt, a breath of comfort seemed to breathe upon him and his children; it proceeded from the wings of his angel mother.

When her child died, the mother's love was changed into love for the whole nation. When Israel was threatened with misfortune, or overwhelmed with sorrow, she always appeared as their guardian angel. When they would no longer have God to rule over them, it was she who prevailed on the prophet to give them a king. When Saul, their anointed king, was passing her grave, he was surrounded with a dazzling light, like that of the sun playing with the waves of the ocean, and began to prophesy. And when the people, driven forth from the land of their fathers into hopeless exile, were passing near her tomb, there was heard a voice of bitter wailing:—" Rachel weeping for her children and refusing to be comforted, because they are not."

And, now, gentle reader, let us say farewell to this land of Palestine, so wonderful in its past history, so beautiful in its present ruins. If you have found me at all a pleasant companion, you will perhaps accompany me, on some future day, to the ancient land of Mizraim. *Au revoir!*

THE END.

R. BORN, PRINTER, GLOUCESTER STREET, REGENT'S PARK.